NEW FOUNDATIONS THEOLOGICAL LIBRARY

General Editor
PETER TOON, MA, M.TH, D.PHIL

Consultant Editor
RALPH P. MARTIN, MA, PH.D

NEW FOUNDATIONS THEOLOGICAL LIBRARY

WITNESS TO THE WORLD

The Christian mission in theological perspective

DAVID J. BOSCH

University of South Africa, Pretoria

JOHN KNOX PRESS
ATLANTA

Copyright © 1980 David J. Bosch
First published 1980

Bible quotations in this publication are from
the New English Bible, 2nd edition © 1970,
by permission of Oxford and Cambridge University
Presses.

Library of Congress Catalog Card Number 79-91241

ISBN 0-8042-3706-0

Published simultaneously by John Knox Press in the United States of America
and (in Marshalls Theological Library) by Marshall, Morgan & Scott
in Great Britain.

John Knox Press
Atlanta, Georgia

Printed in Great Britain

To the Church in South Africa—
'ecumenical' and 'evangelical'
Protestant and Roman Catholic
Black and White

CONTENTS

PREFACE

This is not a book for the expert. Its primary purpose is, rather, to acquaint pastors, missionaries, theological students and interested church members with the problems facing the Church-in-mission today. Some knowledge of the general terrain of theology has been presupposed, and yet an attempt has been made to write in such a way that even those readers who have little background, and theological students in the early stages of their studies, should be able to follow the argument with reasonable ease. Where necessary, reference has been made to other publications so as to enable the reader to pursue points not dealt with extensively in this study.

General introductions to missiology appear to be extremely rare in the English language. The best-known ones are, probably, J. H. Bavinck's *Introduction to the Science of Missions* (1960), B. Sundkler's *The World of Mission* (1965), and J. Verkuyl's *Contemporary Missiology: An Introduction* (1978)—all three, incidentally, translations from Dutch and Swedish originals. General and systematic introductions to missiology, in fact, appear to be something for the continental European rather than for the Anglo-Saxon. Apart from the three books mentioned above, we could refer to the introductions to missiology by G. Warneck, J. Richter, T. Ohm, H. W. Gensichen, G. Rosenkranz (all in German), A. Seumois (French) and A. Mulders (Dutch).

What we offer here is, however, not another 'introduction to Missiology'. It is concerned with the *theology* of mission. A large variety of missiological issues (such as the relationship between 'older' and 'younger' churches, the problem of the cross-cultural communication of the gospel, the evaluation of non-Christian religions—to mention but a few) are not discussed. I have limited myself, rather, to some fundamental questions regarding mission, such as: Why mission? What is the aim of mission? How has the Church, in the course of nineteen centuries, understood her responsibility towards the world? What is the relationship between 'mission' and 'evangelism'? How should we interpret the confusing plethora of answers given today to the question about the Church's mission?

All these are, I believe, questions of fundamental significance. They can, perhaps, all be reduced to one: What does it mean to be the Church of Christ in the world of today? If the following pages stimulate the reader to reflect in a responsible way on these questions, even if this leads to disagreement with me, I will regard my effort as more than worthwhile.

I have attempted to be fair to all theological persuasions. This is, incidentally, also the way in which I try to teach missiology at the University of South Africa. Our students hail from a bewildering variety of theological backgrounds and a rich diversity of racial groups. It is a challenge, but also a privilege, to teach missiology in such circumstances. Hopefully the reader will discover that, in spite of all my attempted fairness, I have not been too hesitant to adopt a viewpoint of my own.

Lastly, I wish to express my gratitude to two friends, my colleague Canon Trevor Verryn of the University of South Africa, and Dr Arthur Glasser of Fuller Theological Seminary in Pasadena, California, who have read the entire manuscript and have given me invaluable advice—which, however, I did not always follow. I also wish to express my indebtedness to Dr Peter Toon and Dr Ralph Martin, general editors of this Theological Library, as well as to the publishers, for including this volume in their series.

Pretoria   DAVID J. BOSCH
September, 1979

PART I

CONTEMPORARY THEOLOGY OF MISSION

CHAPTER ONE

MISSION IN CRISIS

The International Missionary Council (IMC) held its last plenary meeting in Achimota, Ghana, from 28th December 1957 to 8th January 1958. The milestones in the history of the Council were Edinburgh (1910—where it was decided in principle to found the IMC), Jerusalem (1928), Tambaram, near Madras (1938), Whitby, Ontario (1947), Willingen, Germany (1952), and finally Ghana (1958). Three years later, in New Delhi, the IMC was to be integrated into the World Council of Churches (WCC) and thus lose its independent character.

The Ghana meeting was therefore primarily intended as an opportunity for stock-taking and preparation for integration into the WCC. One of the speakers was the German missiologist, Walter Freytag, who discussed the changes in the pattern of Western missions. He was one of the very few who had attended all meetings of the WCC since Jerusalem (1928). He summed up the difference between 1928 and 1958 by saying that, in 1928, missions had problems; by 1958, however, missions had themselves become a problem.

Another two decades have passed since Freytag uttered those words. It has become increasingly clear that his evaluation of the modern missionary situation was correct. Mission is today a greater problem and more disputed than ever.

In his doctoral thesis, *The Theology of Mission: 1928-1958,* Gerald Anderson summarises the situation as follows: In Edinburgh the dominant question was: *How* mission? In Jerusalem it was: *Wherefore* mission? In Tambaram the key question was: *Whence* mission? At the first post-war conference, in Whitby, delegates grappled with the question: *Whither* mission? Finally, in Ghana, the main question was: *What* is mission?

There is undoubtedly considerable schematisation and over-simplification in Anderson's analysis. It nevertheless contains an element of truth to which we should not close our eyes. For the Edinburgh conference, and to a large extent for Jerusalem as well, the questions concerning mission were of a practical nature. How should we embark upon the missionary enterprise? What are we aiming at? Gradually, however, and especially since Tambaram, the questions concerned themselves more and more with matters of principle. Mission was no longer self-evident to everybody. The questions of Willingen and Ghana—Why mission? What is mission?—were not even asked in Edinburgh. Everybody still knew exactly what mission was. It required two world wars to make Christianity aware that not only mission but the Church herself was experiencing a period of crisis unprecedented in her history.

Naturally, even after the two world wars, there were people who believed that the crisis in Church and mission was of a merely transient nature. Even today many adhere to this view. As early as 1951, however, Johannes Dürr warned that it would be a serious misjudgment to believe that we were passing through an extraordinary period and no more, and that we could soon revert to earlier views and approaches as if nothing had changed.[1]

The time for clearcut, easy answers has irrevocably passed. We may, if we so wish, proceed as if nothing has happened and repeat the unmodified answers of earlier generations. The danger then, however, is not merely of becoming irrelevant to the situations in which we live but also of being disobedient to the Lord who has called us to mission.

THE END OF AN ERA

We do not, at this point, wish to review the origins of the present crisis of Church and mission in any detail. Hopefully the full extent and gravity of the crisis will unfold itself gradually as we proceed, especially in the third part of this book. It is nevertheless necessary to indicate some of the elements of the nature and extent of this crisis by way of introduction and paradigm.

The history of the Christian Church (and with it the history of the whole Western world) can be subdivided into three parts: the early Church (the first three centuries), the Constantinian period (from the fourth century onward), and the post-Constantinian or modern era. The Constantinianisation of the Church manifested itself especially in the following characteristics. The small, disparaged community developed into a large, influential Church; the persecuted sect in time became the persecutor of sects and dissidents; the bond between Judaism and Christianity was finally severed; an increasingly close liaison developed between throne and altar; it became a matter of form to belong to the Church; preoccupation with the immortality of the soul replaced the expectation of the coming of the Kingdom of God; the gifts of the Spirit were largely unrecognised; the ecclesiastical offices became institutionalised; the Church became wealthy and no longer quite knew what she ought to do with the message of Jesus (especially the Sermon on the Mount); Christian doctrine and practice became increasingly fixed in rigid moulds.[2]

These elements dominated the Roman Catholic, the Orthodox, and later also the Protestant churches, and remained almost unchallenged until relatively recently. The acceptance of this domination as self-evident is today largely a thing of the past. It goes without saying that the Constantinian era did not come to an end for all countries and communities at the same time. Whereas the dismantling of Constantinianism began in parts of Western Europe as long ago as the Renaissance, there are even to this day regions and communities where for all practical purposes the population still thinks and acts in Constantinian categories.

On the whole, however, this is a thing of the past. The typical power-structure during the golden age of Constantinianism was, in descending order, God—Church—kings—nobles—people. The Renaissance in principle deleted the Church from the list. The American and French revolutions subsequently challenged the divine rights of kings and nobles. Even in countries where no revolutions took place, the monarchy increasingly ceased to play a decisive role. Of the original order only God and people remained. During the periods of the Enlightenment of Rationalism, and of the rise of the natural sciences in the nineteenth century, God, too, was to be eliminated. Only man remained. Instead of tracing back his origin to God, man would now trace it back to the world of plants and animals. His position at the bottom of the God—Church—kings—nobility—people scale had been reversed. Now man held a position at the top: man—animals—plants—objects.[3]

In addition to the termination of the acceptance by all and sundry of the ruling position of the Church and the Christian ethos in society, we must underscore, secondly, the fact of the changed *political* situation of today and the influence this has on Church and mission. During the Middle Ages Christianity was, for all practical purposes, a European affair. The global expansion of Christianity was really to start only in the sixteenth century. This process coincided almost exactly with the expansion of European dominance over the world, inaugurated by the discovery of the Americas by Columbus (1492) and the sea route to India by da Gama (1498). The Vasco da Gama era—as it came to be known—is, however, now irrevocably behind us. In some parts of the world, notably South America, the process of the gradual termination of Western dominance started in the nineteenth century. For most of Asia and Africa it began only in 1947, the year India gained her independence from Great Britain.

The end of the dominance of the 'Christian West' has brought, as an inevitable consequence, far-reaching changes in the way the religion of the West is regarded in the erstwhile colonial territories. In some former colonies missionaries from the West are no longer welcome.

On today's *ecclesiastical* scene we also find ourselves in a totally new situation. Thanks to the global missionary enterprise of the (predominantly Western) churches, there are now younger churches in practically all non-Western countries. However, some of these churches are increasingly refusing to accept assistance, in whatever form, from churches in the West, because such help is regarded as indefensible paternalism and enslavement. In February 1971, John Gatu of Kenya suggested a *moratorium* on missions and missionaries from the West for a period of five years. At both the Bangkok conference of the Commission on World Mission and Evangelism (1973) and the Lusaka meeting of the All Africa Conference of Churches

(1974) the moratorium call was extensively discussed. Its importance moreover is underlined by the fact that the April 1973 issue of the *International Review of Mission* was devoted almost entirely to the moratorium issue.

Fourthly, we find ourselves today in a totally new situation as far as *religion* in general is concerned. Ever since the Church in Europe, towards the end of the Middle Ages, became aware of the large non-Christian world beyond her borders and of her missionary responsibility to that world, she had little doubt that she and she alone carried the only true message and would eventually triumph. This triumphalism sustained itself uninterruptedly until the second decade of this century. Typical of the then dominant spirit is the title of a book published by Johannes Warneck in 1909, *The Living Christ and Dying Heathenism.* Equally typical is a calculation which Lars Dahle, a Norwegian, made in the year 1900. Comparing the numbers of Christians in the Third World in 1800 and 1900 respectively, he was able to develop a mathematical formula which revealed the exponential growth rate of the Church in the nineteenth century. He proceeded to apply this formula to successive decades of the twentieth century and calmly predicted that by the year 1990 the entire human race would be won for Christianity.

The optimism of Warneck and Dahle is today a rarity. In many circles it is tacitly accepted that Christianity will remain a minority religion. In the year 1900 some 36 per cent of the world population were Christian. By 1973 this percentage had dropped to only 26. According to some calculations a mere 16 per cent of the world's population will still regard themselves as Christians by the end of this century. We should, however, not exclude the possibility of a new awakening which may lead to a quite different picture by the year 2000. Renewal movements in the past, such as the sixteenth-century Reformation and the eighteenth-century Evangelical Awakening would have upset calculations, had there been any in those days.

Some would, of course, argue that the real issue at stake is more radical than the mere question whether or not Christianity will be able to hold its own. The prominent Roman Catholic theologian Hans Küng, for instance, takes a hard look at the traditional doctrine that there is no salvation outside the Church *(extra ecclesiam nulla salus)*. At present, he says, Christians are still a minority in the world; can we really say that those now living outside the fold of the Church are lost? Can we, he adds, regard with complacency the past, knowing that in bygone ages millions of people lived in total isolation from the Church, and say that they are all lost? Can we, looking at the future, continue to insist that salvation is to be found in the Church only, when statistics indicate that Christians will constitute a steadily decreasing percentage of the world's population? Küng therefore believes that the time has come to take a fresh look at this traditional doctrine.[4] Others have agreed with Küng. Indeed, across the years there are those who have gone even further in their theological speculations. The non-Christian religions should, together with Christianity, be incorporated into something larger (W. E. Hocking); there should be a complete and whole-hearted 'participation' in one another's religion (W. Cantwell Smith); or non-Christians should be regarded as 'anonymous Christians' and their religions as the 'latent Church' (Karl Rahner)—to mention only a few suggested refinements of the ever more popular universalism.

To underscore the whole problem, attention is sometimes drawn to the fact that the Christian mission has only been really successful—at least in the numerical sense of the word—among the adherents of tribal or primal religions. The oldest and best example of this is Europe where pre-Christian paganism took the form of non-literary tribal religions and where the Church scored extraordinary successes. Similar successes were later to be achieved in Africa, Latin America, throughout the Pacific basin, and in parts of Asia. Wherever—so the argument continues—the Church encountered closed, literary 'higher religions', such as Islam, Hinduism and Buddhism, her progress was almost negligible.

Further, we are reminded of the fact that these religions have themselves become missionary. Some Western scholars have even begun to believe that salvation will come from Asia.[5] The 'spiritual East' rather than the 'materialistic West', so they say, holds the answer to man's deepest needs. Hinduism is no longer confined to India; in the form of the Ramakrishna Mission, Transcendental Meditation, the spread of Yoga, and the *ashrams* of the Hindu saint, Sri Aurobindo, it has appeared in many Western countries. Islam is no longer confined to North Africa, the Arabic world and isolated parts of Asia, but has expanded to parts of the world where it used to be completely unknown. Buddhism is no longer a religion of south and east Asia only; it has penetrated the West, largely in the form of Zen. The conference of the World Federation of Buddhists held in Cambodia in 1961 revealed an energy and missionary fervour which contrasted significantly with that of some of the large modern Christian world missionary conferences.[6] Of special importance, in this regard, are the many new religious movements (notably in Japan, but elsewhere as well) which present a special challenge to Christianity. We mention only Sōka Gakkai, a religion which has risen like a phoenix out of the ashes of post-war Japan and which emphasises inner-worldly salvation and happiness. Many of these movements reveal an aggressiveness which—so some would argue—puts the Christian mission to shame.

All this leads to a final element of the contemporary crisis of Church and mission—the fact that, in many circles, there is a great deal of uncertainty about what mission really is. To some extent this present study in its entirety will attempt to grapple with the problem: What is mission? Each of the elements of crisis already identified—the uncertainty of the position of Church and mission in a post-Constantinian world; the shifts in political power, away from the traditionally Christian West; the call for a moratorium and the other critical voices from Third World churches; and the increasing self-assurance and missionary consciousness among adherents of non-Christian religions—has in certain ecclesiastical circles given rise to the question whether Christian mission work still makes sense and, if it does, what form it should take in today's world. A fortnight before his death in August 1977, Max Warren, long-time general secretary of the Church Missionary Society, lamented the 'terrible failure of nerve about the missionary enterprise' in many circles today.[7] Stephen Neill likewise makes mention of 'a certain failure of nerve and unwillingness'[8] with regard to mission; and Samuel Moffett, a prominent Presbyterian missionary, writes: 'In my father's day coming home was a kind of triumph. The missionary was a hero. Today he is an anti-hero.

Even in Christian churches I am eyed askance as a throw-back to a more primitive era."[9]

This 'failure of nerve' is by no means universally in evidence. Still, even where this is not the case, people are grappling in a new way with the question about the essence of mission. Is it identical to evangelism in the sense of proclaiming eternal salvation? Does it include social and political involvement, and if so, how? Where does salvation take place? Only in the Church, or in the individual, or in society, or in the 'world', or in the non-Christian religions?

Such, then, is the complex situation facing those who would reflect seriously on mission in our day. The picture is one of change and complexity, tension and urgency, and no small measure of confusion exists over the very nature of mission itself. Our task is to enter the contemporary debate and seek answers that are consonant with the will of God and relevant to the situation in which we find ourselves.

MISSION IN DISPUTE

It is, of course, possible simply to ignore the elements of crisis just referred to (many others could be added) and encourage the Church to proceed as if these matters are only of peripheral concern. Merely repeating vigorous affirmations of the validity of the Christian mission without seeking to take the full measure of the present crisis in mission into account, would however certainly be culpable in God's sight. He wants his Church to discern 'the signs of the times'. To ignore the present crisis in mission may only aggravate its magnitude and gravity.

It is, in fact, theologically far more correct and practically far more realistic to regard the Church's missionary enterprise as something that, because of its very nature and being, will always be in dispute. It was an anomaly that there was a time when mission was *not* disputed, and we would have to ask ourselves in all seriousness whether what the Church was engaged in then, could *truly* be called mission—for instance, when mission work in Europe was conducted with the aid of the sword, or when popes literally promised heaven to those who would chase the Muslims from Palestine, or when mission, no matter how compassionately performed, became the companion and handmaid of European expansion in Africa and Asia. And yet even in those unfortunate episodes and epochs signs of true mission were always to be found.

The practical missionary endeavours of the Church always remain, under all circumstances, ambivalent. Mission is never something self-evident, and nowhere—neither in the practice of mission nor in even our best theological reflections on mission— does it succeed in removing all confusions, misunderstandings, enigmas and temptations.[10]

In our theological reflections on mission it is, therefore, a more serious matter than merely one of making a choice between the optimism of an earlier period and the pessimism of today. Neither is relevant here. Theology concerns itself with reflection on the nature of the gospel, and the theology of mission with the question of the way in which the Church spreads this gospel. Putting it differently: the theology of mission concerns itself with the relationship between God and the world in the light of the gospel.

Walbert Bühlmann is therefore correct when he declares: 'It is certainly no anachronism to go on speaking of mission.'[11] Mission is a permanent aspect of the life of the Church as long as the Church is, in some way or another, standing in a relationship to the world. Mission is the traditional and scriptural symbol that gives an answer to the question about the dynamic and functional relationship of the Church to the world.[12] In the words of Emilio Castro: 'Mission is the fundamental reality of our Christian life ... Our life in this world is life in mission.'[13]

CHAPTER TWO

MISSION AND EVANGELISM

THE GEOGRAPHICAL AND THEOLOGICAL
COMPONENTS

Our conclusion at the end of the previous chapter that mission is a 'fundamental reality' of the Christian's life in this world, does not in itself help to explain *what* mission really is. We shall now try to move a step nearer to an answer to that question by investigating the relationship between mission and evangelism.

The tremendous increase in the use of the word 'mission' in recent decades, especially in circles close to the World Council of Churches, appears to be a hindrance rather than a help. The word 'mission' was once as rare in the vocabulary of certain churches as it has become commonplace in our time.

The escalation in the use of the concept 'mission' has indeed had an inflationary effect, for 'mission' has now become the flag under which practically every ecclesiastical (and sometimes every generally human) activity is sailing. Stephen Neill has therefore repeatedly pointed out that if everything is mission then nothing is mission. Walter Freytag likewise referred to the 'ghost of pan-missionism'. This development reached its apex at the Fourth Assembly of the WCC (Uppsala, 1968) where practically everything was brought under the umbrella-term 'mission'—health and welfare services, youth projects, activities of political interest groups, projects for economic and social development, constructive application of violence, combating racism, the introduction of the inhabitants of the Third World to the possibilities of the twentieth century, and the defence of human rights. Small wonder that Donald McGavran, in an open letter, criticised the Uppsala assembly for allowing mission to develop into 'any good activity at home or abroad which anyone declares to be the will of God'.

Since the middle of the seventies the concept 'evangelism', long neglected and under-accentuated in ecumenical circles, gained currency again, partly due to the emphasis it received at the International Congress on World Evangelisation and at the Fourth Roman Catholic Synod of Bishops, both held in 1974. At the Fifth Assembly of the WCC (Nairobi, 1975) evangelism was, as it were, again given place of honour in the ecumenical movement, especially because of the stimulating contribution of Mortimer Arias and the ensuing discussions. Subsequent to this Assembly, however—as often happens nowadays—the concept 'evangelism' has begun to be used as frequently as 'mission' and often in the same all-inclusive sense. It then becomes doubtful whether anything of significance was achieved in calling the Church back to her evangelistic task.

These most recent developments have, nevertheless, made one important contribution: they have broken with the earlier view according to which both mission and evangelism had to do only with the verbal proclamation of the gospel. The one difference, in the older definition, was that the objects of mission and evangelism were distinguished.

Sometimes the difference was deemed to be merely geographical in nature. 'Mission' was something we did in far-off, pagan countries; 'evangelism' was something for our own environment. This difference in meaning was related to the fact that the concept 'mission' in the sense of christianisation came into vogue only gradually, beginning with the sixteenth century. This development coincided with the early period of the European colonisation of Africa, Asia and the Americas. 'Mission' thus presupposed an established Christian Church in Europe which sent missionaries overseas to convert the heathen. In this way the word developed a strong geographical component. Somebody was a 'missionary' if he stood in the service of a church or society in Europe (or another Western base) and was sent to a remote area by that agency. If he worked in the vicinity of his home, he was an 'evangelist'.

Sometimes a theological rather than a geographical difference was decisive. 'Mission' had to do with 'not-yet-Christians'; 'evangelism' meant reviving 'no-more-Christians' or nominal Christians. In practice this interpretation did not differ much from the previous one; after all, the 'not-yet-Christians' usually were in the countries of the Third World and the 'no-more-Christians' in the West. Nevertheless, for some the primary consideration was indeed theological. The Dutch theologian A. A. van Ruler argues that one has to distinguish between the apostolate in the West and in non-Western cultures, otherwise one thinks individualistically and unhistorically. God-in-Christ, he avers, has walked a long way with the peoples of the West and they cannot undo this history, even if they wished to. In Europe God himself is (in a way quite different from that which obtains in Asia) the point of contact for the gospel. A secularised, de-christianised European is not a pagan. The Westerner *cannot*, in fact, revert to paganism, for that has been totally destroyed in Europe. He can never again become pre-Christian (or pagan), but at most post-Christian. For precisely this reason we have to maintain the difference between mission and evangelism.[1]

In Roman Catholic circles this distinction is often still in vogue, albeit without explicitly using van Ruler's arguments. We find this for instance in the documents of the Second Vatican Council. In both the Constitution on the Church *(Lumen Gentium)* and the Decree on Mission *(Ad Gentes)*, the 'not-yet-Christians' are described as objects of mission; albeit the Council fathers refrained from identifying these 'not yet-Christians' with inhabitants of specific geographical areas.

It may, however, also happen that mission and evangelism (both still essentially understood as verbal proclamation) are used as alternatives without distinguishing between the addressees. Hendrik Kraemer and Johannes Hoekendijk for instance both pleaded for an interpretation of mission and evangelism as synonyms: Europe was, just as Asia and Africa, a mission field, with the Church in a minority position. Whether we work among non-believers in Europe or Asia, and whether we call this mission or evangelism, ultimately makes no difference.

In the English-speaking world the two words are likewise often used as interchangeable concepts, apparently without necessarily reflecting any theological considerations. The same guileless usage is still reflected in the name of the World Council of Churches' 'Commission on World Mission and Evangelism'. When this division was created in 1961, its mandate was defined as follows: '... to further the proclamation to the whole world of the Gospel of Jesus Christ, to the end that all men may believe in him and be saved'. Philip Potter thus correctly points out that 'mission', 'evangelism' and 'witness' are, as a rule, interchangeable concepts in ecumenical literature.

IN SIX CONTINENTS

We have already inferred that objections could be raised to all the interpretations discussed above. If one maintains that the difference between mission and evangelism is essentially of a geographical nature, Christians in the West may be accused of persisting in thinking in colonialistic categories and of simply dividing the world into a 'Christian' West and a 'non-Christian' Third World. This distinction is not acceptable any more and in any case both existentially and theologically indefensible. This is one of the reasons why, especially since the meeting of the Commission on World Mission and Evangelism in Mexico City in 1963, ecumenical spokesmen tend to talk about 'mission in *six* continents'. The three continents' view of mission, in which the geographical component was the constitutive element, is thus increasingly rejected.

The attempt to confine mission to work among 'not-yet-Christians' and evangelism to work among 'no-more-Christians' does not provide a solution either. It becomes increasingly difficult to draw this distinction. Is a secularised and dechristianised European, whose parents and grandparents have already lost all contact with the Church, a not-yet-Christian or a no-more-Christian? Van Ruler may be correct in contending that such a person is a post-Christian rather than a pre-Christian. This, however, merely calls for a special approach in communicating the gospel to him; it does not necessitate a separate theological terminology. To this we must add that, increasingly, we have to do with people in Asia and Africa whose grandparents were Christians, but who themselves have been completely secularised and dechristianised. Would we regard them as objects of mission or of evangelism? They are 'no-more-Christians' in an environment made up pre-dominantly of 'not-yet-Christians'.

Would it be preferable then, to use 'mission' and 'evangelism' interchangeably, as the tendency is in many English-speaking churches? Then when an evangelistic campaign is being launched, whether it is in New York or New Delhi, we refer to it either as 'evangelism' or as 'a mission to …'.

This view has some advantages but does not provide a solution to our problem of trying to establish what mission is. Where the first view we discussed absolutises the geographical component, the danger in this third view is that this component may disappear altogether. What the Church does *in* England or Germany is, after all, also 'mission'; therefore she does not *need* to cross geographical and cultural frontiers any more to become involved in mission. Traditionally mission *only* had to do with the non-Western world; that was wrong and one-sided. Today we face the possibility of an opposite one-sidedness. People can argue that mission will have less and less to do with the great unfinished task which, at least for the time being, awaits us especially in the Third World. Church and mission then develop a lamentable myopia and parochialism, and lose the breadth of vision of people like Wesley who could say, 'The world is my parish.'

GOD'S SALVIFIC INTERVENTION

Should we not approach the whole matter of the relationship between mission and evangelism from a completely different angle? We have seen that the traditional view was that these two activities differed only in respect of their 'objects'. Perhaps the difference should be looked for in the nature of the two enterprises themselves. If we concede this, we may define the relationship as follows: Mission is more comprehensive than evangelism.

We have already mentioned that there has of late indeed been a tendency in ecumenical circles to define mission as something more comprehensive than used to be the case. This is in itself a promising development. Two points of criticism may, however, be raised. First, mission may be defined so comprehensively that, in the words of Neill, everything becomes mission. It becomes a collective noun for everything God does as well as for everything Christians believe they should be doing. Secondly, a problem develops in that, since more or less the middle of the 1970s, evangelism has often been defined as widely and comprehensively as mission. And then we are back where we started.

There is even a tendency to widen the meaning of the word 'evangelism' and to narrow the meaning of 'mission'. 'Evangelism' then becomes the umbrella-term 'for the entire manner by which the gospel becomes a reality in man's life', and includes proclamation, translation, dialogue, service, and presence, in other words all the activities, methods and techniques of the Church's involvement with the world, whereas 'mission' becomes a purely theological concept, 'used for the origin, the motivation and the ratification' of all these activities.[2]

In his contribution to the Lausanne Congress (1974) and in his very readable *Christian Mission in the Modern World*, John Stott made a commendable attempt to bring clarity to the whole discussion. He came to the conclusion that 'mission' is a comprehensive concept, 'embracing everything which God sends his people into the world to do'. Evangelism, on the other hand, is less comprehensive and actually constitutes a component of 'mission'. Mission is then defined as 'evangelism plus social action'.

This view undoubtedly has merit, but it does not satisfy in all respects. Evangelism is something more than a mere component of mission and mission is something more dynamic than the sum total of evangelism and social action. It is precisely when we subdivide mission into two such distinctly different components that a battle between the two for supremacy may easily develop. Stott himself is, in some respects, a victim of this. In his chapter on 'mission' he still, with approval, quotes a document of the National Evangelical Anglican Congress that 'evangelism and compassionate service belong together in the mission of God' (p. 27), that the priority of one or the other may be dictated by circumstances (p. 28), and that Jesus' 'Great Commandment' and 'Great Commission' belong inseparably together (pp. 23 and 29). In his chapter on 'salvation', however, social action is relegated to a secondary position. We shall look at this whole problem more closely at a later stage.

We should rather try to explain the relationship and difference between mission and evangelism in another way, while making use of some of the analyses of Stott, and also of others, among them Jürgen Moltmann.[3]

Mission and evangelism have both to do with that aspect of the Church's life where she crosses frontiers towards the world. This is not the only feature of her existence. She is also to be a worshipping presence, providing for the building-up of her members *(oikodomē)* through liturgy *(leitourgia)*, fellowship *(koinōnia)* and teaching *(didaskalia)*. We may therefore not call everything the Church does 'mission' or 'evangelism'.[4]

Mission has to do with the crossing of frontiers. It describes the total task which God has set the Church for the salvation of the world. It is the task of the Church in movement, the Church that lives for others, the Church that is not only concerned with herself, that turns herself 'inside out' (Hoekendijk), towards the world.

Mission thus defined is comprehensive (but not all-inclusive) and comprises more than the proclamation of the gospel. When Jesus begins his public ministry in Nazareth, he outlines it in terms of mission: 'The spirit of the Lord is upon me because he has anointed me; he has sent me to announce good news to the poor, to proclaim release for prisoners and recovery of sight for the blind; to let the broken victims go free, to proclaim the year of the Lord's favour' (Luke 4.18-19). The Mexico City conference, to which we have already referred, rightly described mission as 'the common witness of the whole Church, bringing the whole gospel to the whole world'.

Mission is the symbol of the Church moving towards the world. The Nairobi assembly of the WCC (1975) formulated this in the following words:

> The Gospel is good news from God, our Creator and Redeemer ... The Gospel *always* includes the announcement of God's Kingdom and love through Jesus Christ, the offer of grace and forgiveness of sins, the invitation to repentance and faith in Him, the summons to fellowship in God's Church, and command to witness to God's saving words and deeds, the responsibility to participate in the struggle for justice and human dignity, the obligation to denounce all that hinders human wholeness, and a commitment to risk life itself.

There may be questions about some aspects of this formulation and about the practical implementation thereof by the WCC

itself, but it does give expression to the wholeness of God's
involvement through the Church with the world. It identifies
some of the frontiers the Church should cross in her mission to
the world. These frontiers may be ethnic, cultural, geographical,
religious, ideological or social. Mission takes place where the
Church, in her total involvement with the world and the
comprehensiveness of her message, bears her testimony in word
and deed in the form of a servant, with reference to unbelief,
exploitation, discrimination and violence, but also with
reference to salvation, healing, liberation, reconciliation and
righteousness.

THE CENTRE OF GOD'S MANDATE

What, then, is evangelism? We noted that John Stott defines it
as a component of mission, adding that 'social action' is the
other part. Evangelism is, however, *more* than a mere segment
of mission (which, of course, as segment, may easily be isolated
from the other segment). Evangelisation is, rather, an *essential
dimension of mission.* It is the core of the Christian mission to
the world, 'the centre of the all-embracing mandate of God to
the Church', as Hans Bürki puts it.[5]

John Stott is therefore correct when he argues that
evangelism should not be described in terms of its 'objects' or
results (pp. 37-40), but rather of its *contents.* When he identifies the contents more closely, he rightly does it in the form of
an exposition of the New Testament *kērygma* which, as he puts
it, consists of at least five elements, 'the gospel events', 'the
gospel witnesses', 'the gospel affirmations', 'the gospel
promises', and 'the gospel demands' (pp. 44-54). He explicitly
says (p. 40) that evangelism is more than verbal proclamation.
The preaching of the word should be accompanied by signs of
the approaching Kingdom and a new life in obedience and
community.

Evangelism is moreover, by virtue of the primary meaning of
the word *euangelion,* always the bringing of good news. It
always contains an element of invitation: The God of grace
invites us. The *euangelion* is, however, never good news in
general, but always quite concretely and contextually good news

over against the 'bad news' which threatens and governs the
lives of the addressees.

Evangelism is thus never merely the proclamation of
'objective' truths, but of what Emil Brunner used to refer to as
'truth as encounter'.[6] The person or Church which evangelises
is not only an agent of evangelism but himself a part of the
message. The Church's credibility is of the utmost importance,
not only in order that her evangelistic enterprise may 'succeed',
but to allow her witness to be authentic and to give substance to
it. The gospel takes shape concretely in the witness, in the
Church, and is never a general, objective, immutable revelation.
True evangelism is incarnational.[7] The situation of the person
to whom the gospel is being brought and the involvement, with
that situation, of the one who brings the gospel, concretely
determine the content of evangelism—naturally nurtured by the
Scriptures. The New Testament reveals this pattern in many
ways; the content of evangelism frequently differs, depending on
whether it is addressed to Zacchaeus, or the criminal on the
cross, or the rich young ruler, or Cornelius, or the Ethiopian
official, or Saul in Damascus. Truth is, in each of these
instances, truth-as-encounter. Immediately after his assertion
that evangelism is the centre of God's all-embracing mandate to
his Church, Hans Bürki correctly states: 'But different times
and different societies need different emphasis. In one country
and in one place the city slums are such that suburban
Christians just cannot go on a kind of an evangelistic trip to
"preach the Gospel" to these "poor masses" and then retreat to
their comfortable homes, without blaspheming the love of God.'
If there is no truth-as-encounter, in other words, if those who
evangelise are not themselves part of the message they proclaim,
there is no evangelism.

Now, if we delineate evangelism in this way, it comes close to
the description of *mission* we have formulated above. There
should be no objection to this. Paul Löffler says: 'When
referring to its theological meaning, "evangelism" is practically
identical to "mission". When referring to the evangelistic
witness, "evangelism" more specifically means "the communication of Christ to those who do not consider themselves
Christians" ... Thus, evangelism is sufficiently distinct and yet
not separate from mission.'[8] It also has, like mission, to do with

the crossing of frontiers, but then very specifically with those between belief and unbelief. Emilio Castro adds, '... it will be "evangel" only to the extent that it points to the wholeness of God's love breaking through in the world ...'[9] It therefore remains an essential dimension of mission, in which the crossing of all frontiers between Church and world remains crucial. The one may never be seen in isolation from the other.[10]

CHAPTER THREE

THEOLOGY OF MISSION

FOUNDATION, MOTIVE, AIM

We are specifically concerned with the *theology* of mission, which Anderson describes as a study of 'the basic presuppositions and underlying principles which determine, from the standpoint of the Christian faith, the motives, message, methods, strategy and goals of the Christian world mission'.[1] Our concern here is therefore less with the *how* of mission—the study of which belongs elsewhere—than with the *why*, the *whereto* and the *what*.

To put it differently: in the theology of mission we occupy ourselves primarily with the *foundation*, the *motive* and the *aim* of mission. We could, supposedly, subdivide the theology of mission according to these three aspects. Some missiologists, such as Thomas Ohm,[2] have tried to do precisely that, and with some success. In reality, however, foundation, motive and aim are so intertwined that it would be difficult to treat them completely separately. After all, the motive of mission usually arises from the foundation, whereas both have a decisive influence on the aim. If it is judged, for instance, that the source of mission is to be found in the Church, the motive of mission will also be found there and the extension or planting of the Church regarded as the primary aim of mission. Similarly, if Western Christian culture is considered to be the basis of mission, then the consciousness of the superiority of that culture will function as missionary motive and its expansion as missionary aim. Instead of treating foundation, motive and aim each in isolation, we should therefore rather pay attention to their interaction. The two examples just referred to in any case underline the necessity of careful theological distinctions in our study.

CHURCH AND THEOLOGY

It goes without saying that the *how*, the practice of mission, cannot be ignored in our reflections. Theology and practice ought to stand in a relationship of dynamic, creative tension. The practice of mission constantly needs the critical guidance of the theology of mission, whereas the latter, in its turn, has to take the practice of mission seriously into account, naturally without, in this process, elevating mere efficiency to the highest norm. In this way we have to continue trying to narrow the gap between missionary theology and practice. There exists more than a mere imaginary danger that the two aspects may become so mutually estranged that theological reflection would, almost as a matter of principle, reject any practical application, and practice, similarly, refuse to be guided by theological reflection.

A few remarks, in general, on the relationship between Church and theology may indicate some guidelines for the relationship between the theology and practice of mission.

To begin with, theology never addresses the Church from a safe vantage-point, so to speak. It does not stand on the side-line as objective spectator. Theology is practised in solidarity with the Church. Its primary functions are to explore the nature and content of the gospel and to inquire whether ecclesiastical practice faithfully reflects the gospel. It thus reflects on what the Church ought to be rather than on what she is or in all probability is going to be. Theology knows that Church history often is the history of the grieving of the Spirit rather than of his victories, and that it is unlikely that the future will be very different. Theology nevertheless persists in challenging the Church to become what, in Christ, she already is, and to cease being what she reflects in practice.

This does *not* mean, however, that theology is to be regarded as something elevated above the Church and immune to temptations and mistakes. On the contrary, theology remains an exposed and hazardous enterprise, without any guarantees that its premises and conclusions will be free of error. All theological activities thus remain a knowing-in-part only. They are imperfect and can at best be mere approximations of what they are supposed to be.

It is, furthermore, essential to emphasise that the Church

cannot expect theology to produce results which, according to its very nature and being, it cannot produce. It is, for instance, *not* the task of theology to arouse and stimulate missionary fervour in the Church. True, theology does serve the Church and can also, with respect to the Church's missionary endeavour, help to achieve greater clarity as far as missionary aims and motives are concerned; it may hold up the Church's own history as an example to her; it may help those engaged in mission to compare strategies and methods; it may act as corrective to their wilfulness and onesidedness. It is, nevertheless, outside the province of theology to motivate and activate the Church to engage in mission. To put it differently: not theology, but the Lord of the Church grants the Church faith, vision, fervour and perseverance. Theology cannot make available to the Church weapons and instruments which would make the believer's trust in God dispensable or the Church's activities less hazardous. Theology may and indeed must challenge the conscience of the Church but it may never be used as substitute for any deeds and decisions of faith.[3]

'EVENT CHARACTER' AND 'THEOLOGISING TRAIT'

On occasion theology has been regarded as the instrument that should provide the necessary 'ammunition' for the practice of mission. However, it has also often been true that theology and practice have regarded each other as opponents.

In this connection we refer to an informative article by Herbert C. Jackson on 'The Missionary Obligation of Theology'.[4] Jackson argues that there is a certain tension and even contrast between what he calls the 'event character' of Christianity and the 'theologising trait of religious man'. Where the former is dominant, the latter tends to disappear from the scene, and vice versa. He illustrates his thesis as follows. During the first three centuries of the Christian era, a period of rapid missionary expansion, the 'event character' predominated and pushed aside the 'theologising trait'. During the ensuing five centuries, the period of the seven ecumenical councils, precisely the opposite trend prevailed; it was largely a missionless time.

Taking a similar sweeping view of the subsequent centuries of Church history, Jackson argues that the same phenomenon has tended to repeat itself, in the Roman Catholic as well as the Protestant churches. As regards the latter, for instance, he sees the sixteenth century as a time of theological flowering, chiefly because of the impressive contributions of Luther and Calvin. At the same time it was a period during which any thought of Protestant missionary outreach was conspicuous by its absence. During the missionary revival of Pietism and the Great Awakening the position was exactly the opposite. Jackson then deduces that, apparently, 'practical mission work' and 'theological reflection' are mutually exclusive. Where the one is in the forefront, the other is almost by definition absent.

If Jackson's theory were valid, it would appear that we should throw all 'theology' overboard and dedicate all our energy to the practice of mission. We believe, however, that we are here presented with a false choice. In fact, the New Testament itself disproves the validity of the subsequent development. Paul, after all, combined his extensive missionary activities with correspondingly intensive work in the area of theology. His theology exercised a decisive influence on his practice; conversely, the way in which he tackled practical issues had a clear bearing on his theology. It is, after all, precisely on the frontier where faith meets disbelief that theological reflection takes on its most dynamic form. Martin Kähler thus correctly remarked, as far back as 1908, that mission is indeed the mother of theology.

How, then, do we react to those who chide missionary activists for their lack of theological reflection? Perhaps we should begin by pointing out that theology is not something that can only take shape in systematic form—creeds, conciliar statements and dogmatic treatises. Theology is concerned with the basic presuppositions and underlying principles which give direction to our ecclesiastical activities. Such presuppositions and considerations are *always* present, in any ecclesiastical activity, even if they are not always expressed or formulated systematically. This implies that behind every missionary enterprise in the various periods of missionary revival there was indeed theological reflection, albeit not always formally articulated. Theology was, therefore, decidedly not absent. No mission is possible without theology.

The reverse, however, is possible: theologising without

mission. Here Jackson is absolutely correct. The question, then, is to what extent this can be called *genuine* theology. Authentic theology, after all, does not develop where the Church is preoccupied with herself or where she is desperately erecting defensive barricades on her own soil. What we then get is not theology but rather dead orthodoxy. Salvation becomes a treasure the Church has at her magnanimous disposal, the gospel self-evidently a possession of the Church, the Kingdom of God an institution, and the new life in Christ a good habit.

Authentic theology, however, only develops where the Church moves in a dialectical relationship to the world, in other words, where the Church is engaged in mission, in the widest sense of the word. Internal renewal of the Church and missionary awakening belong together.

The question about the meaning of 'mission' is, therefore, to some extent, simply another form of the question about the Church's understanding of her faith and message. Missiology— and more specifically the theology of mission—is not merely a dispensable theological minor, but belongs, as Hendrik Kraemer correctly remarked, to the 'norm-giving' subjects in the theological encyclopaedia. Missiology, as E. Jansen Schoonhoven puts it, 'is *theologia viatorum*'. It involves all the Church's reflection, evaluation and praise as 'she accompanies the gospel on its way through the nations and the times'.[5]

We have said that every missionary endeavour of the Church has had its theological basis, albeit implicit and unreflected. It is, nevertheless, also necessary to make explicit that which is only somewhere implicit in the background (cf. 1 Pet. 3.15). We have to give expression to it, formulate it, allow it to enter into dialogue, not only with the practice of mission but also with the theological reflection of others. This is necessary for the sake not only of mission but also of theology.

Jackson, in the article referred to, pleads in fact not only for a 'theology of mission', but for a 'missionary theology'. In subsequent chapters we shall point out—as Jackson correctly states—that such a theology has never been developed in any stage of the Church's history, but that nevertheless, here and there, a few buds of such a missionary theology are becoming discernible in the present period. Such a development is possible, however, only where the Church has become aware of the pilgrim character of her existence.

We return, for a moment, to Jackson's primary hypothesis—the fact that, throughout the course of Church history, 'event' and 'theologising' have tended to alternate. The problem that lies behind this is that the Church has always revealed the double form of institution and movement, sometimes more of the one, sometimes more of the other.[6] The tragedy is, however, that only too frequently the two elements oppose or attempt to exclude one another. Then we get a one-sided emphasis either on the institutional and official or on the Church as event and movement. We should not be faced with such a choice, however. There should be a sustained dynamic and creative tension between the two. 'Institution' without 'event' gradually becomes a museum or an asylum. 'Event' without 'institution' dissipates after a short time, or, where this does not happen, the 'event' in any case gradually becomes institutionalised.

In his *The Kingdom of God in America*, H. Richard Niebuhr traced this interaction with reference to American ecclesiastical developments since the Puritans. Greek predilection for abstraction and Roman preference for systematisation in the course of time gave the Medieval Church the appearance of almost complete ossification. The Protestant Reformation, in contrast, was an 'event' which, however, after its spring period, became institutionalised in a similar fashion. Those Puritans and other nonconformists who migrated to North America were, for their part, a corrective to this. But they, in turn, succumbed to the same sequence (cf. Cotton Mather).

There remains, however, a never-ending process of interaction between the static and the dynamic. Whenever the Church, like Israel of old, forgets her pilgrim and event character and wants to settle down in a wayside inn, whenever she forgets that she is not of this world and begins to exercise power in society, there develops an element of unrest within her, which often takes the form of cells, groups, societies, or sects, which challenge the establishedness of the Church. Whenever the Church allows herself to become conformed to the world to such an extent that she abandons or neglects dynamic elements which belong to her essence, all kinds of corrective counter-currents begin to develop. Adventism came as a corrective to the disregard of the expectation of the *parousia*, the pentecostal movement as a protest against the disappearance of the charismata, Darbyism (Plymouth Brethrenism) as a repudiation of the institutionalisation and hierarchical structure of the offices in the Church; the Baptist movement as a rejection of membership of the Church as a matter of course, Marxism as a judgment on the neglect of social justice and on the transcendentalisation of salvation, and Quakerism and Mennonitism as criticism of the acceptance by the Church of violence and war as something normal.[7]

If the institution has no eye or ear for these voices of protest, it denies itself the possibility of renewal and gradually dies of suffocation. If, on the other hand, the renewal movements deny themselves the solidity and breadth of the institution, they become like beautiful flowers without roots, floating on the water and driven to and fro by various winds until they lose their splendour and are washed ashore. Others strive to retain their *élan* and significance by deliberately organising themselves into a 'separatist Church'.

This dynamic interaction between movement and institution is no simple matter. The real tragedy is when the renewal movement pours its white-hot convictions into the hearts of people, only to find that these convictions eventually cool down and become crystallised codes, solidified institutions and petrified dogmas.[8] The prophet then becomes priest of the establishment, charism becomes office, and love routine.

Mission is by definition an element of renewal. Frequently, indeed, practically always, the narrow channel in which the institutionalised Church moves, is too confined for the impetuous missionary current; it then tends to overflow the banks. Sometimes this missionary current becomes a separate stream next to and over against the channel of the institutional Church. When this happens, it is to the detriment of both Church and mission. Institution and movement—these two may never be regarded in mutually exclusive categories. Neither may theology and mission.

CHAPTER FOUR

CONTRASTING MISSIONARY MODELS

POLARISATION IN MISSION

The introductory chapter pointed out that mission is in a crisis today, a crisis more radical and extensive than anything the Church has ever faced in her history. Chapters 10 to 17 will follow the Church on her missionary course through the ages. The background against which the present crisis developed will then gradually become clearer. It would nevertheless be helpful at this stage, precisely for the better understanding of the historical course of mission, to review the dominant contemporary interpretations of mission.

This procedure will entail that, for the time being, we shall not attempt to expose the finer shades and complexities that lie behind the contemporary understanding of mission. We are rather going to try, in somewhat stereotyped fashion, to outline modern missionary theology with the aid of two contrasting models. Granted all the disadvantages of such a method, it does have certain points in its favour. We shall, in this way, at least outline the parameters of a theology of mission and thus construct, as it were, a 'scale' which allows for the full spectrum of contemporary interpretations of the missionary task.

It should of course be remembered that none of the varied interpretations on this scale has simply dropped from the skies. They are, rather, all historical legacies. The roots of the modern missionary controversy should to a large extent be searched for as far back as the eighteenth century, and in some respects even earlier.

At this stage we are going to reduce the differences in the modern theology of mission to only two positions. This is admittedly a scarcely defensible procedure. Reality is much more blurred than this. However, precisely by delineating the two extreme 'wings', it may help to expose more clearly the nature, extent and seriousness of the fundamental differences. The two positions we intend studying more closely, are those usually referred to as the 'ecumenical' and 'evangelical' understandings of mission. We are not suggesting that all views concerning mission may be neatly fitted into either of these two 'camps'. In subsequent chapters we shall argue that such a rigoristic division is untenable. The inadequacy of our terminology emerges moreover from the fact that we cannot possibly declare all 'evangelicals' to be unecumenical or all 'ecumenicals' to be unevangelical. It remains true, nevertheless, that these two terms are today being used almost universally and that we can hardly ignore them.

We have to take the unavoidable risk of naming people. Many missiologists—I am thinking, to mention only a few examples, of Stephen Neill, Lesslie Newbigin, Johannes Verkuyl, Gerhard Rosenkranz, Hans-Werner Gensichen, Gerald Anderson, Bengt Sundkler, Eric Sharpe, Mortimer Arias, John Mbiti, Olav Myklebust—would probably refuse to be categorised simply as 'evangelical' over against 'ecumenical' or vice versa. There are indeed those who could (sometimes admittedly with reservations) be classified as either 'evangelical' or 'ecumenical' and who defend and propagate their respective positions with a considerable degree of consistency. Representatives of the 'evangelical' wing, from the past two decades, would include Peter Beyerhaus, Arthur Johnston, Herbert Kane, Byang Kato, Donald McGavran, Arthur Glasser, and Ralph Winter. Typical ecumenicals would be people such as Burgess Carr, J. G. Davies, Johannes Hoekendijk, Ludwig Rütti, Richard Shaull, M. M. Thomas, and Thomas Wieser.

It is striking that the dividing line does not only separate Protestants, but also Roman Catholics, into two 'camps'. The terminology 'evangelical'—'ecumenical' is not current among Roman Catholics, but the dynamics are the same. In a contribution on 'The Temptation of the "New Christianity" ', an anonymous Roman Catholic author warns his readers against precisely the same theological dangers as an 'evangelical' Protestant would do.[1] Whereas, in the Roman Catholic ecclesiastical structure, the two 'wings' are still being held together organically by their common dependence upon the See of Peter and thus are still able to enter into dialogue with one another, there is in Protestantism a danger that evangelical and ecumenical groups might not only *ignore* but even deliberately *oppose* one another.

The ecumenical viewpoint is today being propagated chiefly in the circles of the World Council of Churches and the evangelical position either as a minority voice within the WCC or by groups who have withdrawn from the WCC or have never belonged to it.

It is not our intention, at this stage, to evaluate the two positions critically, or to express a preference. Naturally such a critical evaluation will *have* to be made at a later stage. We shall therefore return to this in the fourth part of the present study.

THE EVANGELICAL VIEW OF MISSION

Peter Beyerhaus has pointed out that evangelicals do not constitute a monolithic block. There are, he believes, no less than *six* distinguishable evangelical groupings.[2] The first and largest is that of the so-called 'new evangelicals', to which Billy Graham belongs and which attempts to unite all evangelical forces. Over against them we have the separatist fundamentalists which have joined hands in organisations such as Carl McIntire's International Council of Christian Churches. A third group are the 'confessional evangelicals', to which Beyerhaus himself belongs. A fourth category is to be found in the pentecostal and charismatic movements. Fifthly, there are the so-called 'radical evangelicals' who have emerged especially during the Lausanne Congress on World Evangelisation (1974) and among whom Latin Americans such as Samuel Escobar, René Padilla and Orlando Costas are prominent, but also various North American groups, especially Mennonites. They emphasise, on biblical grounds, the necessity of a socio-political involvement. Lastly, there is the group which Beyerhaus identifies as 'ecumenical evangelicals'. They are people who, in spite of often fierce criticism, nevertheless adopt a positive attitude towards the ecumenical movement. Here Beyerhaus mentions Festo Kivengere who, at the concluding communion service of the Lausanne Congress, pleaded with evangelicals to extend the hand of friendship to the WCC. Independently of

Beyerhaus, John de Gruchy distinguishes, in a very readable article, five evangelical groups. His classification tallies, in broad outline, with that of Beyerhaus.[3]

In light of the above it is clear that it will be impossible to give a characterisation of the views of the evangelical movement with which every representative of that movement will agree wholeheartedly. We nevertheless believe that what follows can be regarded as representing, in contrast to the ecumenical, the salient features of the evangelical approach to mission.

The wider interpretation of 'mission' discussed in Chapter 2 tends to be rejected in evangelical circles. Arthur P. Johnston states categorically: 'Historically the mission of the church is evangelism alone', and he chides John Stott for having 'dethroned evangelism as *the* only historical aim of mission'.[4] Harvey Hoekstra regards the introduction of the idea of the 'new mission' and the consequent 'demise of evangelism' as the major proof of the apostasy of the WCC.[5] The fact that John Stott, himself an avowed evangelical, supports a wider understanding of mission than does Johnston and others, proves however that evangelicals do not all see eye to eye on this issue.[6]

The primary motive for mission, according to evangelicals, is to be found in the fact that Christ commanded it (Matt. 28.19-20), and, as the authority of Scripture is accepted without question, this motive is sufficient. Not all evangelicals would, however, concur with Johnston when he says: 'An evangelist committed to the verbal infallibility and full authority of the Scriptures possesses the theological foundation necessary to clearly discern the message and to declare it simply with the power and persuasion given by the Holy Spirit.'[7]

A secondary but equally important motive for mission is to be found in the conviction that, if we do not do mission work, the people who have not heard the gospel will perish eternally. Conversely, if they do hear and accept the gospel, they will enter eternal glory. The gospel is here sometimes understood as primarily 'a subject for belief' rather than 'a way of life'.[8] It is a message which, if 'accepted', guarantees entrance into the Kingdom.

Man's greatest anguish is his lostness before God, his greatest need to be saved from his sins and reconciled to God, his greatest fear for eternal punishment in hell, his greatest hope

for eternal glory in the hereafter. Sin, in this definition, has to
do primarily with man's relationship to God which has gone
wrong. It is, moreover, something personal and individual:
'... the eye of the evangelist is always on the individual, with a
view to motivating personal conversion ... Only individuals *qua*
individuals can be saved.'[9]

Evangelicals tend to regard the world in which we live as
essentially evil, surrendered to the 'prince of this world'
(John 16.11; cf. 1 John 5.19). The Christian may not enjoy this
world; rather he should consistently shun 'the things of this
world'. After all, his citizenship is in heaven. Contact with the
world should therefore be reduced to the minimum.

In the more pronouncedly adventist and dispensational circles
all emphasis lies on the *coming* Kingdom of God. The believer
looks forward with longing to Christ's return. The present is
empty. All that really matters is the glorious future. To
illustrate this by means of a metaphor: The Church is a tiny
lifeboat on a tempestuous sea, busy picking up survivors. The
survivors are hauled into the uncomfortable lifeboat where they
cling together for fear that the waves might toss them out of the
boat. There they huddle, enduring discomfort, cold, damp, or
the scorching rays of the sun. There is little they can do but sail
round and round, looking for more survivors. And their full
attention is riveted on the distant horizon. For one day—nobody
knows exactly when, although all kinds of calculations are
frequently made—a luxury liner will appear and take them to a
safe harbour. They live only for that day. The little lifeboat is
their 'church', but in reality it serves primarily to protect them
against drowning and sharks and to sustain them in view of that
glorious day in the (distant?) future. There is little positive or
dynamic relationship between the lifeboat and the sea. The sea,
the environment, is hostile, evil, and a permanent threat.

Even adventist groups find it difficult, however, to sustain
such a strong futuristic orientation. The portrayal just given
characterises the adventist movement in its early beginnings but
would hardly do justice to all facets of the movement today.

Evangelicals, moreover, reveal a degree of reticence towards
involving themselves with the structures of society: '... there is
no point in tampering with the structures of society, for society
is doomed and about to be destroyed'—as John Stott[10] sums up

this view. Or in the words of Arthur Johnston: '... the goal of Biblical evangelism is not a Christianized world or a Christlike world, but a world evangelization that will bring back the King.'[11] Even John Stott, who defines mission as evangelism plus social action, advocates the primacy of evangelism when discussing the Church's total mission to the world. This should, however, not be taken to mean that evangelicals are devoid of compassion and humanitarian concern. They often reveal greater sacrificial involvement with the existential needs of the victims of society—drug addicts, refugees, the exploited poor, the sick, and so forth—than many ecumenicals who malign them for their lack of social concern.

Most evangelicals would, however, draw a line when it comes to the Church's direct involvement in structural changes in society. Such changes—which are often indeed regarded as desirable by evangelicals—are rather to be viewed as a possible *result* of evangelism. The emphasis is on evolution rather than revolution. The New Testament's attitude to slavery is often cited in this regard. Nowhere in the pages of the New Testament, so the argument goes, is slavery explicitly condemned; and yet, because of the spread of Christianity the whole system was increasingly discredited and eventually abolished. It is for the same reason that evangelicals today involve themselves with education, medical work and schooling in agriculture in their missionary enterprises: this involvement will gradually lead to changes in a nation's entire infrastructure.

There are, however, also those evangelicals who regard such 'services' not as the logical consequence of evangelism but rather as aids to evangelism. Schools, hospitals, orphanages and the like are primarily seen as instruments affording pupils, patients and orphans the opportunity of hearing the gospel. By attending to man's body (for instance in the hospital) or mind (in the mission school), they are preparing him for the gospel. The success of mission schools and hospitals is often judged according to the number of converts they produce.

Because of their reticence in the area of addressing themselves directly to the wrongs in the structures of society—racial discrimination, migratory labour, economic and political exploitation, etc.—evangelicals are often seen as siding with the existing socio-political order. In the expression 'conservative evangelical' the word 'conservative' frequently seems to cover both the theological and political aspects.

As regards non-Christian religions, evangelicals tend to view them as reflecting the involvement of fallen man in the religious quest. In his groping he is prey to the deceptions of Satan, and the systems man devises all too frequently prevent him from responding to Christ's Lordship. A non-Christian religion is a cave in which man hides from God while ostensibly seeking him. If he wants to accept the gospel, he has to turn his back resolutely on his pagan past and embrace the message unconditionally.

The call to mission is often regarded by evangelicals as 'a direct command incumbent upon individual believers based upon the exegesis of the Great Commission'.[12] The authority for evangelism is not derived from the Church, as ecumenicals tend to argue. This emphasis on the individual's calling to mission has been one of the factors that gave birth to the proliferation of evangelical missionary agencies, especially in North America. The supporting base of many of these agencies is not the institutional Church but free associations of individual Christians.

Where the institutional Church plays so little a role in the calling and commissioning of missionaries, it should come as no surprise that often the planting of churches on the mission field receives scant attention. The essential thing is that people are 'won for Christ'; their incorporation into an ecclesiastical organisation is of secondary importance. The Church as institution and organisation may even be considered a handicap to the spiritual growth of converts.

In other evangelical circles the Church is of central importance. Mission is primarily viewed as church planting or extension. What happens inside the church building is what really matters: public worship, baptism, confirmation, prayer meetings; the quality of a convert's Christian life is measured mainly according to his involvement in these activities. The evangelical tendency to withdraw from the world for fear of defilement is, strangely enough, often coupled with the idea of viewing the world as a territory that has to be invaded and its prisoners liberated. In this way parts of the world can be reclaimed for God.

It frequently happens that younger churches established by evangelical missionary enterprises are judged to be immature and hence granted only a limited degree of autonomy. They are regarded as constantly needing the help and advice of the experienced Western missionaries and missionary agencies, especially as regards spiritual matters. A considerable period must elapse before they are judged to be able to decide for themselves what is right and wrong. A degree of trusteeship, which on occasion finds expression in numerous precise and often legalistic prescriptions, is maintained. The final decisions are made in Europe or North America.

MISSION IN ECUMENICAL PERSPECTIVE

If we now, as it were, switch from evangelicalism to the ecumenical position, it is as if we are moving from one planet to another—planets that are often apparently light-years apart! In general terms, the ecumenical position reflects a serious attempt to overcome all the dualisms of the previous view, for instance those between eternal and temporal, soul and body, individual and community, religion and culture, evangelisation and social involvement, vertical and horizontal, salvation and liberation, proclamation and presence, religious and secular, Church and world.

A basic characteristic of the ecumenical position is its openness towards the world. A book by an East German theologian, Hanfried Müller, may serve as an illustration of this: *Von der Kirche zur Welt* (1961). Müller finds the move from the Church to the world exemplified in the life and work of Dietrich Bonhoeffer, the man who started his theological career with a treatise on the Church, *Sanctorum Communio*, the communion of the saints, and concluded it with his letters from a Gestapo prison where the full emphasis was laid on the 'world come of age'. Small wonder that we can detect an explicit Bonhoeffer renaissance behind the modern ecumenical views.

God is not primarily interested in the Church or in saved individuals, as evangelicals tend to say, but in the total human world. The Uppsala Assembly of the WCC (1968) formulated it as follows. Previously, in Luther's case for instance, the basic question of man was where to find the true and merciful God; mission's task was to help man to encounter that God. 'Today the fundamental question is much more that of *true* man.' The aim of mission today is the humanisation of society, by way of service to mankind. Therefore a German Protestant Sunday paper can publish an item with the title: 'India needs help, not mission!' Elsewhere the demand is for 'tractors, not tracts!' Salvation has to do with personal and social liberation from everything that hinders man from attaining a true existence in justice and community. The Church has to serve mankind unselfishly, thus making life on earth more human in every respect. The key concept here, introduced by Hoekendijk, is the Old Testament word *šālôm*, peace, in the sense of harmony in society which, as Uppsala has formulated it, finds expression in 'the emancipation of coloured races, the concern for humanization of industrial relations, various attempts at rural development, the quest for business and professional ethics, the concern for intellectual honesty and integrity'.

In 1964 Manfred Linz published his doctoral thesis *Anwalt der Welt. Zur Theologie der Mission.* In this he analyses German sermons on mission during the period 1900 to 1960. His conclusion is that practically all sermons show that the preacher did not really know what to make of the world. Of course, in a sermon on mission there is bound to be some references to the 'world', but throughout these sermons 'the world' remains singularly anaemic and ill-defined, at most only a geographical entity. Linz then pleads for a corrective. The world has to be moved from the periphery to the centre. Mission should become 'Anwalt der Welt'—advocate for the world. To be a missionary means precisely to be God's co-worker *in* the world. The task of the Church-in-mission is 'to point to God at work in world history' or, more specifically, 'entering into partnership with God in history' (Uppsala Assembly, 1968).

The contemporary secularisation process is in ecumenical circles often judged essentially as positive—even if it may sometimes be necessary to make minute distinctions between concepts such as secular, secularisation, secularism, and secularity.

Involvement with the world may, in a given context, take the form of political or even revolutionary action. This means that mission does not take place in the southern hemisphere only—as many spokesmen of the evangelical view of mission still believe. Rather mission takes place everywhere in the world, in the midst of all those socio-political events which currently reflect the rising tide of expectations and movements for social change to better the lot of the common man. Mission is the total responsibility of the Church for the world. This does not imply that the Church fulfils the same functions as ordinary secular organisations or that she should compete with these. Her task is rather 'to be a source of dissatisfaction and disruption, calling attention to problems, realities, and responsibilities otherwise ignored ... The church as an eschatological community is called to bring the future into the present as an explosive force, to be a sign of the power of reconciliation as it breaks down old barriers and overcomes old conflicts'.[13] Ludwig Rütti puts it as follows: Mission does not take place in the private inwardness of the individual nor in the circumscribed space of the Church, but in the concrete world of the life of man. He, like Hoekendijk, defines mission as the bringing of šālôm, which he describes as getting involved in social processes, permanently exercising criticism of society, and social reform. As such the process of šālôm is universal; it has to be extended to all areas of life and the world.[14]

Directly in line with this lies a statement which Burgess Carr, until 1978 secretary general of the All Africa Conference of Churches, made at a meeting of that body in Lusaka in May 1974: 'We must give our unequivocal support to the liberation movements because they have helped the Church to rediscover a new and radical appreciation of the cross. In accepting the violence of the cross, God, in Jesus Christ, sanctified violence into a redemptive instrument for bringing into being a fuller human life.' He had already said on a previous occasion that it was the explicit aim of the Conference of Churches 'to harness the potential marginal groups ... for agitation and restructuring society ... This is how we perceive the meaning of evangelism and salvation today'.[15]

All this means that the frontier between Church and world, and with it also between salvation history and world history, becomes increasingly vague. In fact, the de-sacralisation of salvation history leads to the sacralisation of world history.[16] What the Church *is*, is unimportant; only what she *does* has value. The Church is at most a hyphen between God and the world. We should therefore not concern ourselves any more with the development of a religious, 'christianised' culture, but rather with secular culture. God is at work *there* rather than in the religious sphere.[17]

As far back as 1964 the central committee of the World Students Christian Federation rejected terms such as 'evangelism', 'witness', 'mission'—and by implication with them also 'Church'—for they all suggest 'the Christian behaviour of speaking before listening, of calling people away from their natural communities into a Christian grouping and of a pre-occupation with the soul at the expense of the whole life'. Over against this the students found the attitude of 'Christian presence' much more acceptable: 'It tries to describe the adventure of being there in the name of Christ, often anonymously, listening before we speak, hoping that men will recognize Jesus and stay where they are, involved in the fierce fight against all that dehumanizes, ready to act against demonic powers, to identify with the outcast, merciless in ridiculing modern idols and new myths.'

Whereas evangelicals seek to apply Scripture deductively—in other words, make Scripture their point of departure from which they draw the line(s) to the present situation—ecumenicals follow the inductive method; the situation in which they find themselves becomes the hermeneutical key. Their thesis is: we determine God's will *from* a specific situation rather than *in* it. The nature and purpose of the Christian mission therefore has to be reformulated from time to time so as to keep pace with events.[18] In the words of the Uppsala Assembly: The world provides the agenda.

Apart from those ecumenicals who put all emphasis on the secularisation of the Church, there are also those who talk in specifically religious categories, but then in such a way that salvation in non-Christian religions is highlighted. These two approaches do not contradict one another; on the contrary, 'secular' and 'religious' ecumenicals complement one another. Just as the dividing line between Church and world grows dim in the first view, so does that between Christian and non-

Christian in the second. If the secular world, outside the Church, is the area of God's activities, the same should apply to the religious world outside Christianity. If it is no longer necessary to transfer people from the world to the Church, it is also superfluous to transfer them from paganism to Christianity. We should therefore no longer accept that the fulfilment of God's plan with the non-Christian peoples depends on the question of whether they get converted to Christianity and join one of its many denominations.[19] The aim of our mission should not be to incorporate people into the Church but rather to liberate them for a saving contact with the best in their own religious traditions; Christian theology should create theological space for the great world religions.[20]

The Christian mission therefore has really no other responsibility in respect of adherents of other religions than to help the Hindu become a better Hindu and the Buddhist a better Buddhist. In our dialogue (for this concept replaces the older idea of 'mission') it may be that the Buddhist becomes a Christian; it is, however, equally possible that the Christian may become a Buddhist or both end up being agnostics (J. G. Davies). Echoing a statement of Paul it can be said that mission means to become godless for the godless, a nihilist for the nihilists, and for those outside the Church somebody outside the Church—omitting, in this process, the 'like' which Paul includes in his exposition in 1 Cor. 9.20-22. In the report of the Bangkok Conference on 'Salvation Today' (1973) the brother who has found the entire traditional language of the Church meaningless and has become 'an atheist by the grace of God' is praised. The Church therefore becomes dispensable and redundant, indeed, even a stumbling-block. The circle is thus completed: The centuries old *extra ecclesiam nulla salus* (no salvation outside the Church) has gradually made way for *extra ecclesiam multa salus* (ample salvation outside the Church), and occasionally here and there already tends towards *intra ecclesiam nulla salus* (no salvation inside the Church).

RECONCILABLE POSITIONS?

The evangelical and ecumenical approaches to mission have to a large extent dominated the theory and practice of mission in recent decades. The polarisation appears to be complete: Proclamation stands over against 'Christian presence', Jesus as Redeemer over against Jesus the Man for others, redemption over against humanisation, the salvation of the soul over against liberation and revolution.

We do not, at this stage, intend making a choice between the two approaches. It is, however, impossible to take no stand at all; we all approach any object of investigation with some preconceived ideas and presuppositions. Nobody is completely objective.

Nevertheless, it is possible, even while holding a view of one's own, to listen to the opinions of others. Theology, after all, is also practised by listening. Especially in controversial matters it is important to try to understand *why* a person or group adopts a specific position. To understand somebody's motive in no way implies approving of his views. As a matter of fact, no meaningful criticism is possible unless we are at least prepared to accept the good intentions of the person with whom we differ.

The tragedy is that the more extreme representatives of the two 'camps' demonstrate little serious desire to enter into dialogue with their opponents. All too frequently there is, on both sides, a surprising eagerness to find fault with one another, coupled with a barely concealed delight at every new 'proof' of the opponent's extremism. Undoubtedly it is the easiest thing in the world to shoot the ecumenical position to pieces, from the evangelical angle, using labels such as 'liberalism', 'neo-Marxism', 'revolutionary ideologies', 'rejection of Scripture's authority', etc. And it is equally easy for the ecumenically minded to denounce his evangelical colleague as 'bigoted', 'conservative', 'old-fashioned', 'on the side of the oppressors', 'blind to man's needs', and so on. Unless we approach one another in humility, we do not help anybody and only intensify the polarisation. True theology can only be practised in weakness, with an accompanying self-critical attitude. When we trace the understanding and motive of mission in Scripture and follow it through the nineteen subsequent centuries of history, we shall become very conscious of the limitations, inadequacy and relativity of our own insights into this great mystery.

PART II

THE BIBLICAL FOUNDATION
OF MISSION

CHAPTER FIVE

A BIBLICAL THEOLOGY
OF MISSION

It is customary, especially in Protestant circles, to open a discussion on the theology of mission with the 'biblical foundations'. An example of this is J. H. Bavinck, who is in his *Introduction to the Science of Missions*, after a brief survey of the nature of the study of mission and the subdivisions of mission theory, proceeds to the 'biblical foundation of missions'.[1] As soon as this 'biblical foundation' has been firmly laid, one may move ahead to elucidate the practice of mission (the descriptive task) and evaluate it critically in light of the Bible (the normative task).

There can be little doubt, in both Protestant and Roman Catholic circles, about the necessity of a biblical foundation for mission. Ferdinand Hahn confirms the consensus in this respect today, but adds that it may not be as self-evident as we might think, for nineteenth-century missionary theology proceeded differently. Gustav Warneck, father of Protestant (and, in fact, also Roman Catholic) missiology, propounded, apart from biblical, dogmatic and ethical foundations for mission, ecclesiastical, historical and ethnological foundations as well.[2] Among early Protestant missionaries, especially pietists and Moravians, serious studies about the biblical foundation of mission were likewise little in evidence.

In traditional Roman Catholic missiology the situation was not markedly different. It attached even less importance to finding a biblical foundation for mission. In the second edition of his *Inleiding in de Missiewetenschap*, Alphons Mulders devotes only ten pages to what he calls 'biblical mission theology'. Even in these pages, however, only a few paragraphs deal with the foundation of mission as such. Much more time, energy and space are devoted to 'traditional', 'dogmatic' and 'moral' missionary theology.[3] In his 927 page-long missiological handbook, *Machet zu Jüngern alle Völker*, Thomas Ohm refers only in passing to the biblical foundation of mission in his chapters on the 'cause', 'origin' and 'aim' of mission.[4] Scriptural data do indeed enter into the discussion more fully in the sections on missionary planning, the missionary call, preparation for mission, the missionary himself, and the various missionary activities, but with the *foundation* as such it has to do only indirectly.

INDUCTIVE OR DEDUCTIVE?

It would be wrong to deduce from the above that Protestant missionary theology is by definition more biblical than its Roman Catholic counterpart. To place a lengthy chapter on the 'biblical foundation of mission' at the beginning of a treatise on missionary theology, is in itself no guarantee that what follows will indeed be more biblical than if such formal reflection is absent. The reason for this is what we all involuntarily read the Bible from within a specific historical and social context and then project our own convictions back into the Bible. This tendency is nowhere more evident than in the many books on Jesus published in the past two centuries. At the beginning of this century Albert Schweitzer published his *The Quest of the Historical Jesus* in which he demonstrated brilliantly how every previous scholar had simply mirrored in the pages of the New Testament his own idea of who Jesus of Nazareth was. Schweitzer's own attempt at a reconstruction of the person and work of Jesus, however, in this respect hardly differed from those of his predecessors. In each instance the 'historical Jesus' proved to be the historian's Jesus. Time and again the Christ of Scripture is simply identified with the Christ of one's own experience.

It is customary to claim, especially in theologically conservative circles such as those discussed in the previous chapter, that Holy Scripture is the only norm of theology. The point of departure here is that theology is to be worked out 'deductively'; first, it has to be established precisely what Scripture says on a specific matter or in a certain pericope, then normative guidelines that apply to the believer in his present situation, have to be derived from this. But from what has been said above, it ought to be clear that the deductive method contains no guarantee that its use will indeed establish beyond doubt what the Bible has to say on specific contemporary matters. We usually presuppose far too readily that we may summon the Bible as a kind of objective arbitrator in the case of theological disputes. In this way we are blinded to the presuppositions lurking behind our own interpretations.

In ecumenical circles, on the other hand, the 'inductive' method is usually used; one takes the actual situation as point of departure (Uppsala, 1968: 'The world provides the agenda') and attempts to read Scripture in light of the situation. The context becomes the hermeneutical key which makes possible his 'correct' understanding of the Bible. Gerhard Ebeling has defined Church history as 'the history of the interpretation of the Bible.' Today there is a tendency to describe the entire world history in these terms. This is the ultimate consequence of an 'inductive' method in theology.

We are, however, faced with a false alternative if we are asked to choose between a 'deductive' and an 'inductive' method. The first is in any case impracticable for, in spite of the most careful research imaginable, nineteen centuries separate us from the most recent biblical document. We have no immediate access to it. Even if our present context does not co-determine our interpretation of Scripture, our historical and theological traditions do. An American Protestant reads the Bible in a way which differs from that of a German Catholic or a Kimbanguist from Zaire. The *second* method is practicable but not justifiable. Historical events and personal or group experience are too ambivalent to serve as key for the interpretation of a biblical text.[5]

What then? Should we try a third method? Actually, no third method exists as a handy, clearly-defined 'recipe'. We can only, with full awareness of the limitations and relativity of 'deductive' *and* 'inductive' approaches, make use of both. As G. Casalis puts it: 'Theology, nurtured by the word of God, reflects on a historical situation in which we are wholly and responsibly involved.' Or elsewhere: 'The situation is not God's word; God's word is not outside the situation; only a reference back to both the analysis (of the situation) and the word permits the discovery of all dimensions of the situation.'[6] It is important to note the word 'permit' in Casalis's statement. It suggests that, even if we follow the 'right' method, we still do not have any guarantee that we indeed interpret either the word or the situation correctly. We have already, in a previous chapter, argued that the practice of theology remains a risk. We can engage in theology only haltingly.

This reasoning is not unimportant for our reflection on the biblical foundation of mission. On the contrary. It explains, for instance, why this chapter is not the first in this book. What happens only too frequently—when missiological publications open with a section on the biblical foundation—is that the author proceeds from the assumption that his readers already know what mission is (their definition tallies with his own!) and that his primary task now is to establish what the Bible has to say about mission, thus defined.

We have proceeded along a different path. By drawing attention to the confusion about the meaning and content of the concept 'mission', we have at least made it possible to listen to what Scripture says about this with a certain degree of openness. We are now aware of the fact that our own definitions cannot without further ado advance the claim of being the only valid ones. We may even discover that not even in the Bible itself is there any carefully defined and unalterable notion of mission, but rather a variety of emphases and approaches within the wider framework of an understanding of mission as God's concern with the world for the salvation of man.

THE BIBLE AS A 'MINE'

The deductive and inductive methods—practised in isolation from or over against one another—have yet another disadvantage. In both instances it can easily happen that, consciously or unconsciously, the reader refers only to the biblical data which particularly appeal to him or provide the 'answers' he is looking for. The evangelical-ecumenical controversy largely springs from this selective use of Scripture. As a result, it inevitably happens that a canon develops within the canon; what is not to the liking of a particular group is simply ignored. In liberation theology circles the Exodus story or Jesus' message in the synagogue in Nazareth (Luke 4.16-20) constitutes such a canon within the canon. In evangelical missionary circles, on the other hand, it may happen that the Great Commission (Matt. 28.18-20) is regarded as the central mandate for mission.

This approach easily leads to the Bible being regarded as a 'mine' from which—in the case currently under discussion, namely that of the biblical foundation for mission—'missionary texts' are with some difficulty excavated and brought to the surface. It is granted that the largest part of the Bible, especially the Old Testament, is undoubtedly 'particularistic'—its focus is largely on Israel—and therefore it hardly provides a basis for a world-wide mission. If, however, we look carefully and persistently among the rocks and rubble we will indeed find genuine gold nuggets. The Old Testament will yield stories of pagans such as Ruth and Naaman who accepted Israel's faith and 'universalistic' expressions in the Psalms and Isaiah 40-66, and the New Testament describes encounters between Jesus and non-Jews. Sometimes no such gold nuggets are visible; then the ore has to be smelted carefully and the hidden gold extracted from it by means of the laborious process of exegesis and hermeneutics.

Let us illustrate what we mean. During the past few centuries the concepts 'mission' and 'missionary' accrued to themselves very specific meanings in the Western world, both Roman Catholic and Protestant. It is therefore obvious that, if the reader approaches the Bible with this meaning in his subconsciousness, he will feel attracted to those texts which correspond to his preconceived view.

The beginning of the modern missionary era coincided with the beginnings of the European discovery of the world beyond its shores. By that time Europe was completely christianised. 'Pagans' were people who lived in distant countries across the ocean. 'Mission' meant going to them; 'missionaries' were the people who went. 'Mission' thus developed a strong geographical component. After all, the Great Commission (Matt. 28.19) explicitly says: 'Go ye therefore ...' The locality, not the task, decided whether someone was a missionary or not; he is a missionary if he is commissioned by the Church in one locality to go and work elsewhere. The greater the distance between these two places, the clearer it is that he is a missionary.

A second element was added to the geographical. Because the moden missionary movement largely coincided in time with the Western colonisation of the non-Western world, it, unintentionally and unnoticed, became intertwined with elements of Western feelings of superiority, power, knowledge, and the paternalistic idea of the haves bestowing on the have-nots. Mission was therefore understood in the typical activistic Western categories of the crossing of—preferably remote—geographical frontiers, to impart to peoples of inferior cultures something they did not possess.

If theologians with these preconceived ideas about what mission is or ought to be, study the Bible, it is to be expected that they, at least as far as the Old Testament is concerned, will come to the conclusion that the Old Testament reflects an 'entirely passive character' with regard to mission. Indeed, the idea of a going out to evangelise the nations is almost entirely absent from it.[7] The sole exception in the Old Testament, some people would grant, is the book of Jonah. Here we certainly have a story which conforms to our traditional Western view of mission: a prophet journeys to a distant country to proclaim the message of Yahweh to a heathen people.

JESUS OF NAZARETH AND MISSION

As regards the New Testament, the four Gospels are usually also seen within this 'particularistic' framework. The idea of a mission to heathen appears to fall outside Jesus' field of vision. Adolf von Harnack was one of the first theologians who, early in this century (1902), interpreted the Gospels accordingly. He argued that none of the Gospel sayings which had traditionally been understood to refer to a mission among Gentiles, could be traced directly to Jesus. They are all of a later origin.[8] The views of Harnack and others caused many in missionary circles either simply to ignore critical theology, or to try, in an apologetic way, to 'save' mission as understood traditionally in the Western Church (compare the contributions of Karl Bornhäuser, Max Meinertz and Friedrich Spitta, all within only a few years of the first publication of Harnack's study).

We are not suggesting that Harnack and those who followed or opposed him, used the Bible as a 'mine' from which they

unearthed texts in support of their respective positions. It is
nevertheless true that, first, they tended to get bogged down in
small details where the preferences of the researcher only too
often played a decisive role, and secondly, they accepted as
axiomatic the traditional Western definition of mission as point
of departure.

In the light of remarks in previous chapters from which it
appears that mission may with equal justification be defined
differently and more broadly, we want to employ a different
method, namely, that of trying to establish the central thrust of
the message of Scripture.[9] We would, of course, have to take
cognisance of the shades of difference and variation of scriptural
data in this regard. It would be an unjustified over-simplification to believe that all biblical authors agree in the
minutest detail.

Our emphasis, in this investigation, will be on the biblical
foundation of mission. This will, for instance, imply that in our
discussion of the data of the four Gospels, the attitude of the
historical Jesus to a mission to Gentiles will not be of decisive
importance for our subject. To me this represents something of
a shift away from an earlier position when I still believed, like
Meinertz, Spitta and others, that the positive attitude of the
historical Jesus towards the Gentile mission was basic to a
scriptural foundation of mission.[10] Today I would put it
differently: although the question about Jesus' attitude towards
an eventual Gentile mission undoubtedly has theological implications for our understanding of his ministry, this is of no more
than secondary importance for our present investigation into a
biblical foundation for mission. To anticipate our conclusion:
there would have been a Gentile mission in the post-
Resurrection period even if the historical Jesus had had no
contact with non-Jews and had said nothing about them. That
he did indeed encounter non-Jews and said some remarkably
positive things about them, should not be interpreted as a *motive*
for the Church to engage in mission but rather as a *result* of the
essentially missionary dimension of God's revelation in him.

It is this essentially missionary dimension, in both Old and
New Testaments, which we now want to expose, paying
attention to the following elements:

God's compassion, and its meaning for the foundation of mission; the historical character of the biblical revelation; the missionary dimension of the suffering of the witness; mission as God's work.

CHAPTER SIX

GOD'S COMPASSION

THE ELECTION OF ISRAEL

In the Old Testament God reveals himself as the One who among other characteristics has compassion on the poor, the oppressed, the weak and the outcast.[1] Israel's election is to be attributed to this divine compassion, not to any good qualities Israel might have possessed. One of the most moving descriptions of this is to be found in Ezek. 16.3-6: Israel is portrayed as the child of an Amorite father and a Hittite mother, who, after birth, was discarded in the open field, unwashed and uncared for. Yahweh, however, had compassion on this foundling: 'Then I came by and saw you kicking helplessly in your own blood; I spoke to you, there in your blood, and bade you live.'

This is why the Exodus event ('I am the Lord your God, who brought you of Egypt, out of the land of slavery'; Exod. 20.2) became the corner-stone of Israel's confession of faith. It is this compassion for the unworthy which distinguished Yahweh from the other gods. He is 'father of the fatherless, the widow's champion ... (He) gives the friendless a home and brings out the prisoner safe and sound' (Ps. 68.5-6). The people of Israel are therefore challenged: 'Search into days gone by, ... and ask if any deed as mighty as this has been seen or heard ... Or did ever a god attempt to come and take a nation for himself away from another nation, with a challenge, and with signs, portents and wars, with a strong hand and an outstretched arm, ... as the Lord your God did for you in Egypt in the sight of you all? You have had sure proof that the Lord is God; there is no other' (Deut. 4.32, 34-35). Whereas the gods of the predominantly hierophantic religions stressed order, harmony, integration and the maintenance of the status quo, the violation of which would provoke their fury, Yahweh revealed himself as the God of change, the God who comes to the rescue of the poor and the needy.

The basis for God's election of Israel was to be found throughout in his spontaneous and unmerited mercy (Deut. 7.6-8). Time and again the prophets reminded the people of Israel that their election could not be attributed to their own extraordinary character but solely to God's compassion. Problems were, however, not wanting and in the course of time the covenant was perverted into something it was never intended to be. Instead of God's faithfulness to Israel being contingent on her obedience to his law, the Israelites came to feel that God was unconditionally committed to preserving Israel because of their superiority to the heathen nations. In Jeremiah's day, this distortion became the central issue in his confrontation with the false prophets.

In what came to be known as Late Judaism, the reconceptualisation went as follows: Abraham was chosen, it was suggested, not on the basis of God's grace but because of his own achievements. Not only was he the father of Phoenician and Egyptian astrology; he was also the first missionary who gathered crowds of proselytes around himself. The story of the Sinai covenant was also revised. God, so the new version went, had offered his *tôrâh* in all (that is, seventy) languages to the peoples of the earth. Only Israel, the most insignificant nation—the very last to whom God had come with his offer— accepted the *tôrâh* and thus saved God from embarrassment. Now the Gentiles had no excuse any more; indeed, God had offered them the *tôrâh* so that they *could* not have an excuse any more and Israel's reward might be doubled. Just as the Gentiles, since Sinai, bore an indelible stamp as God's enemies, so Israel was marked as the people and friend of God. The *tôrâh* bestowed upon Israel a particular character which made her practically independent of God. Yahweh, after all, *needed* Israel; without her he would have been a God without worshippers. If Israel had refused the *tôrâh*, the earth would once again have become 'without form and void' (Gen. 1.2). God's kingship was derived from Israel, not vice versa. *Israel* had elected *God*, saved him in his distress, made him into what he is. Since the Sinai covenant he is therefore not called 'the God of all nations' any more, but only 'God of Israel'. Israel was a 'holy people'; this holiness was, however, no longer what it used to be in the Old Testament, a gift from God. It was an attribute of Israel. The quality of holiness was inextinguishable; even if Israel sinned, it remained God's people. Thus human attributes supplanted divine grace.[2]

Since the earliest times, but especially from the eighth century BC onwards, the prophets unleashed passionate polemic against the development of these tendencies. Not only should Israel have attributed her total existence to God's compassion and mercy; God also expected of his people a similar compassion towards others.

The purpose of election was service and where this was withheld, election lost its meaning: 'For you alone have I cared among all the nations of the world; *therefore* will I punish you for all your iniquities' (Amos 3.2). Election primarily conveyed neither privilege, nor favouritism, but rather responsibility. Israel, who had been a stranger in Egypt, had to have compassion on the stranger in her midst. The constitutive element here was neither the ethnic, nor the biological, nor the cultural; the stranger who lived in Israel had to be accepted completely and without reserve. The same paschal and burnt offering regulations applied to him (Num. 9.14; 15.14), also the same right of sanctuary (Josh. 20.9). Nor was Israel permitted to lose sight of the fact that essentially she had no advantage over the nations around her: 'Are not you Israelites like Cushites to me? says the Lord. Did I not bring Israel up from Egypt, the Philistines from Caphtor, the Aramaeans from Kir?' (Amos 9.7).

THE BOOK OF JONAH

It is in this respect that the book of Jonah gives us a matchless object lesson of Yahweh's compassion.[3] We have already called attention to the tendency to regard this book as a missionary document par excellence since it seems to tally remarkably with the traditional understanding of mission as the crossing of geographical frontiers.

If we look at it more closely, however, we find little that resembles the popular missionary story. In such narratives the author usually portrays a heroic missionary convinced of his missionary calling, who goes to a distant land, encounters unimaginable hazards, but gradually overcomes them. Out of his preaching a young church develops and much attention is given in the narrative to the quality and spiritual life of the new Christians.

The book of Jonah differs radically from such missionary stories. It says precious little, for instance, about the reaction of the Ninevites. We are tempted to ask: did their conversion last? The book appears to be hardly interested in that aspect, so our question remains unanswered.

The concern of the book is rather with Jonah himself—a 'missionary' without a missionary's heart—and through Jonah with Israel. The message God directed him to proclaim to the Ninevites—the rapacious enemies of the Northern Kingdom—involved no call to embrace the faith of Yahweh. It was one of impending judgment, not of grace. The entire story is a holy satire, because the pagans—recipients of the message of God's wrath—did what Israel—recipients of the message of God's mercy—so frequently refused to do: they turned to God in penitence. And yet, because Jonah understood something of God's grace ('I knew that thou art a God gracious and compassionate, long-suffering and ever constant, and always willing to repent of the disaster!'—Jonah 4.2; cf. Exod. 34.6), he tried to subvert God's plan. He was not going to allow the Ninevites to be pardoned!

The emphasis of the Jonah story is therefore not on the conversion of Nineveh; it is a call to Israel to allow themselves to be converted to a compassion comparable to that of Yahweh. The story's missionary significance does not lie in the physical journey of a prophet of Yahweh to a pagan country but in Yahweh's being a God of compassion—a compassion which knows no boundaries. What is being castigated is Jonah's and Israel's exclusivistic appropriation of God's favour and compassion to themselves. As Verkuyl puts it: 'Why is Jonah really so angry? For no other reason than that God is treating those outside his covenant the same as he is those within', and then adds: 'The book ends with an unsettling question which is never answered.'[4]

THE MINISTRY OF JESUS

Compassion is also the essence of the New Testament message, especially that of Jesus. The church in mission is sometimes embarrassed by the fact that, according to the Gospels, Jesus said very little about Gentiles and had little contact with them. The impression is created that this state of affairs considerably narrows the basis of mission. The real basis for mission in Jesus' ministry should, however, be looked for elsewhere—in his boundless compassion. It was *this* that distinguished him from all contemporary groups—Pharisees, Sadducees, Zealots and Essenes—and not the idea of a Gentile mission as such. The Pharisees after all also had a missionary programme. Jesus even said that they were prepared to traverse sea and land to make *one* convert (Matt. 23.15). So the difference did not lie here.

Unlike the other teachers of his day Jesus did not recruit disciples to teach them the *tôrâh*, but in order that they might 'follow' him. He questioned traditional Jewish values at decisive points, especially by turning to the outcasts of society and by proclaiming to them the message of God's compassion. Simultaneously he radicalised the ethical demands of the *tôrâh* by focusing on the command to love, especially to love the enemy. And in his miracles his concern was with the totality of human need—poverty, sickness, hunger, sin, demonic oppression.

It is striking to note the way in which the people on whom Jesus had compassion are described. They are referred to as the poor, the blind, the cripple, the leprous, the hungry, those who weep, the sick, the little ones, the widows, the captives, those who are last, those who are weary and heavily burdened with religious legalism, the lost sheep. It is equally striking that, whereas these descriptions suggest boundless compassion, the Pharisees refer to the same categories of people as 'sinners' and 'the rabble who know nothing of the Law'.[5]

Time and again the concern here is with people who are pushed to the periphery or even excluded from Jewish society—Gentiles, naturally, but also Samaritans, women, children, lepers, the tax-gatherers and women of bad reputation. Jesus even entered the homes of non-Jews. He told the parable of the lost son, in which he cut at the root all human justification by works and pride of achievement; he also told the story of the good Samaritan and thereby exposed all national Jewish self-righteousness and pride of descent. He asked the young lawyer: 'Which of these three do you think was neighbour to the man who fell into the hands of robbers?' And the lawyer grudgingly had to admit the compassion of the despised Samaritan: 'The one who showed him kindness' (Luke 10.36-37). The most radical and revolutionary demand, as illustrated by this parable, is the call to love the enemy (Matt. 5.44; Luke 6.27-29). Especially Luke, the evangelist who, more than the others, emphasises the element of forgiveness in Jesus' ministry, brings this to the fore. This kind of love resists all forms and expressions of racial pride within the disciple's heart.

VENGEANCE SUPERSEDED

In this respect we pay attention to the pericope in Luke which has more or less become the key text of the modern theology of liberation: Luke 4.16-30. Joachim Jeremias and Walter Grundmann[6] have argued that the storm of protest which developed in the synagogue in Nazareth during Jesus' preaching should in all probability be ascribed to the fact that Jesus had dared to omit any reference to the 'day of the vengeance of our God'.

Unlike Matthew and Mark, Luke places this episode at the very beginning of Jesus' public ministry. In this unique event the entire future pattern of Jesus' ministry unfolds itself. Jesus reads from Isa. 61.1-2—a text that the synagogue regarded as messianic. In contrast to John the Baptist, who announced the Kingdom as near, at the very door, Jesus now categorically states: '*Today*, in your very hearing this text has come true.'

Just as important as the announcement of the presence of the Kingdom is the way in which Jesus quotes from the Isaiah scroll. He deliberately breaks off before the words, 'and a day of the vengeance of our God' (Isa. 61.2) and returns the scroll to the servant. In the synagogue preaching of that day it was customary to put the whole emphasis precisely on these words—God's vengeance on his (and therefore Israel's) enemies. Jesus, however, does the unimaginable: He reads only the portion on grace, not the one on vengeance! This was unforgivable, especially as it implied that the same attitude might be expected of his followers.

Jeremias and Grundmann argue that this omission determined the entire subsequent course of events in Nazareth. They
believe, however, that verse 22 has usually been wrongly
translated, for instance: 'There was a general stir of admiration;
they were surprised that words of such grace should fall from
his lips'. It should rather be translated: 'They protested with
one voice and were furious, because he only spoke about (God's
year of) mercy (and omitted the words about the Messianic
vengeance)'.[7] The next sentence concurs with this translation:
' "Is not this Joseph's son?" they asked.' In other words: he
never studied; he is no rabbi; how dare he proclaim the dawn of
the new era, and who gives him the authority arbitrarily to
truncate Scripture by omitting the reference to divine
vengeance?[8]

That Jeremias is probably correct in his exegesis of the
events in Nazareth also emerges from a comparison with what
we find in Luke 7.22-23 (par. Matt. 11.5-6).[9] Jesus here quotes
freely from three Isaiah pericopes: Isa. 29.18-20, 35.5-6 and
61.1-2. In all three instances there is reference to the
eschatological day of vengeance (Isa. 29.20; 35.4; 61.2) which
Jesus, however, omits from his message to John the Baptist.
This can hardly be unintentional. Therefore the added remark:
'... and happy is the man who does not find me a stumbling-
block' (Luke 7.23; Matt. 11.6). In other words: Blessed is
everyone who does not take offence at the fact that the era of
salvation differs from what he has expected, that God's
compassion on the poor and outcast has superseded divine
vengeance!

We could quote other examples of this compassion in Jesus'
ministry. Compassion may indeed be called *the* key concept in
his total ministry. The above examples however will have to
suffice. In light of this Martin Hengel is correct when he says
that the ministry of Jesus was hardly less 'missionary' in nature
than that of his disciples after Easter. He also quotes with
approval Erich Grässer, who says: 'The Church saw in Jesus
the archetype of the missionary.'[10]

What we have said here about Jesus' compassionate ministry
as foundation for mission is not the same as identifying
sympathy as missionary motive. During the rise of Pietism
sympathy was a particularly dominant motive for mission. E.

Jansen Schoonhoven reminds us that even today there are many
supporters of mission who believe that, on the 'mission field',
there are only lamentable creatures, permanently haunted by
fear, people who exist in spiritual and bodily misery. For
Western Christians who hold such views it may come as a rude
awakening to hear a conservative theologian such as Karl Heim,
a man who wholeheartedly supported the Church's world-wide
mission, saying: 'Maybe Buddhists often live more happily and
harmoniously and die more peacefully than many Christians.'
Sympathy of the nature referred to above thus hardly provides a
solid basis of mission—it is too sentimental and moreover
emerges from Western man's feeling of superiority. Biblical
compassion is something entirely different and indeed provides a
genuine source of mission.[11]

To summarise: in both Old and New Testaments God
reveals himself as the One who has compassion on the less
privileged, the marginal figures, and the outcasts. He is the God
of grace. If we look for a biblical foundation for mission we will
find it in this essential element of biblical religion as a religion
of mercy and compassion, rather than in incidental references to
encounters between members of the biblical covenant people and
the surrounding nations. A religion in which compassion
occupies so central a position, cannot but be a missionary
religion. Verkuyl is correct when he discerns in all our Lord's
encounters with Gentiles 'Jesus itching with a holy impatience
for that day when all the stops shall be pulled as the message
goes out to the Gentiles'.[12]

With this observation of Verkuyl we have, however, already
touched upon a second element of a biblical foundation for
mission, to which we now turn our attention.

CHAPTER SEVEN

GOD AND HISTORY

THE RELIGIOUS DIVIDE

Apart from the biblical message of compassion there is another element which is of decisive significance for a biblical foundation for mission—the fact that the biblical religion, in Old *and* New Testaments, reveals throughout an *historical* character. And history, in order to he history, has to be *specific*, localised, particular. It is precisely this, however, that becomes a problem for people who are looking for a biblical foundation of mission. The Old Testament especially has always caused embarrassment for the Church in mission because of its apparently completely one-sided concentration on Israel. The Old Testament is 'particularistic'. People say this almost with regret, as if they would have liked to add: 'We should so much have preferred the Bible to concern itself not only with Israel, but with all of humanity, from the very beginning.' It therefore appears that the fact that the Bible reveals a historical religion, is a stumbling-block rather than a help for a missionary foundation. On the surface a religion which is built on eternal, universal values appears to be more appropriate for such a purpose. But what do we mean when we claim that the religion of the Bible in its essence reveals an historical character?

In spite of many differences, the ancient religions of Egypt, Babylon and Canaan had many fundamental characteristics in common. They found expression in ritual practices which were primarily related to problems experienced by a predominantly agrarian population, practices in which the king as earthly representative of the gods played an important role. Such a ritual pattern usually included the following: a dramatic presentation of the death and resurrection of the fertility god, a sacred battle against the powers of chaos, a triumphal procession, the accession to the throne, and then the sacred nuptial. All these religions contain a strong cyclical element based on the sequence of the seasons, year by year. By way of a re-enactment of primordial events the mythical time is 'brought back'. In this way the status quo is stabilised.[1]

Undoubtedly the Old Testament canon contains many elements that were originally part of the ancient Near Eastern religious world. These in turn were adapted by its writers. Because of its uniqueness, the self-critical element in Israel's religion precluded complete identification with the nature cycle and preserved it from becoming a victim of religious ritual tied to the seasons—new life, maturity, ageing and decay, and then once again resurrection and new life. Faith in Yahweh challenged this cyclical view; even in the Wisdom literature the cycle was replaced by the (historical) dimensions of cause and effect.[2] Yahweh is God of *history*. The biblical cult is an 'exodus celebration', ever again a new journey into the future. Its concern is not with festivals of remembrance or with a return to a one-time appearance of God in mythical, primordial time (a hierophany), because man is not caught up in a passive commemoration, directed to the past. The Bible speaks predominantly in terms of personal relationships, it uses 'encounter terminology' and hardly ever treats any question abstractly or as an aspect of general concepts. This is what Daniel T. Niles meant when he said that the biblical revelation could not be taught, but only proclaimed: 'The Christian evangelist announces that something has happened which is of both immediate and ultimate significance ... The adherents of other religions ... expound the teachings of their own religions as the true interpretation of the meaning and responsibilities of life.'[3] Bishop Lesslie Newbigin tells of the astonishment of a devoted and learned master of the Ramakrishna Mission when he discovered that Newbigin was prepared to stake his entire faith as Christian on the essential reliability of the New Testament historical records about Jesus: 'To him it seemed axiomatic that such vital matters of religious truth could not be allowed to depend upon the accidents of history. If the truths which Jesus exemplified and taught are true, then they are true always and everywhere, whether a person called Jesus ever lived or not.'[4]

The danger of becoming overwhelmed by the ahistorical cultic forms of the religions of surrounding peoples constituted a permanent threat to the Old and New Testament believers. In the early period this threat came especially from the Canaanite fertility cults as personified in the Baalim and the Asherim. In the New Testament period it usually assumed the form of the Greek mystery religions or Gnosticism, which agreed in at least one respect: their ahistorical understanding of reality.

There is indeed an element of legitimacy in the idea of the cultic repetition of what has once been. Israel's festivals were such cultic re-enactments of the exodus, the entry into Canaan, etc.[5] The presence of Christ in Holy Communion is another example, as is Kierkegaard's idea of the status of the Christian as 'being contemporary with Christ'. However, when the cyclical thought-pattern takes over and the historical character of biblical revelation and of the life of the believer in the present makes room for the idea of eternal, immutable and timeless truths, one has left the soil of biblical revelation.

An equally unacceptable companion to ahistoricity is the tendency to 'over-historicise'. This may happen in two ways. First, where it is maintained vigorously that biblical revelation has to do with historical events, but the historical correctness of every detail of the story in the remote past must be clung to desperately. It then follows that the story becomes so completely *static*, with the emphasis on eternal immutables, that it becomes more important to preserve the historical correctness of the original event than it is to move into the future and act in light of that event. The Bible then becomes an oracle. Conservatism and dead orthodoxy then become more important than taking the risk of stepping into the future and devising new 'models' of obedience.

Where the one form of over-historicisation leads to a hyper-accentuation of the past, the other puts all emphasis on the future. We find an example of this in apocalypticism. Within the framework of utopian categories an overwhelmingly glorious future is expected, a future which bears no resemblance to the drab and dreary present. No attempt is made to change the present dismal conditions. All that remains is to sit and wait for the dawn of a new day—as the Qumran community did in their settlements near the Dead Sea.

The two contrasting forms of over-historicisation are in reality closely related. In both instances the present is left empty. God is regarded as active either only in the past or only in the future. And because the present is empty, genuine missionary involvement is possible in neither case. Mission implies something new happening in the here and now. Mission is, by definition, an eminently historical event. This becomes clear when we compare the early Christian Church with the Qumran community. The latter, like the early Church, also understood itself as the salvation-community of the end-time. But the two communities drew contrasting conclusions from this consciousness: the Church understood herself as a missionary movement whereas the Qumran community withdrew from the world and shied away from all missionary involvement.[6]

GOD BEGINS SOMETHING NEW

Our thesis is that precisely the historical character of biblical revelation is of essential significance for a biblical foundation for mission, however paradoxical this may appear. The Old Testament concentration on Israel, far from reflecting a non-missionary dimension, is in reality the very opposite. History has to be specific, or it is no history. Without this element of specificity the salvation of Yahweh would have been ahistorical. A careful reading of the Old Testament indeed reveals the specifically missionary significance of Yahweh's dealings with Israel.

Abraham's call (Gen. 12.1-3) already indicates this. With Abraham God embarks upon a history. The patriach is snatched from the cyclical stanglehold of the Amorite and Sumerian religious world and called to journey into the unknown—an event that symbolises that what follows in Abraham's life is truly 'history', something new, where something different may happen at any time, a transcending of the predictability of the cyclic thought-world.

What is more, the history of Abraham's calling refers back to the Babel episode in Gen. 11.1-9 (in fact, Abraham's genealogical register follows immediately after the story of the tower, 11.10-32). In Babel man's attempt to procure salvation fails miserably. Thereafter God begins something new. What Babel has lost, is promised and guaranteed in the history of Abraham's election. Gen. 12 follows on Gen. 11—the history of

Israel is a continuation of God's dealings with the nations. Precisely as the elect the patriarch, and with him Israel, is called into the world of nations. Every one of the Yahwist's Abrahamic stories in some way or the other touches upon the relationship between Abraham (and thus also Israel) and the nations.[7] Yahweh creates history by breaking out of the circle of eternal return and going, with his people, into the future, with Abraham out of Ur, with Israel out of Egypt, en route towards the nations.

History is, however, always something ambivalent—a matter which will be discussed more fully in a later chapter. Even biblical history does not escape this problem of ambivalence. It is not 'salvation history' in the sense of a clearly reconstruable, progressive course, a logical and consistent unfolding of events, a calculable project. It is, on the contrary, a history full of gaps, which is enacted on different levels.

One of the elements of tension in the Old Testament is to be found in the ambivalence of the concept 'Israel'. Israel is God's people in the world and at the same time an ethnic and political entity. Because of Israel's struggle for existence—a small nation surrounded by powerful empires—it was, humanly speaking, difficult for them to impart a message of love and generosity to the surrounding nations. There was always a tendency automatically to regard political enemies as religious opponents as well; it was, in fact, practically impossible to distinguish between these two types of opponents. Israel as people of God and Israel as political entity largely overlapped, but never entirely, because there was always the awareness: '... not all descendants of Israel are truly Israel' (Rom. 9.6). Precisely because of this partial overlapping it remains difficult, however, to 'read' Israel's history. The contrast between the two 'faces' of Israel did not always emerge as clearly as it did in the ministry of the prophets Isaiah, Jeremiah and Amos. Hence, the ambivalence of Israel often obscured the missionary dimension of the calling and existence of the 'true Israel'. This means that we cannot shake off the problem of history and its interpretation; it is only in the abstract ahistorical world of ideas that we can keep our categories of distinction pure and unadulterated.

JESUS AND ISRAEL

As in the case of the Old Testament stories, missionary enthusiasts are often embarrassed by the absence of absolutely clear and indisputable references to a Gentile mission in stories about Jesus of Nazareth. Once again, however, history is specific, not general. Here it is specific in the extreme: God's revelation is incarnated and concentrated in the history of this one Man. In his entire ministry he remains true to Israel; after all, 'It is from the Jews that salvation comes' (John 4.22). This does not, however, mean that his ministry is without meaning for the rest of the world. On the contrary. His very concentration on Israel—or to express it differently: precisely the historical specificity of his ministry—has cosmic-missionary significance. As Bengt Sundkler puts it: 'He was "universalist" precisely because, in fact, only because he was "particularist".'[8]

The significance of this historical specificity of Jesus for mission becomes even more apparent in the role the city of Jerusalem plays in his ministry, especially according to Luke's account. After only one third of his Gospel has run its course, Jerusalem emerges as the goal of Jesus' journey (9.51). From that moment onward, virtually the whole story unfolds under the rubric 'En route to Jerusalem'. During the following ten chapters he is bound for Jerusalem, apparently continuously (read in sequence Luke 9.51; 9.53; 13.22; 13.33; 17.11; 18.31; 19.11; 19.28 and 19.41). Only then does he reach the city. The words which mark the start of this journey are exceptionally solemn: 'As the time approached when he was to be taken up to heaven, he set his face resolutely towards Jerusalem' (Luke 9.51). 'Geographically' Jesus journeys to the temple, to Jerusalem and his death; 'theologically' he is bound for the nations. In the final analysis he himself would take the place of Jerusalem and the temple (John 2.19-21).[9] As the 'New Jerusalem' he himself becomes the place of encounter with the nations. 'The Old Testament Scriptures locate the meeting with the nations in Zion, since, in the age of promise, God appointed Jerusalem to be the scene of His revelation. The Gospel teaches us that God calls us to meet Him in Jesus Christ. Messiah has taken the place of His City ...'[10] Paul would express it differently, but with essentially the same meaning: 'God was in

Christ reconciling the world to himself' (2 Cor. 5.19). Christ became both the final High Priest and the final sacrifice.

The history of Jesus of Nazareth gradually unfolds itself. However, it belongs to the ambivalence of this history—of *any* history, as we have in fact indicated—that not everybody can 'read' it. In this respect the Gospels use the concept *kairos*, in the sense of decisive moment, fateful hour, extraordinary opportunity, turning-point in history. John's Gospel uses *hōra*, hour, in more or less the same sense. So all the Gospels agree: there are people who recognise the *kairoi* and others who remain blind. They may forecast the weather correctly but are unable to judge 'this fateful hour' (Luke 12.56). To Jerusalem Jesus says that the city will be destroyed 'because you did not recognize *God's moment* when it came' (Luke 19.44).

History is *filled time*, now, in the present. This is being said in many ways, and precisely the awareness of this forms the basis for the early Church's involvement in mission. If the present is empty, as the Pharisees, Essenes and Zealots believed, then you can only flee into the memory of a glorious past recorded in codes (Pharisees), or you can, with folded arms, sit and wait for God's vengeance on your enemies (Essenes), or you can play God yourself by violently liquidating the empty present thus trying to make the utopian future a present reality (Zealots), or you can enter into an uncomfortable compromise with the status quo (Sadducees). But if the present is filled; if Isa. 61.1-2 has come true, 'today, in your very hearing' (Luke 4.21); if 'the Kingdom of God has already come upon you' (Luke 11.20); if it is no more necessary to call out that God's Kingdom is 'here' or 'there', because in the person of Jesus it is already 'among you' (Luke 17.21); if many prophets and kings have longed to see and hear what you now see and hear (Luke 10.24); if the 'strong man', the devil, is bound and his house ransacked (Matt. 12.28; Luke 11.21-22); if Satan falls out of the sky like lightning and the demons submit to the disciples (Luke 10.17-18); if the Son of Man has authority to do what even the Messiah according to Jewish expectations could not do, namely, to forgive sins on earth (Mark 2.10); if even 'the least' in the newly inaugurated Kingdom is greater than John (Matt. 11.11); if the One in our midst is greater than Jonah or Solomon (Matt. 12.41-42); then those who partake of this 'new history', cannot possibly go the way of their contemporary Jewish religious groups. They can only let themselves be taken along by Christ into the future, not as soldiers fighting in the vanguard, but as 'captives in Christ's triumphal procession' (2 Cor. 2.14). If you participate in this historical event, you are involved in the world, which means: you are engaged in mission.

In the period after Easter—when Jesus was no longer present in the flesh among his disciples—the awareness of living in a *kairos* did not change. On the contrary, it was broadened and deepened. Initially there was, understandably, the danger that the present might once again be experienced as empty and bleak. And there was the possibility that the disciples, in accordance with the Pharisaic model, would yield to the temptation to live on memory only and to codify the traditions regarding Jesus of Nazareth as a 'new law'. Actually, this was, in a way, what happened in Ebionitic Christianity. There was, likewise, the danger that, in accordance with the Essene model, they would fix their eyes on the *parousia* and let the world go its own way. There was yet another danger, that, under the influence of Gnosticism, the historicity of Jesus might be regarded as insignificant and even become a stumbling-block; in this way the new message might dissipate into the Greek spiritual world of ideas.

Two convictions, or rather two events which became part of their experience, protected the early Christians against this flight into the past, or into the future, or into the world of ideas—that Jesus was raised from the dead and sent his Spirit to remain with his disciples. These pivotal events gave them the consciousness that the present was still filled, that, because of these events, they were irrevocably involved with the world and therefore with mission. Jesus' resurrection and the gift of the Spirit are referred to as *aparchē*, first-fruits, and *arrabōn*, pledge (cf. 1 Cor. 15.20, 23; 2 Cor. 1.22; 5.5; Eph. 1.14). Indeed, the Church herself, on the basis of this double event, is the 'first-fruits' (Rom. 8.23, Jas. 1.18) and 'new creation' (2 Cor. 5.17; Gal. 6.15). The old order has passed, the new has already begun (2 Cor. 5.17). In Resurrection and Holy Spirit the early Christians had a manifestation of the fact that the new era had indeed invaded the old. They knew, of course, that the Kingdom still had to come in its fullness. However, Christ's resurrection and the coming of the Spirit were clear signs that it already made sense to live according to the standards of the 'coming age'.

It is within this context that the more specific New Testament sayings about mission should be seen. Of course, this does not imply that all New Testament authors understood mission in exactly the same way. Neither did they interpret the reality of the 'new era' in an absolutely uniform fashion. Once again, history is ambivalent and the accents of our experience and interpretation of history vary. History is dynamic; therefore one person can bring to the fore something which another accentuates less or even omits completely.

THE GREAT COMMISSION

Today it is widely accepted that the so-called Great Commission (Matt. 28.18-20) should be regarded as the key to the understanding of the entire Gospel of Matthew. The missionary command, together with sayings such as those of Matt. 24.14 and 26.13 stand, however, in contrast with 'particularistic' statements such as those in 10.5-6 and 15.24-26, according to which the disciples had to confine their mission to 'the lost sheep of the house of Israel' and not 'throw the children's bread to the dogs'. We have already argued that 'particularism' and 'universalism' are not mutually exclusive but rather inclusive. It is therefore unnecessary to explain the contrast between the two sets of sayings by feebly stating, 'Matthew prefers to counteract' (B. H. Streeter), or by averring that the tradition changed Jesus' universalistic sayings into particularistic ones (F. Spitta), or vice versa (M. Goguel).

We ought rather to establish how the evangelist himself understood and used the sayings of Jesus in his own context and with an eye on his specific (Jewish Christian?) readership. For those reading the Gospel today the Church's world-wide mission is self-evident whereas its limitation to Israel in Matt. 10.5-6 and elsewhere calls for an explanation. For the original readers the situation was exactly the opposite: the mission entrusted to them, so they believed, was the command to go to Israel only. Hence, it was the universal mission that required explanation.[11] If we keep this in mind, the structure of the Gospel and its culmination in the Great Commission becomes clear.

Matthew opens his Gospel with the genealogy of Jesus. He includes four women who were probably all pagan and in addition remind us of moments of sin in the history of the elect people (Tamar and Bathsheba). He contrasts pagan astrologers with Herod as representative of the Jewish people (Matt. 2) and the faith of a pagan army officer with that of the Jews (8.11-12). He reports Jesus' visit to pagan and semi-pagan areas (Tyre, Sidon, Gadara), relates parables such as those about the tenants of the vineyard (21.33-44), and concludes his Gospel with a missionary command—all this against the background of Jesus' matchless compassion on all who are held in contempt (see our previous chapter).

It is within this broad context rather than in isolation that we should read sayings such as Matt. 10.5-6 and 15.24-26. Within the total framework of the Gospel their apparently absolute prohibition of a Gentile mission is relativised. The mission to Jews retains validity—though it almost appears as if Jesus' lament over Jerusalem severs the possibility of the Jewish mission at the root (23.37-38). After Easter, however, this is set within the wider context of world mission.

Looking more specifically at the Great Commission itself, it would be irrelevant to ask whether we have here the exact words of the risen Christ. History is not a matter of bare facts but of appropriating and assimilating what has happened. To quote Jesus' words literally has in itself little meaning. To make them one's own is another matter, but in this process those words inevitably acquire the stamp of the narrator of the event concerned. We have long since accepted the validity of this in the case of John's Gospel. It applies to the Synoptics, however, with scarcely less force than to John. All the Gospel writers 'made present' in their own way the stories handed down to them. To say the same thing in their own context as Jesus had done decades earlier, they often had to say it differently.

It is therefore not strange that the Great Commission reveals in every detail the evangelist Matthew's specific language and style. *Mathēteuein* (to make disciples), *tērein* (keep), and *entellesthai* (command) are typical Matthean concepts. The key word is *mathēteusate*, make disciples. For Matthew Jesus is the rabbi *sui generis*, the incomparable. Therefore the theme of discipleship, of following, is central in this Gospel. For example, in Matt. 8.23 ('and his disciples followed') this is mentioned explicitly, but omitted in Mark and Luke. (See also 12.49.)[12]

According to Matthew, Jesus is also King. In no other Gospel is the 'Kingdom of heaven' as prominent as in Matthew's. In the first chapter he announces Jesus as the royal descendant from the line of David who appears on the scene as Immanuel, 'God with us' (1.23). In the final verses of the last chapter it is this same Jesus who says, 'I am with you always' (28.20), and he says it as King. Scholars such as Otto Michel have argued that here we probably have an enthronement hymn which (as is also the case with Dan. 7.13-14) is modelled on the pattern of an ancient Eastern coronation liturgy. Other scholars deny this parallel, maintaining that we should rather read Matt. 28.18-20 as an official decree of Jesus as King. An analogy is found in 2 Chr. 36.22-23 where Cyrus issues a decree permitting the Jews to return to their land. The resemblance in literary form and choice of words is indeed striking. More important is the observation that, as 2 Chr. 36.22-23 concludes the Hebrew Bible, Matt. 28.18-20 was intended by the evangelist as the conclusion of the story of the 'new testament' of Jesus Christ.[13]

Matt. 28.18-20 may be interpreted in other ways as well, but it remains undeniable that, however we explain the *structure* of the text, we have here to do with a mandate which, on the basis of Jesus' authority here and now ('in heaven *and* on earth', v. 18) is instructing the disciples that a totally new era has been inaugurated which implies their involvement in a world-wide mission. The word *oun* ('then', 'therefore', v. 19) ties this missionary responsibility indissolubly to the authority granted to Jesus (v. 18). The Great Commission, says Max Warren, is not an ethical demand, but a person: 'Jesus ... is the Great Commission.'[14]

Traditionally the Great Commission has not been understood

in the way we have outlined it—at least not in Western
Protestantism and Roman Catholicism. *There* the full emphasis
was on the aorist participle *poreuthentes*, usually translated as
imperative, 'Go ye therefore'. The activist Westerner found this
translation attractive; it was, moreover, the only translation that
made sense to him during the golden age of Western consciousness of superiority. The 'go ye therefore', the crossing of
geographical frontiers, was the dominant element in the
missionary command, whereas the 'make disciples' tended to
assume a subordinate meaning.

Within the overall context of the Matthean ending the 'go ye
therefore' is, however, of only secondary importance. To
illustrate this, let us look at an imperative construction which
Matthew frequently uses and which Adolf Schlatter elucidates
as follows: 'When two actions are connected with a single event,
Matthew puts the aorist participle of the preparatory actions
before the aorist of the main verb. This sentence construction is
so common that it may be designated a characteristic of
Matthew's style.'[15] In 28.19 the aorist participle *poreuthentes* is
used in conjunction with the aorist imperative *matheteusate*.
Practically always when Matthew uses the verb *poreuomai* (go,
journey) in this type of construction, e.g. in 9.13; 11.4; 17.27;
and 28.7, it has this unaccentuated meaning. The 'go' is in each
of these cases in a certain sense pleonastic and could even have
been omitted. The crossing of geographical frontiers is no key
idea here. The full accent is on *mathēteusate* which, as already
indicated, is in any case a key concept in Matthew.[16]

What have we attempted to achieve with this exegetical
exercise on Matt. 28.18-20? We simply wanted to show to what
extent we, in looking for a biblical foundation for mission, read
our own presuppositions into the text instead of allowing the
text to say what it intends to say within its own context.

Like Matthew the other evangelists also put the foundation
of mission in their own way within the context of their and their
readers' experience of the events concerning Jesus of Nazareth.
A few remarks in this connection will suffice. For *Mark* the
concept *keryssein* in the sense of proclaiming authoritatively is
of special importance. He describes vividly Jesus' conflict with
the powers of evil as well as his victory over them. Although the
missionary command in Mark's ending (16.15-18) is a later

addition, it reflects the same understanding as the rest of the Gospel. Mark's concern throughout, from 1.1 onward, is with the *euangelion*, the good news of salvation. Therefore Mark's rendering of the Great Commission is not to be looked for in the unauthentic ending of his Gospel, but in 13.10: '... before the end the *euangelion* must be proclaimed to all nations'.

Luke, the 'Gospel of the poor', which always has an eye for the less privileged and for those who have been pushed to the periphery of society—the women, the 'lost' (Luke 15), the tax-gatherers and Samaritans—emphasises the message of forgiveness and the possibility of new relationships. It is therefore understandable that in its rendering of the Great Commission (24.46-49) conversion and forgiveness are central.

John sees everything, including mission, from the perspective of Christology. The mission of the Son by the Father establishes contact between God and the world; the mission of the Church continues this contact: 'As the Father sent me, so I send you' (20.21). As with Jesus, so too with the disciples this does not only apply to mission (20.21; 17.18), but also to mutual love and service (13.34; 15.12) as well as unity (17.11; 17.22-23). In the Church, among the disciples, it should become clear who and how God is. The Church is God's bridgehead in the world.[17]

In spite of all mutual differences in approach and emphasis, there is in all four Gospels—and indeed in the entire New Testament—an unmistakable basic unity of witness as regards the foundation of mission. The coming of Jesus of Nazareth was 'fulfilled' the time (Mark 1.15); 'the term was completed', 'the time was ripe' (Gal. 4.4; Eph. 1.10). In this fulfilled, historical period the Church lives and labours; she contributes to the 'filling' of the time by means of her missionary involvement in the world. God does not send 'ideas' or 'eternal truths' to the nations. He sends people, historical beings. He incarnates himself in his Son, and through his Son in his disciples. God becomes history, specific history, mundane history, in the followers of Jesus en route to the world.

CHAPTER EIGHT

MARTYRIA IN OLD AND NEW TESTAMENT

Research into Isa. 40-55 has shown that here the 'universalistic motif' in the historical unfolding of the Old Testament revelation reaches a high-water mark.[1] What is remarkable is that these chapters deal with Israel in exile. And it is in this extraordinary combination of suffering and missionary involvement that we find the third important element of a biblical foundation of mission—an element which, moreover, relates closely to the two already discussed.

Completely contrary to what Israel always imagined, it now appears that the possibility of witness finds expression not in national triumph but in national adversity. This applies especially with regard to the *'ebed Yahweh*, the servant of the Lord: to be God's witness in the world does not only imply witness by word of mouth but also silent suffering for the sake of others. Isa. 53 thus reveals both the highest and deepest dimensions of mission in the Old Testament. In Exod. 19.6 Israel was called a 'kingdom of priests' and with that assigned a priestly function in the midst of the nations. The priest does not rule; he serves. Isa. 53 shows that, on occasion, this service may take the form of innocent suffering for the sake of others. The priest, as it were, becomes himself the sacrifice which he lays on the altar.

Israel believed that she could truly achieve God's purpose for herself only as long as she was powerful and was feared and respected by the nations. What is remarkable, however, is that, the mightier Israel became, the less was there an indication of a missionary dimension to her existence—the nations moved into the background, they remained at a distance. We have here, once again, an example of the ambivalence of the concept 'Israel', as political entity and as God's people.

Conversely, the more Israel was stripped of all earthly power and glory, the more clearly her prophets spoke of the missionary dimension of her existence. Deutero-Isaiah deals with a period in her history when she was, politically speaking, completely insignificant. She had apparently failed miserably in playing any significant role as a priestly presence among the nations. She had become the refuse of the earth, abhorred by every people, a slave of tyrants (49.7). Nevertheless, precisely at this moment of deepest humiliation (and self-humbling) there was the possibility of kings and princes bowing down, 'because of the Lord who is faithful, because of the Holy One of Israel who has chosen you' (49.7).

This one Old Testament example will have to suffice. As the idea of mission reached its highest (and deepest) point in the period of Babylonian captivity, especially in the person of the suffering servant, so the New Testament highest and deepest point is reached in the suffering of the Son of Man, especially on Golgotha, where he gave his life as ransom for many (Mark 10.45). What appeared to be disaster was, in reality, God's road to victory. It is for this reason that the suffering servant of Isa. 53 was, since the earliest times, regarded as the archetype of Jesus of Nazareth. Not in Jesus' successful preaching to the masses, neither in the sometimes over-whelmingly positive reaction to his miracles, but in his suffering and death he became the true Missionary.

For the Church-in-mission, already in the New Testament period, this had consequences of vital importance. To follow the Rabbi of Nazareth did not mean studying the *tôrâh* under his supervision but identifying with his suffering. This becomes nowhere more apparent than in Paul's second epistle to the Corinthians.[2] Here Paul rejects the conduct of the hawkers (2.17) who define mission in the categories of demonstrable success and triumphalism. In contrast, he is a captive (2.14) who glories in weakness (12.9). In fact, weakness *(astheneia)*, affliction *(thlipsis)* and suffering *(lypē)* are key concepts in this letter in which Paul defends his apostleship against 'those superlative apostles' (11.5; 12.11) who recommended themselves to the Corinthians. Unlike them he has this treasure in an earthen vessel (4.7) a fact to which his suffering testifies abundantly (6.4-10; 11.23-28). Moreover, suffering and affliction are *normal* experiences in the apostle's life, but for those who can only think in success categories, they remain a *skandalon*, a stumbling-block. The difference between the Pauline mission and that of his opponents in Corinth lies in the Cross. Second Corinthians presents an indisputable identification of mission with the Cross—not only Christ's but also the apostle's. As in the case of the Colossians Paul rejoices in suffering, completing, in his flesh, 'the full tale of Christ's afflictions still to be endured, for the sake of his body which is the church' (Col. 1.24).

For today's Church-in-mission it will not be different. The imagery of 'salt', 'light', and 'yeast', which Jesus sometimes used, all express, in one way or another, the idea of permeation and the crossing of frontiers. Elton Trueblood observes about these three metaphors: 'The most surprising thing is that each of these is frustrated in its true function whenever it is *saved*, because the essence of each is that it is radically expendable'.[3] One of the deepest elements of God's compassionate search for man, says N. P. Moritzen, is the indispensableness of the weak witness, the powerless representative of the message. The people who are to be won and saved should, so to speak, always be able to crucify the witness of the gospel.[4] It is here where the theological and practical justification for the idea of 'the Church for others' is to be found. In May 1944, Dietrich Bonhoeffer wrote from prison, on the occasion of the birth of his godson, that a Church which today fought for her own survival only, as though that were a goal in itself, was unfit for bearing the word of reconciliation and salvation to mankind. For a time at least the Church, instead of speaking many words, should become powerless and silent and our being Christian should consist of two elements only: intercession, and the doing of justice.

Of course, Bonhoeffer wrote these words at a time when the Church in Germany had been largely silenced. Her prophetic utterances of Barmen days had ceased. Silent witnessing can therefore not be made universally applicable. Bonhoeffer's real point is, however, that witnessing and suffering go together. The Greek word for witness is *martys*. From this our word 'martyr' is derived, for in the early Church the witness often had to seal his witness *(martyria)* with his blood. 'Martyrdom and mission—so experience teaches us—belong together. Martyrdom is especially at home on the mission field.'[5] Bonhoeffer's words should therefore not be taken as a plea for quietism. We hear, for instance, the German churches stating in their Stuttgart Declaration a few months after the collapse of the Nazi regime: 'We accuse ourselves for *not witnessing more courageously*, for not praying more faithfully, for not believing more joyously, and for not loving more ardently.'

CHAPTER NINE

GOD'S MISSION

THE 'SERVANT OF THE LORD'

A careful reading of both Old and New Testaments reveals that God himself is the subject of mission. This, then, is the fourth characteristic of the biblical foundation of mission. We have here to do with *missio Dei*, God's mission—an aspect we now intend examining briefly, in close relation to what we have discussed in the preceding chapter. The *martyria*, the witness by word and deed, has its ultimate origin not in the witness himself, but in God. To this we must hasten to add, however, that the witness himself is in no way excluded here. He is part of God's mission. But God remains the author.

One of the ways in which the Old Testament in particular has given expression to this conviction, is by laying much emphasis on what God rather than man does, almost to the extent of suggesting that man is inactive. That this is not the intention will hopefully become clear.

It has for a long time been customary to refer to the 'Servant of the Lord' in Isa. 40-55 as the missionary par excellence. This interpretation flows from the centrality of the concept 'witness' in those chapters.[1] The 'servant' is, however, not an active missionary sent out to the nations. The verb '*yôṣî*' in Isa. 42.1 is not to be translated as 'carry out', 'bring to', but rather as 'cause to become visible'. The NEB translation of this verse is therefore preferable: '... my servant ... will *make justice shine* on the nations'. It is not the servant's own activities which are emphasised, but the fact that *God* works in and through him. He is, we are told, brought into the courtroom to witness in the case between God and the nations. He is, however, a very remarkable and, according to our standards, useless witness, for he can neither see nor speak (Isa. 42.18-20; 43.8-13). The purpose of this metaphor is, once again, not to say that the witness is indeed blind and deaf, but that, in the final analysis, Yahweh himself is the Witness.

The 'servant' of the Lord in Isa. 40-55 is a paradigm of Israel. Israel's election and existence has no goal in itself. Through Israel God is busy with the nations. Her election is a prolepsis, an anticipation. In and through her God stretches his hand out to the world. His salvific activities in Israel are a sign and signal to the nations. She is called to be 'a light to all peoples' (Isa. 42.6). God intends doing more than merely restoring the tribes of Judah and bringing back the descendants of Israel: 'I will make you a light to the nations, that my salvation may reach to earth's farthest bounds' (Isa. 49.6).

For many years it has been customary to argue that the Old Testament views mission centripetally—the nations coming towards Israel—whereas the New Testament understanding of mission is centrifugal—from the centre, Israel or the Church, missionaries move outward, into the world. It is undoubtedly true that the Old Testament views mission predominantly in centripetal categories. This is however not exclusively so. The metaphor of light in Isa. 42.6, 49.6 and elsewhere, is particularly appropriate to give expression to both a centripetal and a centrifugal movement. A light shining in the darkness draws people towards it, centripetally, yet at the same time it goes outward, crossing frontiers, allowing, in the words of Isa. 49.6, God's salvation to reach 'to earth's farthest bounds'.

In the Old Testament Israel's missionary significance lies, however, predominantly within the framework of centripetal categories. This explains the centrality of Jerusalem or Zion in the Old Testament's universalistic passages. This theme has experienced a significant development in the Old Testament, as R. E. Clements shows. The earliest model was that of Israel as an imperial power bringing peace, prosperity and justice to those over which she ruled. After the division into two kingdoms the idea was modified and re-appeared in a much more directly religious form, as we may see from the picture of the pilgrimage of the nations to Mount Zion to hear God's law (Isa. 2.2-4; Mic. 4.1-5). There are still overtones of the nations' sub-servience to Israel in these visions, however. Only in Isa. 40-55 the servant-master image is finally reversed; now *Israel* is regarded as the servant who has to make God's truth and righteousness known to the nations.[1] God himself remains the real 'missionary', but Israel—in as far as she is God's obedient servant—is most directly involved in this. The summons in Isa. 2.5 also reveals this: 'O people of Jacob, come, let us walk in the light of the Lord.'

In light of the above we should add, therefore, that the dominant characteristic of the Old Testament understanding of mission is not that it is centripetal. Rather the centripetal category is employed to give expression to the conviction that *God*, not Israel, is the author of mission.

Zech. 8 gives classical expression to this. It is Yahweh who, after the exile, gathers his scattered people from the nations (vv. 7-8) and instructs them (vv. 9-19). The nations observe this and spontaneously express the desire also to go to Jerusalem. As many as ten men 'from nations of every language' will pluck the robe of a Jew and say: 'We will go with you because we have heard that God is with you' (v. 23). It is not Israel's faith, example and witness that act as a magnet here; it is God's faithfulness to Israel that causes the nations to come. And yet, not for a single moment does this suggest that Israel's faith, example and witness are dispensable. Far from it. Once again, therefore, Israel herself is fully involved in God's mission to the nations. She was a pagan whom God elected to salvation; but she retains her new and special position as 'non-pagan' only in so far as she accepts and lives up to her responsibility in the world. Primarily this means remaining true to Yahweh; but then this implies remaining true to the world, in letting her light shine forth, in being an example to the world, indeed, in witnessing by word and deed.

GOD AND MAN AS COMPETITORS?

We have so far looked at only the Old Testament in our discussion of the biblical understanding of mission as God's mission. Does this characterisation also apply to the New Testament? Unfortunately the view according to which the Old Testament understands mission centripetally and the New Testament centrifugally has unnecessarily clouded this entire issue. As mission is usually, in the Western world, understood in centrifugal categories, a remark such as that of Horst

Rzepkowski is understandable: 'The decisive difference between the Old and New Testament is mission.'[3]

It is, of course, undoubtedly true that the New Testament understanding of mission differs fundamentally from that of the Old Testament. This we have attempted to explain in Chapter 7. It would, however, be wrong to find the real difference between Old and New Testaments in the centripetal-centrifugal distinction. At least three observations can be made to establish that that distinction is a relative one.

First, the centripetal missionary dimension is by no means confined to the Old Testament but characteristic of the New Testament also. Astrologers came from the East to Jerusalem to look for the Saviour of the world (Matt. 2). Simeon refers to the deliverance which God has prepared 'in full view of all the nations: a light that will be a revelation to the heathen ...' (Luke 2.31-32). Quoting Isa. 56.7, Jesus referred to the temple as 'a house of prayer for all the nations' (Mark 11.17). The cleansing of the temple moreover suggests that the restoration of Israel should precede the pilgrimage of the nations to Jerusalem. The Roman army officer coming to Jesus (Matt. 8.5) and the Greeks travelling to Jerusalem to see Jesus (John 12.20) give expression to the same idea: Salvation is to be found in Israel and the nations who wish to partake of it, should go there. After all, 'it is from the Jews that salvation comes' (John 4.22). The world's salvation can be consummated at one place only—in Jerusalem; this explains the prominence of this city in all four Gospels, especially that of Luke (the non-Jew!).

Secondly, we have to point out that the centripetal-centrifugal distinction may easily lead to 'true' mission being understood as only centrifugal, as this suggests the crossing of geographical boundaries and proclamation to pagans by word of mouth. We have, however, argued both that the crossing of geographical boundaries constitutes one element only of what the Bible understands by 'mission', and also that mission is more than oral preaching to pagans.

Thirdly, there is a tendency to understand mission in the Old Testament as entirely and exclusively 'God's work'; this implies that New Testament centrifugal mission, in which man is ostensibly more actively involved, might then be labelled 'man's work'. With this, however, we enter a very slippery area where

God's activity excludes man's and vice versa. Then God and man become competitors. However, John Deschner's observation here is to the point: 'This is a perversion because it suggests that God's activity is the enemy of human freedom, ... and the more you emphasize God's activity the less you can emphasize man's ... The Christian knows that the more he lets God have his way with him, ... the more he is free to forgive, love and serve his neighbor. In the light of the gospel (and the Old Testament!), ... the more we recognize that the church's mission is God's activity, the more we may properly speak of it as our activity.'[4]

Some of Jesus' contemporaries indeed believed that God's work, by definition, excluded any human involvement. Jesus' ministry has also been interpreted within this framework by some theologians. Albert Schweitzer judged that Jesus thought in wholly apocalyptic categories and expected within his own lifetime the arrival of the Kingdom in its ultimate form. Schweitzer founded his theory of 'consistent eschatology' on Matt. 10.23: 'I tell you this: before you have gone through all the towns of Israel the Son of Man will have come'. This apocalyptic expectation of Jesus, Schweitzer believed, excluded any idea of mission. Jesus adopted an 'expectant universalism' according to which specific pagans—those whom God himself had called and prepared in his own mysterious way—would be 'revealed' at the inauguration of the messianic era. The idea of a Gentile mission was unthinkable for Jesus as this would imply man taking into his own hands what God had reserved for himself.

Somewhat like Schweitzer, Joachim Jeremias argues that the proclamation of the gospel to all nations in Matt. 24.14, Mark 13.10 and 14.9 has no reference to 'human mission work'. Referring to Rev. 14.6-7, Jeremias contends that these sayings of Jesus suggest that God's final victory in the last hour will be announced to the nations of the world by an angel. That will be the sign for the eschatological pilgrimage of the nations to Mount Zion. Jeremias continues: 'Thus we see that the incorporation of the Gentiles in the Kingdom of God promised by the prophets, was expected and announced by Jesus as God's *eschatological act of power, as the great final manifestation of God's free grace*.'[5]

The problem with Schweitzer and Jeremias is their assumption that Jesus believed that God's work excluded man's. This interpretation has frequently been advocated in the course of nineteen centuries of Church history and we shall return to it. We want to put it categorically, however, that this is a false conception that cannot but be detrimental to the Church. The Bible speaks with a disarming candour here. The disciples are seed (Matt. 13.38) and at the same time labourers bringing in the harvest (Matt. 9.37-38); they are members of the flock (Matt. 10.16; Luke 12.32; John 10.1-16) but also shepherds (Matt. 10.6; John 21.15-7); they are in need of absolution (Matt. 18.23-27) but can also give absolution to others (Matt. 16.19; 18.18; John 20.23). God has revealed to them the 'secrets of the Kingdom' (Matt. 13.11), yet they have to seek the Kingdom (Matt. 5.20; 6.33; Luke 13.24). They are God's children (Matt. 17.26), yet have to become that by loving their enemies (Matt. 5.44-45). They have received eternal life (John 3.16-17; 11.25-26) yet still have to go through the gate that leads to life (Matt. 7.14). Because they have done what Jesus expected of the rich young ruler, they are 'perfect' (Matt. 19.21; cf. Mark 10.28), yet have to keep watch and pray so that they will not fall into temptation (Matt. 26.41). The believers must work out their own salvation in fear and trembling, for(!) it is God who works in them (Phil. 2.12-13). Therefore Paul can, quite unselfconsciously, call them 'God's fellow-workers' (1 Cor. 3.9). The key to these apparently complete paradoxes lies in the New Testament expression 'in Christ': 'By God's grace I am what I am, nor has his grace been given to me in vain; on the contrary, in my labours I have outdone them all—not I, indeed, but the grace of God working with me' (1 Cor. 15.10).

If, however, we regard God and man as competitors and put God's work over against man's, we soon land ourselves in one of two untenable positions. If we emphasise only the one side, our faith adopts the blind, unbending characteristics of fate; if we emphasise only the other side, we become fanatics and arrogant Zealots.

There is, as the examples quoted from Scripture indicate, a dialectical and creative tension between God's work and man's, and any attempt to explain it by means of a balanced formula or to codify it precisely in a dogma, risks destroying its tender mystery. To recognise this is of the utmost importance for the biblical foundation of mission.

IN CHRIST

Many scholars have underlined the remarkable fact that the so-called 'Great Commission' (Matt. 28.18-20 and parallels) seems to play no role in the New Testament Church herself, because it is never repeated nor referred to. Two reasons may perhaps be suggested to explain this silence. First, the Great Commission is not a commission in the ordinary sense of the word. It is, rather, a creative statement in the manner of Gen. 1.3 and elsewhere: 'Let there be ...'. Or, as Newbigin puts it, with reference to Acts 1.8: 'The word, "You shall be my witnesses", is not a command to be obeyed but a promise to be trusted.'[6] It was a promise, however, that could only be perceived in the act of obeying, as Peter discovered when he visited Cornelius and said in amazement: 'I *now* see how true it is that God has no favourites ...' (Acts 10.34). Paul referred to it as a 'mystery', a 'secret' only now revealed to him in the act of preaching the gospel to all people, 'that through the gospel the Gentiles are joint heirs with the Jews, part of the same body, sharers together in the promise made in Christ Jesus' (Eph. 3.6).

A second reason for the silence about the Great Commission in the early Church lies in the fact that a mission to the Gentiles was never at issue in the early Church—despite the views of scholars such as Ferdinand Hahn, Ernst Käsemann, and others. Heinrich Kasting has convincingly refuted their arguments and shown that the Gentile mission was never a point of controversy in the early Church. Opinions differed only on the way in which Gentiles were to be brought into the Church, especially on the question of circumcision.[7] In these circumstances a reference to a 'missionary command' would have been irrelevant.

Both these considerations demonstrate that mission in the New Testament is more than a matter of obeying a command. It is, rather, the result of an encounter with Christ. To meet Christ, means to become caught up in a mission to the world.

Mission is a privilege in which to participate. Thus Paul introduces himself to the church in Rome as somebody who, through Christ, has 'received the *privilege* of a commission in his name to lead to faith and obedience men in all nations' (Rom. 1.5). Mission, for Paul, is the logical consequence of his encounter with the risen Christ on the Damascus road.

Similarly, in the so-called 'christological hymn' (Phil. 2.6-11), there is no reference to a missionary command. And yet, the world-wide mission falls clearly within the purview of the hymn: '... that at the name of Jesus every knee should bow ... and every tongue confess, "Jesus is Lord"' (vv. 10-11). Mission is therefore, according to the New Testament, a predicate of Christology. This is how it appears in another early Christian hymn: 'He who was manifested in the body, vindicated in the spirit, seen by angels; who was proclaimed among the nations, believed in throughout the world, glorified in high heaven' (1 Tim. 3.16). Similarly, in 2 Cor. 5.18-20 and Eph. 2.14-18 mission is christologically founded as the message of the reconciliation of the world with God; the 'service of reconciliation', entrusted to the Church, proceeds from the fact that Jesus, with regard to Jews and Gentiles, has broken down, 'in his own body of flesh, the enmity which stood like a dividing wall between them', thus creating 'out of the two a single new humanity in himself'.

The Church, therefore, is involved in mission because Jesus was given a name above all names (Phil. 2.9), and declared Son of God by a mighty act in that he rose from the dead (Rom. 1.4); because God was in Christ reconciling the world to himself (2 Cor. 5.19) and Jews and Gentiles to one another in a single body to himself through the cross (Eph. 2.16). If the Church is 'in Christ', she is involved in mission. Her whole existence then has a missionary character. Her conduct as well as her words will convince the unbelievers (1 Pet. 2.12) and put their ignorance and stupidity to silence (1 Pet. 2.15). 'God's scattered people', to whom 1 Peter is addressed (cf. 1.1), are a chosen race, a royal priesthood, a dedicated nation, and a people claimed by God for his own. This new status in Christ has a clear purpose: to proclaim the triumphs of him who has called them out of darkness into his marvellous light (cf. 1 Pet. 2.9). Because of this new life in Christ, mission 'happens', so to speak, for we read about unbelievers calling upon the Christians for an explanation of the hope that is in them (1 Pet. 3.15). This hope was so conspicuous, that the unbelievers became both curious and jealous. To put it in Pauline language: this was the way in which God spread abroad the fragrance of the knowledge of himself (2 Cor. 2.14). Wherever the apostle lived, spoke and acted as 'Christ fragrance', something happened to the surrounding people.

In this and the preceding chapters we have discussed four elements of a biblical foundation for mission. We could have added more elements but have confined ourselves to these four, partly because they are usually not considered as belonging within the framework of a biblical theology of mission. We believe, however, that they are of decisive significance. We could add that they are all merely different aspects of the same theme, because they are all very closely interrelated. The God who has compassion on stranger, orphan and widow in Israel, and through Jesus of Nazareth on all discarded people, is also *par excellence* the God of history who uses the history of Israel as arena for his activities among the nations and the history of Jesus as gateway to the world. He is also—precisely as compassionate God and God of history—the One who turns all human categories upside down: he uses the weak, the suffering, and those of no consequence as his 'witnesses' in the world. In the final analysis it is he himself who works among the nations, through Jesus Christ, in whom the believers exist and live.

PART III

THE THEOLOGY OF MISSION
THROUGH THE AGES

CHAPTER TEN

THE HISTORICAL PERSPECTIVE

In the preceding chapters we paid attention to the foundation of mission in biblical revelation. We have, however, so far said very little about what 'mission', defined within this biblical framework, is supposed to be in practice. There is always the danger that practice (any practice, not just that of mission) may go its own way and reveal little of the source which gave it birth—an unfortunate development indeed.

It nevertheless remains difficult to relate foundation to practice. Regarding our present subject it would, however, be possible to say that the early Church, in her purest form, understood her missionary responsibility in a way at least reminiscent of the biblical guidelines we have uncovered. She saw herself as part of God's compassionate dealings with the world, conscious of the fact that God—as so frequently in the past, so now again in the history of Jesus of Nazareth—has begun something new and has now involved his Church in this. She knew that mission was no triumphal procession in a worldly sense but would unfold itself according to Paul's confession: 'When I am weak, then I am strong' (2 Cor. 12.10) —a statement which Ernst Fuchs calls the most famous paradox in the New Testament. The Church also knew that she could not tackle this superhuman task in her own power; she was involved in it, indeed, with complete surrender, but she also knew that this was nothing but a normal outflow of the fact that she shared in the resurrection of Christ and had received the Holy Spirit. Mission was the activity of the indwelling Christ.

The four elements we discussed in the preceding chapters indicate, as it were, only the parameters of mission, the 'space' within which the Church was to conduct her mission. These elements, fused together, were the leitmotive which characterised the missionary consciousness of the early Church. They were the roots which authenticated the fruits.

We could conceivably proceed directly from the biblical foundation of mission to our own time and situation, asking what the biblical leitmotive might teach us today. This would, however, be an unwise procedure, for various reasons. We therefore insert—between the biblical foundation and our reflection on mission in the modern world—a section in which we survey the way in which the Church, in the course of the past nineteen centuries, has understood her missionary role. Missiology, like any other branch of theology, always has a *critical* function. It is both normative and descriptive. In its normative function it provides guidelines for the way in which mission *ought* to be undertaken. In its descriptive function it critically evaluates the way in which mission has in fact been understood and carried out through the centuries. There is a temptation to regard this second function as unimportant. The two functions are, however, intimately related. It is impossible really meaningfully to discuss the way in which the Church ought to express her missionary calling without taking careful cognisance of the way in which she has in fact been doing this.

A study of mission through the ages may, for instance, teach us a lesson in reserve. Churches and missionaries expose themselves to grave danger whenever they isolate their own missionary activities from the current of nineteen centuries of Church history. A lack of historical perspective all too easily causes people to draw direct lines from the Bible to their own missionary practice, oblivious of the degree to which their interpretation of the Bible might be conditioned by their situation. They then remain blissfully ignorant of the deficiencies of their own enterprise and tend to regard it as the only correct one, perfectly in harmony with what the Bible teaches.

If however we study the historical course of mission—its heights and depths, its glory and guilt, its victories and defeats—we become more modest as regards our own understanding and efforts. We recognise their limitations and relativity. We then realise that we should not have been what and where we are had it not been for the tens of thousands who have preceded us. Our judgment then becomes milder, not only as regards our contemporaries who approach mission in a way different from ours, but also as regards our predecessors who, in other centuries and under different conditions, tried in their

own way to remain true to the biblical understanding of
mission. That we today can in many (not all) respects see better
and further than they, is not due to our own ability and
perceptiveness. We are in fact—in the words of Lucan, a first
century Latin poet—nothing but dwarfs sitting on the shoulders
of giants and therefore able to see further than our predecessors.

Another important reason for research into the understanding
of mission in the course of history, one that relates closely to
what we have just said, is that we need history to interpret the
present and prepare ourselves for the future. In the words of H.
Richard Niebuhr: 'In this respect, Christians of the twentieth
century are like the biblical Israelites who needed to remind
themselves in every period of crisis of their deliverance from
Egypt, of their wanderings in the desert and their ancient
covenant with Jehovah, not only that they might have con-
solation but even more that they might find direction.'[1]

All efforts to interpret the past are, therefore, indirectly
efforts to understand the present and future. For this reason few
subjects are as important as history, and it is a tragedy that, in
many educational institutions, it is either neglected or (what is
worse) taught incorrectly. Among young people today there is a
tendency to draw a solid line immediately behind their heels,
ignore everything that lies in the past, and turn their faces
exclusively to the future. Such people, however, enter the future
without a compass. The response to this error naturally can not
be to direct all attention entirely to the past, to history. Who
would use a compass only to find out from where he had come?

For the theologian, and indeed, for every Christian, it is
important to know history—and Church history as imbedded in
world history, an unalienable part thereof. We always stand
between 'ancestor cult and self-idolisation'[2], in other words, we
either absolutise our own denominational history or act as
though we are the first who know how God's work in the world
ought to be done. Only a detached study of Church history can
open our eyes to this double danger. We need Church history in
order to read our Bibles. In this sense Gerhard Ebeling is right
when he defines Church history as the history of the interpretation of Scripture. This in no way suggests that it will
always be a 'correct' interpretation. History, including Church
history in particular, remains an ambivalent matter.

Church history is, in a sense, the continuation of biblical history, a further unfolding of God's involvement in the world. Because of the presence of the Lord in the midst of his people, the Church can be regarded despite her incompleteness and sinfulness as the continuation of Jesus Christ, of his incarnation in the world. This history has, however, an ambivalence which the biblical revelation does not have. It is the history of the members of the body of Christ, and this does not, without further ado, implicate the Head of the body in a straightforward way in every aspect of each episode.

Regarding mission in particular, history reveals a variegated picture. Sometimes mission was nothing less than the entire church en route towards the world, and at other times it was a special and isolated enterprise of small groups alongside the institutional Church. Sometimes mission went hand in hand with the suffering and self-sacrifice of the missionary witness, and at other times with violence and even the power of the sword. At times the Church-in-mission was viewed as a 'fifth column' within the sociopolitical structure, and at other times as an accomplice of the state. Mission was sometimes regarded as the spread of a Christian counter-culture, and at other times as the ideal vehicle for the spread of a 'Christian civilisation'. The Church grew as a result of the unpretentious witness, in word and deed, of many ordinary, unnamed Christians, but also as a result of organised, massive campaigns against the 'Kingdom of the evil one'. At times the emphasis was on the salvation of individuals before the day of judgment, and at other times the establishing and nourishing of a church superseded the expectation of the Kingdom. Sometimes efforts were made to detect traces of God's revelation and points of contact for the gospel in other religions, at other times such religions were rejected as satanic and attacked tooth and nail. In some circles the Church-in-mission became involved in society in the widest sense of the word, in others she withdrew into a ghetto and lived in isolation from the 'world'. Sometimes indigenous manpower was utilised right from the start, at other times the missionary agency monopolised and controlled all activities for an indefinite period. In some instances efforts were made to convert entire tribes or similar homogeneous groups to Christianity, in others the policy was rather to win individuals who then, as 'first-fruits', could as it were represent the entire group. At times the work was done thoroughly, preceded by careful study and marked by extraordinary commitment; at other times the word was sown in great haste after which the missionaries moved on to new regions. In some circles mission was understood as the unfolding of God's involvement in the world; in others as a suprahistorical, apocalyptic enterprise that had to ripen the world for the day of judgment. Along these and similar paths, false tracks, roundabout routes and byways mission ran its course through the centuries.

In her missionary involvement the Church was frequently confronted with tensions and temptations which frustrated and sometimes totally sabotaged her mission. We must mention some of these.

First, the Church's own spiritual inadequacy and accompanying uncertainty about the foundation, aim and method of her calling in the world had a paralysing effect on her involvement. There was, furthermore, the perennial problem of the relationship between Church and state, a problem which repeated itself in many different forms. There was, thirdly, the less pressing but none the less essential issue of the Church's attitude to social questions: slavery, the position of women, race relations, the attitude of Westerners towards people of the Third World, and the discrepancy between the rich and the poor. Lastly, there was the problem of the attitude of the Christian mission to other religions.[3]

We could no doubt add other issues. The four we have mentioned nevertheless virtually cover all aspects of the involvement of the Church-in-mission in the world. History is, however, a dynamic process and this complicates matters; the four fields of tension time and again present themselves in new forms, so that yesterday's solutions may be irrelevant today and today's legitimate action out of date tomorrow.

We do not intend presenting an historical survey of the Christian mission. We are interested, rather, in the way mission was understood in various periods. There are many books on the history of mission and occasionally such books do indeed refer in passing to the 'theology of mission' through the centuries.[4] An especially praiseworthy enterprise is the comprehensive series in German on 'Church history as the history of mission', of which two volumes have been published to date.[5] Even here, however, the more specific 'theology of mission' appears to be of subordinate interest. It would therefore appear that in this respect a large area still lies fallow. The excellent bibliographies published in the first two volumes of *Kirchengeschichte als Missionsgeschichte*[6] also reveal this lacuna. Thorough research has been done on missionary personalities from the periods covered by the two volumes, on missionary methods, motives for accepting Christianity, specific regions and peoples, linguistic problems, geographical expansion of the Church, the cultural influence of Christianity, relations between Church and state, the influence of pagan religions on Christianity, etc. Relatively little, however, has been done on the ways in which the Church in various countries and periods interpreted her missionary responsibility. To detect her 'theology of mission' we are therefore dependent upon almost incidental remarks strewn throughout the various works of research. A praiseworthy exception is offered by Gerhard Rosenkranz, who in his *Die christliche Mission: Geschichte und Theologie* reviews the entire theology of mission from the perspective of nineteen centuries of Church and mission history.

Our purpose is much more modest than Rosenkranz's who, moreover, offers much more than the theology of mission in his book. In the overall design within which we place this section we must necessarily limit ourselves considerably. We intend merely to sketch the outlines of the theological understanding of mission through the centuries, making use of test samples from history. In so doing we shall not dwell at length on particular theological statements on mission since the earliest period of Church history, although this is the way in which our subject has usually been treated. Thomas Ohm for instance concentrates exclusively on the theological contributions to the theory of mission of people such as Clement of Alexandria, Chrysostom, Ambrose, Augustine, Gregory the Great, Bernard of Clairvaux, Thomas Aquinas, Raymond Lull and many others in more recent times.[7] Naturally we should not be able to ignore such contributions. We are, however, interested in a rather different dimension which Ohm leaves completely untouched: the way in which the Church, and at a later stage the 'Christian government', have understood their missionary responsibility. This means that we shall not look for the theology of mission exclusively in written documents but very specifically also in the activities of the Church in various periods and in different circumstances.

CHAPTER ELEVEN

THE EARLY CHURCH

THE AMBIVALENCE OF THE CHURCH

The notion that the Christian Church was an ideal community in all respects until the beginning of the fourth century and that the 'Fall' of the Church began with the dawn of the Constantinian era, is a myth. The New Testament already proves this, as may be deduced from Paul's first letter to the Corinthians and the letters to the seven churches in Asia Minor (Rev. 2-3). At no stage has the Church been perfect.

The Church has, since her birth, been a peculiarly ambivalent body. She is *in* but not *of* the world. She always moves 'between salvation history and history'.[1] She is a sociological entity like any other human organisation and as such susceptible to all human frailties; at the same time she is an eschatological entity and as such the incorruptible Body of Christ. Seen through the eyes of the world she is usually under suspicion, disreputable and shabby; in the light of eternity she is a mystery. The resurrected Christ breathed his Spirit into a very earthy and common group of people. Thus the Church became an inseparable union of the divine and the mundane. Sometimes the one aspect is more in evidence, sometimes the other. We can be utterly disgusted, at times, with the earthiness of the Church; at other times we can be enraptured by the awareness of the divine dimension in the Church. Usually, however, it is the ambivalence that strikes us: the Church as a community of people—good people, weak people, hesitant people, courageous people—on their way through the world, dust-stained but somehow strangely illuminated by a radiancy from elsewhere.

In a previous chapter we referred to the tension between 'movement' and 'institution' which is peculiar to the Church. In the early years of her existence she was pre-eminently 'movement'. We are tempted to idealise the years of her youth and in this process close our eyes to the dangers to which a 'movement' is susceptible. It can so easily dissipate. Therefore the institutional element has to be added; this is not simply a sign of decay but a protection and preservation. However, where the institutional aspect begins to eclipse the dynamic aspect of the movement, the creative tension disappears and petrifaction sets in. There were signs of this at a very early stage in Church history, a development which had sad results for the understanding of mission in this period.

The gospel could, for instance, become a *new philosophy*, merely a variant of contemporary Greek philosophical schools. The early Christian apologists were especially tempted, in their polemic against the philosophers, to present the Christian faith as the oldest or most reasonable or most practical religion. Such an approach indeed revealed an aggressive universalism, but one frequently devoid of any missionary dynamic.

The gospel could also become the most novel variety of the Greek *mystery religions* where baptism and Holy Communion could be interpreted as the cultic activities of the specially initiated living in other-worldly ghettos.

Another perennial danger was for the gospel to become a new *gnosis*, a religion of redemption by means of 'true knowledge', which could guide the soul out of the darkness of the created world towards its eternal home in light, a religion according to which the world is remote from God, sin is interpreted as being trapped in matter and mission means showing man a way out of the world.

The Church could also, in her efforts to remain at all costs true to the Jewish people, allow the gospel to develop into yet another variety of the contemporary Jewish movements. This is what happened, to some extent, with the *Ebionites*, where Jesus tended to be considered a rabbi or prophet, greater and better than the rest, indeed, but in essence hardly different. Mission then meant recruiting disciples for his 'school'.

The gospel could also be absorbed by *apocalypticism*, as happened in Montanism, where 'having the Spirit' became the prerogative of an elite group and mission consisted in admitting as members the elect who were merely waiting for the imminent end of the world and Christ's return.

These five interpretations of the gospel—to which more, such as Manichaeism, could be added—were all in the course of time repudiated as heresies. The inevitable result of this, however, was that the Church for all practical purposes immunised herself against the elements of truth in each of these heresies. This would remain a permanent dilemma for the Church: for the sake of sheer survival she had to reject every heresy, but in each case this happened to her own detriment. Every heresy contains an essential element of truth. It is this which makes heresies so potent and attractive. We can all cope with lies. It is much more difficult to handle half-truths. Deprive the heresy of its element of truth and you have deprived it of its power. If you reject it and immunise yourself against it you are inevitably harming yourself.

SPIRIT AND OFFICE

In her preoccupation with her own survival the Church suffered in many ways, especially as regards her conception of her mission in the world. 'Church' and 'mission' became two entities next to and sometimes over against one another. Originally they were practically synonymous. The founding of the Church and the beginning of mission coincided (Acts 2). Mission was mission-of-the-Church and Church was missionary Church. In the course of time, however, as one congregation after another was established and experienced 'growing pains', there developed a tendency to concentrate on parochial problems and neglect the relationship of the Church to the world. Ecclesiology developed a weight of its own. In a famous essay on 'The Church in Missionary Thinking', Hoekendijk puts it scathingly:

Ecclesiology has been a subject of major concern only in the 'second generation'; in the 'first generation', in periods of revival, reformation or missionary advance, our interest was absorbed by christology, thought-patterns were determined by eschatology, life became a doxology and the Church was spoken of in an unaccented and to some extent rather naïve way, as being something that 'thank God a child of seven knows what it is' (Luther).[2]

Paul polemicises passionately against the danger of a narrow ecclesiology. In his letters to the Corinthians, Galatians, Ephesians and others he contends for the sanctification of the Church, but he does it specifically in view of her involvement in the world. None of the images of the Church in the New Testament, concerning which Paul S. Minear did such outstanding research—people of God, flock, house where God dwells through his Spirit, new creation, one new man in Christ, salt of the earth, light of the world, bride of Christ, saints, children of God, and many more—describes the Church as a body which exists only for its own sake.

In the course of time, however, the apostles, prophets and teachers began to make room for bishops, elders and deacons. This meant, at least potentially, that the Spirit gave way to the office. Apostolicity—originally a symbol of the Church's involvement in and obligation towards the world—became, in the context of 'apostolic succession', the hallmark of bishops with an 'impeccable pedigree' (Hoekendijk) or a guarantee of purity of doctrine. The bishop became the sole channel through which the current of sacramental grace could flow. The official Church became bulwark and custodian of the orthodox faith over against heretics (Irenaeus); outside this Church there was no salvation (Cyprian). She adorned herself with the divine and indelible qualities of authority and sanctity.

PAROUSIA OR IMMORTALITY?

One of the most serious problems the early Church had to face lay in the fact that the return of Christ, expected in the immediate future, did not take place. Traces of this expectation are discernible in many New Testament passages (cf. for instance John 21.22-23). The second epistle to the Thessalonians is intended to put in a wider perspective this expectation of the end which Paul had portrayed in the first epistle. It had, in many cases, led to inactivity. Now the message is: the end will not come immediately. The way in which 2 Pet. 3.8 counteracts the cynical remarks of the scoffers (that the *parousia* has now been delayed so long that there is no point in still expecting it), namely, by reminding them that with the Lord one day is like a thousand years and a thousand years like one day, appears to be a complete abandonment of the dynamic tension of the early Christian eschatological expectation. Nevertheless, both 2 Thessalonians and 2 Peter placed their 'apologies' for the apparent delay of the *parousia* within the context of a dynamic understanding of history. Nowhere in the New Testament did apocalypticism completely win the day because nowhere was the present regarded as empty. Time and again mission proved to be the Church's dynamic involvement in the world, her response to the question about the significance of the interim period. The Church was never allowed to escape either into a supra-temporal 'eternal' existence, or to sit on her hands waiting for the end. It was her mission which protected her against a fate comparable to that of the Qumran community and similar religious groups, for her mission moored her to history in the process of being fulfilled.

By the second century there was a noticeable relaxation of the creative tension in which the Church of the first century had lived. The hereafter was increasingly interpreted as something outside time. Hell was proclaimed as a constant threat; to escape it, the faithful had to do many good works, pour forth many prayers, and invoke the intercession of many saints. This led to the despising of *this* world. Official Christianity tended to become a religion of redemption, modelled on the mystery religions. The emphasis was on salvation *from* the earth rather than on renewal *of* the earth. Involvement in the world took the form of mere charity. All emphasis was laid on the immortality of the soul which Lactantius designated the 'greatest good'. The consecrated bread in the Eucharist became a *pharmakon athanasias*, a 'medicine of immortality'.[3] Thus eschatology was spiritualised; in its turn this led to a moralism which spread like blight over Christianity's entire expectation of the future.[4]

Did this lead to the cessation of all missionary involvement? No, because in spite of all these signs of spiritual declension the Christians somehow remembered that, as the 'third race', they had a calling to fulfil. The sporadic persecutions by the state reminded them that they were pilgrims who fitted nowhere. This could easily have led to their total withdrawal from public life. Nevertheless it was precisely the persecutions which, time and again, reminded them of their involvement in the world, politically, socially, and otherwise, and preserved them from encapsulation.

The early Christians also had the awareness of the presence of the Spirit. In modern theological research the close connection between the Holy Spirit and mission was for a long time not recognised. Roland Allen was one of the first modern scholars seriously to draw our attention to this.[5] Harry Boer devoted an exegetical study to the subject.[6] On the one hand the missionary dimension of Pneumatology expressed itself in the activities of itinerant charismatic preachers who launched a 'world-wide missionary programme', especially in Asia Minor and Syria.[7] On the other hand it evinced itself in the daily lives of ordinary believers.

This last facet is of extraordinary importance to the way in which the early Church understood her existence in the world as mission. Each aspect of her life, including her 'purely religious' activities, had a missionary dimension. Both baptism and Holy Communion had such a dimension, by virtue of their origins.[8] Church leaders were chosen not simply with an eye to internal parish responsibilities, but also with an eye to outsiders; they had to have 'a good reputation with the non-Christian public' (1 Tim. 3.7).

In a world which Rosenkranz describes as 'macabre, lost in despair, perversity and superstition'[9], Christian churches emerged as something entirely new, as 'faultless children of God in a warped and crooked generation, in which you shine like stars in a dark world' (Phil. 2.15). The testimonies of enemies of the Church, such as Celsus, frequently mentioned the exceptional conduct of Christians. The fact that they were such ordinary people made their behaviour so much more remarkable. We read in a famous pericope in the *Letter to Diognetus*:

> Christians are not distinguished from the rest of mankind either in locality or in speech or in customs. For they dwell not somewhere in cities of their own, neither do they use some different language, nor practise an extraordinary kind of life ... While they dwell in cities of Greeks and Bar-

barians ... and follow the native customs in dress and food and the other arrangements of life, yet the constitution of their own citizenship, which they set forth, is marvellous, and confessedly contradicts expectation. They dwell in their own countries, but only as sojourners ... Every foreign country is a fatherland to them, and every fatherland is foreign ... They find themselves in the flesh and yet they live not after the flesh. Their existence is on earth, but their citizenship is in heaven. They obey the established laws, and they surpass the laws in their own lives ... So Christians are kept in the world as in a prison-house, and yet they themselves hold the world together.

Michael Green attributes the missionary dimension of the lives of the early Christians to their example, fellowship, transformed characters, joy and endurance.[10] In a lengthy and penetrating chapter, and with reference to Matt. 25.42-43, 45, Adolf von Harnack describes the early Church's 'gospel of love and charity' as a witness that included alms, care of widows, orphans, the sick, prisoners, mine-workers, the poor, slaves, and travellers.[11] Conversion to Christ manifested itself not in a change of sentiment but in a new way of life that arrested attention in the events of every day. Precisely in this way conversion was understood and put within a missionary context.

THE CHURCH AND THE JEWS

We have to pay attention, briefly, to one more facet of the way in which the early Church interpreted her mission. We refer to her attitude to the Jews. The Christian Church arose out of Judaism, as a Jewish sect. For a considerable period she was regarded—especially by the Roman authorities—as a mere variation on the Jewish theme.

We have every reason to accept that the earliest Christians, the majority of whom were Jews, went out of their way to evangelise the Jews. According to Luke, Paul repeatedly began his preaching in Jewish synagogues (cf. Acts 13.14; 14.1; 17.1-2; 17.10; 18.4). Paul reminded the Gentile Christians that they were cut from a wild olive and against all nature grafted into the cultivated olive, Israel (Rom. 11.24). He asserted that they used to be strangers to the community of Israel and outside God's covenants (Eph. 2.12) but were now made 'joint heirs' (Eph. 3.6). He also described the gospel as God's saving power first for the Jew (Rom. 1.16). By all this he underscored the centrality of the Jews in the eyes of the early Christian converts. Yet there are in the New Testament, especially in the Gospels, statements which later on could easily be used to exclude Jews from salvation in Christ. In a very short period the early Church passed through three stages: from a proclamation exclusively to Jews (cf. especially Acts 11.19) to a mission to Jews and Gentiles, and ultimately to Gentiles only.

Until AD 85 many Jewish Christians participated in synagogue worship. The anti-Christian decrees of that year however made any further participation impossible. The break with Judaism was nevertheless not yet final. It became so only after the second destruction of the temple by the Romans whose armies suppressed the revolt of Simon bar Kochba. After that event no Jew was ever again elected bishop of Jerusalem. The epistle of Barnabas (*circa* AD 113) and Justin's *Dialogue with Trypho the Jew* (soon after AD 150) for all practical purposes excluded Jews from the Church's field of vision. In the writings of Tertullian and Cyprian we encounter the view that, at most, individual Jews could be converted. This too was finally to disappear with the anti-Jewish edicts of Emperor Theodosius in AD 378.

The whole process was inevitable, although tragic in many ways. Christians regarded themselves as the 'true Israel' and the *tôrâh* as something of the past. They accepted Jesus as the expected Messiah and with that placed themselves diametrically opposite rabbinical Judaism which rejected him. Salvation through this Jewish Jesus was proclaimed, without regard to persons, to members of all nations (Gal. 3.28; Col. 3.11).

It was not that the Christians *added* certain elements to the Jewish faith. It was rather that they appropriated many things that were dear to Judaism and reinterpreted them. Harnack is right when he says, 'The Gentile Church stripped it (Judaism) of everything'.[12]

For a time a number of Jewish-Christian churches tried to maintain themselves. They could, however, do it only by perverting Paul's concentration on Israel into a limiting of salvation to Israel, but in so doing they signed their own death-warrant.[13] Increasingly estranged from their fellow Jews and by their own decision cut off from a missionary contact with Gentiles, they could not but pine away and eventually disappear. It is not inconceivable that it was into these encapsulated Jewish-Christian communities that certain inter- pretations of the Old Testament gained access—views such as the one that the gospel need not be proclaimed to Gentiles as God himself would bring them in by means of a direct, divine intervention in the last hour—a distorted understanding of Isaiah 2.2-4 (Mic. 4.1-4).

CHAPTER TWELVE

THE CONSTANTINIAN ERA

CHRISTENDOM AND MISSION

In the previous chapter we dissociated ourselves from the view according to which Emperor Constantine and the period of Church history linked with his name is one-sidedly held responsible for all negative developments regarding Church and mission. We argued that these developments could in embryo already be detected in the early Church described in the New Testament.

In spite of this remark it has to be admitted that a new era dawned with Constantine's victory over Maxentius at the Milvian Bridge near Rome on 28th October, AD 312. Few, if any, events in history had such a far-reaching and lasting effect on the Church. The phenomenon known as Europe has its origin here, as has the idea of the 'Christian West' or 'Christendom'. Constantine's victory has consequences up to this day. In fact, it is only in recent decades that the full significance of those events at the beginning of the fourth century has begun to dawn upon us. For mission and the understanding of mission the events of those fateful years had equally drastic implications, especially in view of the fact that the founding and constituting of Europe may be called a fruit of mission.[1]

The Edict of Milan (AD 313) was the first to guarantee to Christians religious freedom equal to that enjoyed by pagan cults. It was followed by various measures which increasingly favoured Christianity, a process which found its culmination in AD 380, when Emperor Theodosius declared the orthodox faith, as represented by the Bishop of Rome and the Patriarch of Alexandria, the only religious form permitted in the Empire. Pagans and heretic Christians were thus lumped together and branded as enemies of the state. The doctrine of the Trinity, interpreted in orthodox fashion, became a state law. Anybody who refused to accept it was not only a heretic but also an anarchist. The first heretic was executed as early as AD 385. Where, prior to Constantine, it involved a risk to be a member of the Church, it now became dangerous not to be a member. Church affiliation became a matter of course.

One of the most important consequences of the 'Constantinian turning-point' was that the Church lost her pilgrim character. In the light of the New Testament the Church-in-mission may never be completely at home in the world (cf. Heb. 13.13). She is, according to her very nature, a community on the move, a fragment of God's Kingdom in the world, not identical to the Kingdom and yet closely related to it. In the centuries before Constantine, in spite of many adaptations to the world and increasing haziness about her mission, she remained pilgrim. The hostile—or, at best, tolerating—attitude of the Roman authorities helped to remind the Church that she fitted nowhere but remained a stranger in this world.

All this changed with Constantine. The eschatological expectation abated. The Kingdom was spiritualised and internalised. The Church made herself at home in the world as dispenser of salvation. She became the self-designated 'extension of Christ's incarnation', which Braaten rightly interprets as 'the most conservative possible model of eschatology'. He continues: 'All important events in God's history with the world have already occurred. The church has only to sit on its past and raise up leaders to function as guardians of the treasury of salvation stored in the documents of Christian antiquity.'[2]

THE TRIUMPH OF THE GREEK SPIRIT

The fact that the early church expanded especially on Greek soil surely also played a role—quite apart from the influence of the Constantinian era. In some circles today there is a tendency to contrast radically the Greek and Hebrew minds, as though the one is everything the other is not. This is undoubtedly an exaggeration. Yet the observation that we have here two different world-views has· sufficient validity to warrant the thesis that the migration of the Church from the Hebrew to the Greek world had important consequences for the understanding of Church and mission.

For Israel God lived. For the Greeks he was an immortal

Being. Ontology was important to the Greeks. Exod. 3.4, in the Hebrew original, does *not* attempt to define Yahweh. He remains the inscrutable. The Septuagint changes the Hebrew to *egō eimi ho ōn*, thus defining Yahweh as eternal Being. This shift towards ontology eventually led to the doctrine of the thirteen 'attributes' of God. The early Christian message regarding God who disclosed himself, gradually became a rigidly static orthodox dogma about the being of God in three hypostases. Ontology dominated the drawn-out christological controversies. Revelation was not God's self-communication any more but the transmission of 'truth' which could be codified in unalterable formulas.

Unlike the Hebrew *yāda'*, which means knowing-as-experience, the Greek *ginōskein* emphasises intellectual and rational knowledge. The Hebrew *dābār* refers to word *and* event, both containing the element of historical movement, of being open and dynamic. *Logos*, however, is not the same as *dābār*. It is much more static. The emphasis here is on the visual rather than the auditive aspect. The visual, the image, is always more static and unalterable than the spoken word. The Greeks are therefore concerned with 'idea' and 'theory', both words derived from verbs meaning 'to see'. 'To know' here means 'to have seen' and the greatest good lies in being able to 'see God' (cf. Matt. 5.8; John 17.24; 1 John 3.2; Rev. 22.4). Even the concept history—Greek *historia*, derived from *histōr*, eyewitness, which ought to suggest something dynamic—becomes something static in the Greek world.

Ecclesiologically this Hellenising development meant that the Church became a precisely definable entity, with clearly identifiable boundaries. The Church-in-movement became the established Church in orthodox form outside of which there was no salvation. In future 'mission' would simply mean church extension. Being baptised into the Catholic Church meant becoming a 'Christian'. The Church was the hierarchical institution under the supervision of bishops. The few remaining missionaries regarded themselves as ambassadors of the pope whose task was to incorporate new converts into the Church.

Of course this whole development did not come about suddenly. Neither did it take place without protest, as we shall see. Nevertheless, in the course of time, it undoubtedly became the dominant trend, as can be seen in the person and work of Augustine and in the way he was to be interpreted. Chrysostom and others judged that the gospel was proclaimed by the apostles in the entire world (a view which, incidentally, would be held in some Protestant theological circles until the eighteenth century). Augustine did not agree. His understanding of mission, as his view of the Church, contained a dynamic element: the Church is *communio sanctorum*, communion of the saints, the eschatological community of salvation sent into the world. She is also *civitas Dei*, the 'City of God' on earth, the Kingdom, the institution of salvation that grows organically and does not need to lure pagans to her as the heretics do. The first view of the Church, which is forcefully present in Augustine's writings, was to grow paler in the subsequent period. In fact, for Augustine even the *civitas Dei* was not explicitly identical to the visible Roman Catholic Church. This is, however, the way in which later generations were to interpret Augustine.

MISSION AS CULTURAL PROPAGANDA

The view according to which mission is to be understood as cultural propaganda has its origin in the Constantinian era. It is a view that would dominate the interpretation of mission for centuries, even up to our own time. To grasp the extent of this shift in the image of mission it is necessary to remind ourselves that the early Church in no circumstances understood herself as a bearer of culture. After all, she operated in the *oikoumenē*, in other words, within 'civilisation', in contrast to the 'barbarian' areas outside. She thus laboured on soil saturated with culture. Rather than propagating 'culture Christianity' the early Church lamented the decadence of contemporary education and culture on many points. Cultural influence by the Church was out of the question, more so because she originally worked almost exclusively on the periphery of society, among slaves, women and strangers, in other words, among people who had no particular influence on the shape of society. The Greek cultural world, including Greek philosophy and paganism (cf. Celsus!) held the Church in contempt.

All this changed after Constantine. The Church consciously

became a bearer of culture and a civilising presence in society. The fact that the real expansion of the Church in this period no longer took place among civilised Greeks and Romans (they were by now already christianised) but among the barbarian tribes of the Germanic world, added to the idea that Christianity represented a superior culture. It was understandable that this period could produce no Celsus: after all, only Christians were civilised and educated!

The early Church took the pagan religions seriously. This attitude disappeared in the Constantinian era. The Church's claim to truth was absolute. The gods of the barbarians were demons or 'nothings' behind which satanic powers hid themselves. The pagan cults were devil-worship. The point at issue here was not just conversion to Christ but the clash of two worlds, one of which was *a priori* superior to the other. In the Middle Ages people were never referred to as 'Christians' and 'non-Christians', but as *fideles* (believers) and *infideles* or *perfidi* (unbelievers). *Fides*, faith, was something only Christians possessed. Thus nobody would ever have thought of talking about *fides pagana* or *fides Judaica*. Pagan religions were referred to as *ritus, superstitio, error,* or *lex* (law).[3]

Adherents of such 'superstitions' could therefore easily be impressed with the aid of ecclesiastical vestments, crosses and ceremonies. Proclamation could consist of a comparison between the omnipotence and value of the Christian faith and the powerlessness and futility of pagan error. Common law also discriminated against pagans. Occasionally the opinion was even expressed that pagans were without any rights whatsoever. Usually, however, they were accorded 'natural rights' as 'creatures', but then in such a way that it was usually a lesser right than that enjoyed by Christians. As soon as they were baptised, the situation changed and they were accepted as Christian brothers *and* as citizens enjoying equal rights.

MISSION AS 'DE-PAGANISATION'

Baptism was increasingly regarded as the decisive watershed between Christianity and paganism. It imparted an indelible character. Mission was thus increasingly understood almost exclusively as preparation for baptism, which was usually administered after a minimum period of instruction, sometimes even without any such preparation whatsoever. Once baptised, people were without further ado regarded as Christians.

Normally the missionary process passed through two stages, de-paganisation and christianisation, the first negative, the second positive. This is still evident in the baptismal vow with its two poles: *abrenuntiatio diaboli* (renouncing the devil) and *confessio fidei* (confessing the faith). Baptism primarily had to do with the first and was increasingly regarded as act of submission to the hierarchical institute. From the moment of baptism people ceased to be objects of mission and became objects of ecclesiastical discipline. The scope of the missionary's responsibility gradually shrivelled to a much reduced programme of proclamation; that of the ecclesiastical disciplinary power however was extended to something almost all-inclusive. Inner conviction became less and less important; it was a distant goal which would be attained perhaps only after several generations. The baptismal event in itself was decisive, not the inner acceptance of the gospel. Even if baptised under protest, one became a *fidelis* (believer), because of the guaranteed efficacy of baptism. Once baptised, a person could be gradually moulded with the aid of the practice of penance and other coercive measures. Thomas Aquinas could therefore say that what mattered in the last instance was 'a simple, obedient acceptance of the Church's teachings, even without any real knowledge of their contents'.[4]

This approach had yet another implication. Whereas, in most instances, there was still a degree of reticence as regards the possibility of using coercion to christianise pagans, the official attitude towards heretics and lapsed Christians was totally different. They were baptised, and therefore—whether they understood their baptism or not, indeed, whether they were baptised of their own free will or not—they had to conform to what was expected of the baptised. Augustine, one of those who pleaded for a more positive and milder approach to pagans, was relentless and intolerant when it concerned the 're-catholisation' of Donatists and other heretics and apostates. He applied without reserve the words, 'compel them to come in', in Luke 14.23 to these people. The religious roots of both the Crusades and the Inquisition are to be found here. Thomas puts it as follows in his *Summa Theologica*: 'Unbelievers who have not yet accepted the faith, Jews and pagans, should under no circumstances be forced to become believers; but heretics and apostates should be forced to fulfil what they have promised.'

CONVERSION BY COERCION

To understand the role of coercive mission we have to pay attention to the implications which the close link between Church and state had for understanding mission. The Church historian Eusebius, for instance, attempts to give an explanation of the new situation since Constantine. Polytheism, he says, was overcome by the monotheism of the Jews, polyarchy by the monarchy of the Romans since Augustus. The Christian emperor Constantine, ruler of the world, was now called to lead the world back to God and in this process the united empire was an important instrument.

Indeed, the emperors themselves would, from time to time, attempt to equate the unity of the empire with the unity of the Faith. The *Henotikon* of Emperor Zenon in 482, the *Ekthesis* of Heraclius in 638 and the *Typos* of Constantius II in 648 were all measures in which the interests of Church and state were intimately united.

Small wonder then that inhabitants of countries outside the Roman Empire regarded the Church with great suspicion. The Aramaean Christians in the Sassanid Empire were for instance viewed as a fifth column of the Roman Empire. King Sapor II put it succinctly: 'They live in our territories but share the sentiments of Caesar.' Several Christian groups who were not prepared to subscribe to the official orthodox doctrine found asylum in territories outside the borders of the Roman Empire where they were welcomed precisely because of their resistance to the orthodox faith and therefore to the Roman Empire. This applies especially to Nestorians and Monophysites.

After 755 Pippin, and subsequently Charlemagne, used the formula *fideles Dei et nostri* (those who are faithful to God and us) in various documents. This self-evidently implied the obverse: disloyalty to God and emperor went hand in hand. Charlemagne especially was of the opinion that Church and state should support one another. His famous letter to Pope Leo

III testified to this; in it he described the defence of Christianity by force of arms as his responsibility, and Leo's as that of Moses who interceded with raised arms and prayers for the armed conflict against pagans. With the same axiom with which citizens of the Holy Roman Empire were called believers, the peoples beyond the borders were branded unbelievers. From 776 onwards the annals of the empire regularly mentioned that the Saxon pagans were fighting *adversus christianos* (against the Christians).[5]

Initially this interpretation would not lead explicitly to a direct holy war against pagans. Augustine, for instance, was consistently opposed to any form of forced conversion of pagans. He could say, nevertheless, that it might be advisable to prepare for the proclamation of the gospel among pagan peoples beyond the borders of the empire by subjugating them militarily. The peaceful preaching of the gospel could then proceed unhampered under the benevolent protection of the empire. In this way the idea of the 'indirect missionary war' was born and the foundation laid for the close relationship between Church and mission which characterised the much later colonisation programme of the European powers.[6]

From here there was only one step to the direct missionary wars and conversions by force under Charlemagne and others. Yet even in Charlemagne's campaigns the first and foremost concern was to subject people to him and only in the second place to the Christian God. Baptism was a *consequence* of military conquest, a secondary event. To put it differently: baptism was, in Charlemagne's view, the inevitable seal on the subjugation of the Saxons. Deportations on a massive scale and genocide (such as the execution of 4,500 Saxons at the River Aller in 782) served this purpose. History would repeat itself, as when, in about the year 1000, Olav Tryggvason christianised the Norwegians by force, or when a crusade was launched against the Wends, a Slavonic tribe, in 1147. In each case Jesus' words in Luke 14.23, 'Compel them to enter', were misused to justify the ruler's actions.

The Crusades against the Muslims had nothing to do with mission. When Pope Urban proclaimed the first Crusade, he did not for a moment consider the possibility of converting Muslims. If, in Crusade literature, references occur to

Christianity being 'enhanced' or 'extended', this referred to the expansion of the Christian empire and sphere of influence, and only in exceptional cases to the possible conversion of Muslims. Nevertheless the Crusades were nothing but a logical outflow of the idea of the 'holy war' which had been developing since Augustine. Crusades against Muslims, wars against pagan tribes on the borders of the empire, and military expeditions against heretics such as the Albigenses and Waldensees were all variations on the same theme.

In the same context we refer to the attitude of Church and state to the Jews during the Middle Ages—one of the most unsavoury chapters in the history of Europe. As Amnon Linder points out,[7] the attitude towards Jews was for a long time ambivalent. On the one hand there was an attitude of tolerance, due to the theological influence of Paul and Augustine, further stimulated by Pope Gregory I; people who held this view, accepted the possibility of a voluntary conversion of individual Jews. Then there was the attitude of condemnation which increased hand over fist from the beginning of the Constantinian era. Jewish proselytism and intercourse with Christians were prohibited. Jewish revolts were violently suppressed and synagogues destroyed. The Jews were held responsible for Christ's crucifixion: they were 'murderers of God'. Forced conversion to Christianity was frequently the only alternative to expulsion, expropriation and the death penalty—an alternative, moreover, which they were not always offered. In the early Middle Ages these two attitudes still existed side by side. In subsequent centuries however the mild attitude would for all practical purposes disappear.

MONASTICISM AND MISSION

It goes without saying that the views just discussed did not in all respects apply to the Church in all her parts. In every period of Church history and in all countries there were those who did not conform to the general pattern—bishops, priests, ordinary Christians. Nowhere, however, did the protest against the decay in the Church become as evident as in monasticism. As the world increasingly penetrated the Church, those who regarded themselves as the true Church forsook the world and lived in seclusion and sacrifice as monks and ascetics. E. R. Hardy is right in asserting that, after persecution had ended, the monk replaced the martyr as expression of unqualified Christian witness and protest against worldliness.[8]

Frequently the protest was more in evidence than the witness. This was the case for instance both with the Celtic monasteries which were not founded primarily as missionary centres, and with many monks in the eastern part of the Roman Empire and neighbouring territories. And yet, precisely in their protest against the secularisation of the Church, there was a missionary dimension which often had an active missionary involvement as logical consequence. In the east the monks were the spiritual descendants of the itinerant charismatic preachers of the pre-Constantinian era—people such as Hilarion in Palestine, Abraamius in Lebanon, Anthony in Egypt—who through the unity of word and deed combined monasticism and mission. As Neilus put it: 'A life without speech is wont to avail more than speech without the life.' He himself pleaded for a combination of both.[9] In this, monastic mission differed fundamentally from the typical mission of the bishops of the period who, as princes of the Church, were primarily interested in mission as masonry reinforcing remaining weak spots in the ecclesiastical edifice.

For the Irish monks *peregrinatio* (pilgrimage into the unknown) was in the first place an expression of ascetic homelessness and a component of the Christian discipline of penance. Celtic 'Wanderlust' undoubtedly also played a role. Mission remained a by-product. As G. S. M. Walker puts it: '... the (Celtic) urge to travel was turned into Christian channels, so that pilgrimage became associated with mission, and both were subordinate to the spiritual perfection of the monk.'[10]

It was different in the case of the Anglo-Saxon monks after the seventh century. Whereas mission was, for the Irish, an unplanned consequence of their travels into foreign territories, *peregrinatio* was from the start mission for the Anglo-Saxons. In the face of the imminent end of the world, constrained by the command, *Ite, docete omnes gentes* ('Go and teach all nations', Matt. 28.19), and in close liaison with their home church, they embarked upon a world-wide mission. In yet another important aspect they differed from the Irish. Where the latter were concerned about forming local groups of believers, the Anglo-Saxons regarded themselves as ambassadors of the pope with the commission to incorporate the newly converted into the hierarchical Church outside of which there was no salvation. Rosenkranz puts it thus: 'From itinerant preachers the Irish developed into missionaries, the Anglo-Saxons however developed from missionaries into church planters.'[11]

It should not surprise us that the monks, in spite of all their protestations against the prevailing worldliness of the Church, still remained children of their time in their missionary approach by accepting the close connection between Church and state which partly produced the worldliness which they rejected. Willibrord, Boniface and others addressed themselves first to the nobility. The great decisions were taken by the princes, not by the common people. In this way Willibrord—to mention but one example—prepared the way for co-operation between the papacy and the Carolingian dynasty in Frisia. The close link between these missionary monks and the state consistently proved to be both a necessity and a burden for their missionary enterprise.[12]

The significance of the monastic movement can, nevertheless, hardly be over-emphasised. Europe sank into chaos in about AD 450 and remained in turmoil for many years. Tribal incursions and migrations virtually destroyed the fabric of society. The most creative response of the Church to the challenge of the times took the form of monasticism. The disciplined and tireless life of the monks turned the tide of barbarism in Western Europe. Of these, perhaps the most famous was Winfrith, better known as Boniface, a man who, to quote Christopher Dawson, 'had a deeper influence on the history of Europe than any Englishman who has ever lived'.[13]

We should also mention the immense impact of the Benedictines in this regard. One of the best descriptions of the often unobtrusive way in which they went about their mission comes from the pen of Newman:

St Benedict found the world, physical and social, in ruins, and his mission was to restore it in the way not of science, but of nature, not as if setting about to do it, not professing to do it by any set time, or by any rare specific, or by any series of strokes, but so quietly, patiently, gradually, that often till the work was done, it was not known to be doing. It was a restoration, rather than a visitation, correction or conversion. The new work which he helped to create was a growth rather than a structure. Silent men were observed about the country, or discovered in the forest, digging, clearing and building; and other silent men, not seen, were sitting in the cold cloister, tiring their eyes and keeping their attention on the stretch, while they painfully copied and recopied the manuscripts which they had saved. There was no one who contended or cried out, or drew attention to what was going on, but by degrees the woody swamp became a hermitage, a religious house, a farm, an abbey, a village, a seminary, a school of learning and a city.[14]

What was true of the Benedictines was true of Celtic monasticism as well. In fact, independent Celtic monasteries were founded all over Europe and beyond. Between 550 and 1200 such monasteries were established all the way from Skellig Michael, off the west coast of Ireland, to Kiev in the Ukraine.

These communities may be regarded as forerunners of the more explicitly missionary orders of the late medieval period, such as the Franciscans and Dominicans. Together with people such as Ramón Llull (Raymond Lull) these missionaries for instance condemned the Crusades in no uncertain terms. They had grasped something of the vision that mission had to do with quiet commitment and suffering. To be a witness for Christ among Muslims could involve risking one's life. Llull put it as follows: 'Missionaries will convert the world through the proclamation of the gospel, but also by shedding tears and blood and through much suffering as well as a bitter death.' He sealed these words with his own example when he died as martyr in Bugia in North Africa in 1315, at the age of eighty-five.

Most of the monastic missionaries of the Middle Ages laboured within the boundaries of the Roman Empire or in countries the rulers of which were Christian. In most of Asia, however, the Church always laboured as a non-recognised minority in a pagan environment, even though there were periods when she enjoyed the favour of the authorities. Large parts of the Byzantine Church lost their privileged position during the Middle Ages and were subjugated by Muslim governments. In fact the profound differences between Western and Eastern Churches in the understanding of mission have their roots here, to some degree at least. The Western Church was active, aggressive, and imperious. In the Eastern Church liturgical forms and ceremonies played a more prominent role; they were meant to lure the pagans to the Church. The Eastern Church wished to dispense gifts rather than dominate. She therefore also succeeded in surviving even where the political tide turned against her and she could tolerate the continued undisturbed existence of paganism in close proximity to her. In the West, however, the political situation, together with Cyprian's teaching that there was no salvation outside the Church as well as Augustine's emphasis on predestination and judgment, introduced an element of perpetual disquiet in the Church: she could not remain inactive as long as there were, within her reach, people who were still outside the walls of the Church.[15]

CHAPTER THIRTEEN

FROM ALEXANDER VI
TO PIUS XII

COLONIALISM AND MISSION

The *corpus Christianum* or 'Christendom', that is to say the Christian society which developed in the Constantinian era and in which Church and state were indissolubly bound together, did not go unchallenged. It did however survive some severe shocks, such as the rise of Islam which robbed both Church and Christian state of all of the Middle East, North Africa, and Spain. A potentially more serious calamity was the schism between the Eastern and Western Churches in 1054. However, since this division followed mainly geographical lines, it hardly disturbed the equilibrium of the Western Church. The Eastern sister Church, such as the Russian and Greek Orthodox, went her own way; the Roman Catholic Church in the West went hers.

Much more far-reaching, and for the understanding of mission much more important, were the events around 1500. It was, in the first place, the Age of *Discovery*, which suddenly freed Europe from its isolation and opened the way to the far west, east, and south. It was also the age of the *Renaissance* and of *Humanism*, of the dawning of man's autonomy, of burgeoning individualism, and of modern science. Thirdly it was the age of the Protestant *Reformation*, the first movement seriously to question the undisputed hegemony of the Roman Catholic Church in western Europe.

The development of missionary thought in the churches of the Reformation will be the subject of a subsequent chapter. Here we direct our attention only to the way in which Rome interpreted mission from the pontificate of Alexander VI to that of Pius XII—that is, from the discovery of America and the seaway to India, to the death of the last Tridentine pope immediately prior to the Second Vatican Council.

During the fifteenth century Spain and Portugal were the two leaders of geographical exploration. To stabilise the balance of power between them, Pope Alexander VI divided the world beyond Europe in 1493 and 1494, in such a way that both Americas, with the exception of Brazil, would fall within the sphere of Spanish influence while Portugal would have a free hand in Brazil and in virtually all of Asia and Africa. The political division also implied a division as regards the ecclesiastical spheres of influence. It thus went without saying that the Spanish church, in close cooperation with the Spanish crown, would assume responsibility for the incorporation of the peoples of the Americas into the Church.

By this time the Christian West's superiority-feeling had already reached its peak. No local church in Europe could still undertake any mission work in its own neighbourhood since the only remaining pagans now lived far across the ocean. Mission thus became the task of travellers to distant lands. In this way the Western understanding of mission took shape. Missionaries had to travel from Europe to 'savages', to people who were permanently dependent upon their help and guidance. It was an enterprise of the state church and could be undertaken only in countries where the government concerned was also the colonial authority. Stephen Neill sums up:

> Whether we like it or not, it is the historic fact that the great expansion of Christianity has coincided in time with the world-wide and explosive expansion of Europe that followed on the Renaissance; that the colonizing powers have been the Christian powers; that a whole variety of compromising relationships have existed between missionaries and governments; and that in the main Christianity has been carried forward on the wave of western prestige and power.[1]

With this the process inaugurated by Constantine's accession to power was carried to its logical conclusion. The Spanish *conquista* (conquest) of Central and South America was in equal measure a subjugation of the Indians to the Spanish throne and to the Roman Catholic Church. Under the cloak of christianisation an unscrupulous exploitation of the indigenous population, coupled with an unparalleled genocide, was launched.

Even here, however, something of the New Testament understanding of mission survived. Priests such as Antonio de Montesinos, Bartholomew de Las Casas and many others unknown to us intervened on behalf of the victims of the cruelty of the *conquistadores*; they did this well aware of the fact that they were courting fierce opposition and even martyrdom. Later, in the seventeenth century, it was especially the Jesuits who cast in their lot with that of the Indians in Paraguay. Thus even in that dark hour, when mission resembled its biblical original less than ever, something of Christ's compassion was present in some of his ambassadors. Las Casas for instance totally rejected conversion by force—completely contrary to a tradition the roots of which went back to the period even before Charlemagne. *Compellere intrare*, as the Latin Bible of his time translated Luke 14.23, meant, so he argued: '*Persuade* them to enter'. Mission is only mission if it enables people freely to decide to follow Christ. He was concerned with the total need of Indians. For a period of fifty years he intervened with the Spanish throne on their behalf. According to his calculations, between twelve and fifteen million Indians were the victims of the Spanish conquerors.

CHURCH-CENTRED MISSION

In the year 1622 Pope Gregory XV called the *Sacra Congregatio de Propaganda Fide* into being. There could now be no further doubt that mission was not merely a matter for the established Church, but very specifically for the Chair of Peter. Missionary Orders and Congregations were welcome to embark on all kinds of enterprises, and a growing number were founded. It should be noted that by this time the spontaneous missionary endeavours of the early Celtic monks, as well as the role of wordly rulers, in sending out missionaries, were now things of the past. Mission had both its origin and goal in the Church. In the foundation, motive and aim of mission the Church in her hierarchical structure stood in the centre.

To achieve the aim of mission the world was divided into two parts: the area of the established European Church, and the missionary territories of the non-Christian world. The concern behind this action was to give official sanction to the extension of the Western ecclesiastical system which had earlier been given a fixed doctrinal and juridical shape at the Council of Trent (1545-1563).

At the beginning of the twentieth century two 'schools' of missiology developed—at Münster and Louvain. These were to be associated respectively with the names of J. Schmidlin and P. Charles. Münster emphasised the conversion of pagans as the central aim of mission whereas Louvain focused on the implantation of the Church. The two views do not, however, differ as much as is often suggested. Ultimately, in both views, the Church remained central. Schmidlin for instance, the main proponent of the first view and to some extent a student of Gustav Warneck, the father of Protestant missiology, explicitly criticised Protestant mission for being 'in reality churchless'. He argued that a subjectivistic appeal to the Great Commission, as was customary in nineteenth-century Protestantism, did not offer an adequate foundation for mission. For Catholics, however, he said, this problem had long been solved by means of the doctrine of the visible Church and her hierarchical constitution. In the final analysis the pope was the subject of mission. It therefore came as no surprise that the four great papal missionary encyclicals of the twentieth century increasingly proved that the differences between Münster and Louvain were largely academic.

The effect of the Reformation and the Council of Trent on mission theology can be readily found in this concentration on the Church. Over against the view of the Reformers that the true Church was, in the final analysis, invisible, Rome laid ever more emphasis on the visibility of the Church. The Church was viewed as analogous to an earthly kingdom, with the right to exercise authority as a central element. An exponent of this view was Cardinal Billot, probably the most influential Roman Catholic systematic theologian during the first quarter of the twentieth century. His most important work on this topic was *De Ecclesia Christi*. In the first section he developed elaborate arguments in favour of the Roman Catholic Church as the only true Church. The second (and largest) section dealt with ecclesiastical authority, the pope, bishops and councils. The third section concerned Church and state. Adrian Hastings remarks that the whole book reveals a thoroughly juridical and even worldly image of the Church.[2] Laity and even priests appear nowhere except as 'objects' of authority. Not a word is said about the missionary dimension of the Church.

There is an inexplicable anomaly here. Although Roman Catholic mission is ecclesiastical through and through, official ecclesiology has hardly ever paid any attention to it. A. Seumois rightly complains that, even after World War II, many able theologians occupied themselves mainly with speculative theology; they were apparently too proud to leave their ivory towers of scholasticism in order to attend to the missionary dimensions of ecclesiology.[3] The Second Vatican Council was to change this state of affairs, but this is the theme of a later chapter.

Behind the view of the Church as the source of missionary practice lies the question of its role in the foundation of mission. Schmidlin, founding father of modern Roman Catholic missiology, distinguished between a 'supernatural' and a 'natural' foundation. He reasoned that the first refers to a foundation derived from the sources of revelation (Scripture and Tradition) and from doctrinal truths. The second refers to the conviction that (a) the absolute character of Christianity emerges from an objective comparison with other religions, (b) the cultural achievements of mission are of high standing, and (c) the missionary past and present incontestably affirm the claim of the Christian religion to universality.

CHAPTER FOURTEEN

FROM MARTIN LUTHER
TO MARTIN KÄHLER

THE REFORMERS AND MISSION

When the Protestant Reformation shattered the centuries-old unity of the Western Church, each of the fragments into which the Church disintegrated found it necessary to identify and legitimise itself. In the Protestant churches the pure proclamation of the word, the correct administration of the sacraments, and (in some cases) the exercise of church discipline were regarded as the 'marks of the true Church'. In contrast, Rome at the Council of Trent (1545-1563) found the identity of the true Church in her unity and visibility. In both cases the definition of the Church was determined by what, according to the body concerned, was absent in the opposing group. In neither case was the Church defined by virtue of her involvement in the world, as was done in the New Testament. Following Rome, the Reformers also did not discuss Holy Communion in terms of mission, but in terms of the presence of Christ in bread and wine.[1]

On a crucial point the Reformers introduced no real change over against Rome: the area of the relationship between Church and state. This relationship was redefined in a more nuanced way, yet with little fundamental difference. The old, monolithic Christendom merely gave way to different fragments of Christendom, Roman Catholic, Lutheran, Reformed, and Anglican. Typical of this is Art. 36 of the Belgic Confession which described the responsibility of the government in the following terms: 'Their office is not only to have regard unto and watch for the welfare of the civil state, but also that they protect the sacred ministry, and thus may remove and prevent all idolatry and false worship, that the kingdom of antichrist may be thus destroyed and the Kingdom of Christ promoted. They must therefore countenance the preaching of word of the gospel everywhere, that God may be honoured and worshipped by every one, as he commands in his word.' The argument seems to have been that because Roman Catholicism was wrong, the close tie between the Roman Catholic Church and the state was also wrong, whereas a similar tie between the Protestant Church and the state was right, because Protestantism was right.

We are not suggesting that the Reformation produced nothing new. Indeed, we believe that three of its characteristics should be identified and underscored since they are of importance for our survey of the development of the missionary idea. The Reformation introduced a new emphasis on the sovereignty of God, a new awareness of the reality of grace, and a re-discovery of hope, not as a vague, purely metaphysical reality but as a reality in this world. These three elements stood in mutual tension: sometimes one dominated, sometimes another. All three had however one element in common: they emphasised God's sovereignty, his grace, and the Christian hope as *present* realities. Eschatology was for them neither apocalypticism as was the case with many groups on the periphery of the Church down through the centuries, nor pure spiritualisation, which so frequently characterised eschatology in the Roman Catholic Church. H. R. Niebuhr puts it thus: 'The new movement was impatient not only with the system of mediators of divine rule and grace but also with the deferment of the fulfilment of life's promise. Its word was "now". Justification was now to be apprehended; assurance of salvation was now to be received; the rule of Christ was now to become effective.'[2] For Calvin, says Chaney, 'eschatology was written in the present rather than the aorist tense'.[3]

Of course there were differences among the Reformers. Luther and his colleague Melanchthon in some respects thought almost entirely apocalyptically and believed that the Last Day was imminent. Mission—in fact, any form of world involvement—was therefore by no means self-evident to them. Yet Luther rejected as 'fable' the idea that the apostles had divided the world geographically between them and completed the evangelisation of the world. In several statements he emphasised the need for proclaiming the gospel to pagans in Europe and elsewhere. He thus revealed, in his theological thinking, a creative tension between the depravity of the world and the Christian's calling.

Calvin was clearer still on this point. Richard Marius compares the two Reformers and concludes: 'Luther never tried to make much of this present world, and a worldly age cannot make much of him. The Calvinists expected the world to endure, and they believed themselves to be the instruments of God to convert it. ... Calvinism has taught us that we are to make something of this world; ... Calvinism has implanted in both the British and the American traditions a perpetual dissatisfaction with our successes and a restlessness with the ways things are ...'[4] In his classic, *Christ and Culture*, H. R. Niebuhr discusses Luther under the heading 'Christ and culture in paradox' and Calvin under 'Christ the Transformer of Culture'; he describes Luther's view as one of 'mere endurance in the expectation of a trans-historical salvation', whereas Calvin saw Christ 'as the converter of man *in* his culture and society, not apart from these'.[5]

For Calvin, the Christ who was exalted to God's right hand was pre-eminently the *active* Christ. Calvin subscribed to an eschatology in the process of fulfilment. For this he used the term *regnum Christi*, the Kingdom of Christ. He regarded the Church as intermediary between the exalted Christ and the secular order. It fitted completely into this framework that Calvin should co-operate in the selection of two of the twelve missionaries whom Gaspar de Coligny sent to Brazil to found a Christian colony—the first Protestant overseas missionary enterprise, which, however, soon failed.

No other organised overseas missionary efforts were launched in the early years of Protestantism. To Cardinal Bellarmin, leading figure in the Counter-Reformation, this was conclusive proof of the heresy of the Reformers: 'Heretics are never said to have converted either pagans or Jews to the faith, but only to have perverted Christians.'[6]

Bellarmin and others who agreed with him naturally judged Protestantism in light of the current Roman Catholic conceptions of mission. If, however, we bring the New Testament understanding of mission into play, the situation changes somewhat. Mission is surely more than dispatching special ambassadors to remote countries. As far as the Reformers were concerned, Europe, too, was a mission field. Mission is the Church crossing frontiers into the world, but they judged that the world had entered the Church. They thus saw their primary task within the borders of historical Christianity. Trained preachers left Geneva and other Reformed centres—frequently in secret—for France, the Netherlands and Scotland; the Roman Catholics in these countries were, after all, objects of mission. Mission—even where the term itself was not used—was moreover understood more broadly than merely crossing the frontier between faith and unbelief (here, rather, wrong belief). Other frontiers, such as the social and cultural ones, were equally important.

By saying this we do not intend completely to exonerate the Reformers as though they knew precisely, in theory and practice, what mission was supposed to be. Far from it! Certain elements in their historical circumstances and their theology had a crippling effect on their understanding of mission. We refer for instance to their view on Church and state, which resembled that of Rome. The Peace of Augsburg (1555) with its famous clause *cuius regio eius religio*—freely translated, 'each country has to follow the religion of its ruler'—confirmed the current state of affairs. As all overseas colonies at that stage were Roman Catholic possessions, any Protestant missionary ventures there were *a priori* excluded. This was only to change when Protestant countries won their own colonies.

The fact that both Luther and Calvin regarded themselves as living in a period of darkness and suffering constituted an additional obstacle. Calvin produced a theology for a Church under the Cross, for he believed he lived in the era of antichrist. He believed that conditions for a fuller realisation of Christ's Kingdom would improve at a later stage; only then would the Church experience phenomenal growth.

PETRIFIED THEOLOGY OF MISSION

Whereas the Reformers largely succeeded in holding differing, almost contradictory elements in theology and practice in a dynamic, creative tension, their successors largely lost this ability. Increasingly, theology concentrated on the Church herself, especially on the past and on correct doctrine. The

Reformation which began as a fresh wind and dynamic new movement foundered in preoccupation with establishing state churches, defining codes of pure doctrine, and conventional Christian conduct. In Lutheran orthodoxy in particular, mission disappeared completely beyond the horizon of Church and theology. Orthodox theologians no longer saw, as Luther did, a challenge in the decadence of the world, but rather withdrew into the dogmatically demarcated reserve of pure doctrine.[7]

They betrayed a remarkable degree of fear of any optimism regarding the improvement of the world. Their doubtlessly accurate awareness of the power of selfishness and sin in the world led them to believe that any attempt at improvement was doomed in advance to failure. J. H. Ursinus and Gottfried Arnold especially exuded this dark pessimism and tired melancholy.[8]

Philip Nicolai who laboured towards the end of the sixteenth century, in other words about a century before Arnold, still had a strong eschatological or rather apocalyptic emphasis. The Last Day was imminent. He expected it in 1670. He thus believed that there was no time left for a world-wide missionary effort.

To reconcile his views with Scripture, however, Nicolai had to prove that the Great Commission had already been carried out, otherwise, according to Matt. 24.14, the *parousia* could not take place. Thus we find here the third element of orthodoxy's interpretation of mission—in addition to pessimism and apocalypticism there was the notion that the apostles had already carried out the Great Commission; there was, therefore, no remaining obstacle to Christ's return. We have already encountered this view among the Church Fathers. However, Nicolai knew a world geographically considerably larger than that of which the Church Fathers had been aware, and realised that he had to furnish proofs of the global spread of the gospel. He did this by evaluating Roman Catholic mission astonishingly positively, in spite of his severe criticism of the papacy. Roman Catholic missionaries were, in fact, unwillingly and unintentionally 'Lutheranising' the pagans! Legendary reports about missionary expansion in Abyssinia, the spiritual power of the Mar Thoma Christians in India, the growth of the Church in China, Japan and South America (the Jesuit mission), a Christian kingdom in the Congo, the 'vast empire of the

Christian king of the Moors', and the conversion of 80,000 Muslims, all taken together, provided him with ample proof that the gospel had indeed already been proclaimed everywhere.

Nicolai's blunt statement that we should not embark upon mission on our own accord, confronts us with a further element in Protestant orthodox theology. God does not chase us to and fro. We should remain where he had put us. We are not supposed to traverse the world looking for mission fields. If the German princes should found their own colonies they would have to see to it that the colonised people be evangelised; but this had nothing directly to do with the Church's taking the initiative.

More than half a century later, when Justinian Welz, influenced by Paracelsus, pleaded for mission (1664), it was Johann Heinrich Ursinus, Lutheran superintendent of Regensburg, who opposed him with arguments reminiscent of Nicolai's. A missionary society as proposed by Welz would be a work of Satan, as man would here presumptuously be usurping God's work, as the Roman Catholics were doing with their missionary orders. Welz's proposals were therefore unwise, impracticable, and indeed godless.

The fact that the continental Reformation rejected the 'apostolic succession' also, in practice, contributed to the obstructing of mission. The status and labours of the first apostles were unique, unrepeatable, and limited in their temporal aspect. They had no successors. They planted the Church once for all. It is precisely on this point that both Roman Catholics and Anglicans (as represented in Adrian Saravia) attacked continental Protestantism. 'You have no right to do mission work because you reject the doctrine of apostolic succession, and according to your own theology the apostles' office and work were unrepeatable!'

A final element in the orthodox Protestant understanding of mission, which likewise emerged in Ursinus's polemic against Welz, lay in the conviction that some peoples were impervious to conversion. Ursinus argued that he was indeed in favour of a missionary venture among pagans, but then such pagans should not be savages with hardly a trace of humanity, such as the Greenlanders, Lapps, Japanese, Tartars, or American Indians! 'To sum up, they should not be headstrong blasphemers and

persecutors of the Christian faith. God's holy things should not
be cast before such swine.' Here we have the ultimate in
Western cultural snobbery, religious pride and ethnocentrism,
and this despite the Protestant concern for credal orthodoxy.
Lurking behind this easy dismissal of any sense of missionary
obligation was a distorted understanding of predestination.

'SECOND REFORMATION' AND MISSION

The same elements we encountered in Lutheran orthodoxy were
also to be found in Reformed orthodoxy, usually however in a
less extreme form. Anglo-Saxon Calvinism in particular
embarked quite early—and with a conscious appeal to its
Calvinistic roots—upon a comprehensive missionary enterprise.
That however is the subject of another chapter. For the present
we will confine ourselves to continental Calvinism.

Less than half a century after Calvin's death, at the dawn of
the seventeenth century, a movement which became known as
the 'Second Reformation' began in the Netherlands. People such
as Witsius, à Brakel and J. Heurnius protested against the
deadness and formalism of orthodoxy. They emphasised the
double work of the Holy Spirit: renewal of man's inner life *and*
renewal of the 'face of the earth'. The soteriological and
theocratic elements in Calvinism converged in this movement
and laid a firm foundation for a theology of mission. In 1648
Heurnius wrote his *An Exhortation, worthy of Consideration,
to Embark upon an Evangelical Mission among the Indians.*
This was 174 years before William Carey's *Enquiry*, the
content of which showed remarkable similarities to Heurnius's
book. Heurnius himself went to Indonesia as missionary. Others
followed. Between 1622 and 1633 there was even a seminary for
the training of missionaries in Leyden. Hoornbeek, Teellinck
and others supported the enterprise.

The famous Gisbertus Voetius, a leading figure at the Synod
of Dort (1618-19), also came from the circles of the Second
Reformation. In his *Politica Ecclesiastica* he indicated important guidelines for a theology of mission. God himself is the
causa efficiens prima, the 'true, effective ground' of mission, and
he executes his work through the Church. The Church herself,
not a spiritual order or missionary society, is to be the agent of

mission. As regards the *aim* of mission, Voetius distinguishes three facets. The immediate aim is *conversio gentilium*, the conversion of pagans. This aim is, however, subordinate to a more distant goal, *plantatio ecclesiae*, the planting of the Church. The supreme and ultimate goal of mission is *gloria et manifestatio gratiae divinae*, the glorification and manifestation of divine grace.

In its initial stages the Netherlands Reformed mission had to be carried out within the framework of Dutch colonial politics. This led to its being subordinated to the pastoral care of the colonists and subject to the authority of the East Indian Company. The result, in many ways, was a very superficial missionary effort. It does credit to many Dutch theologians and missionaries, however, that as a matter of principle, they did not regard mission as a responsibility of the state. Unfortunately they were unsuccessful in awakening any real missionary interest in the rank and file membership of the Church.

THE ANABAPTIST VIEW OF MISSION

In the so-called 'Radical Reformation' mission was understood in a way that differed in many respects from the views of Luther, Calvin, Zwingli and their successors. This development is so crucial for the understanding of mission in our own time that we have to discuss it briefly.

We have to distinguish, of course, between the revolutionary Anabaptist groups associated with Thomas Müntzer and Jan Matthys, and those who pursued a non-violent way and are today mainly known as Mennonites (the name was derived from Menno Simons, a Dutch ex-priest who did much to reorganise the scattered Anabaptist groups). Although the two groups had similar roots—they both championed a far more radical break with Rome than the other Reformers—their ways parted early, mainly because of their contrasting views on violence.

The Anabaptists are sometimes considered as the forerunners of the modern Protestant missionary movement. They were among the first who regarded obedience to the Great Commission as obligatory on all believers. This was a direct outflow of their ecclesiology.[9]

Their goal was the restoration of the early Christian local churches as communities of believers, born again and sanctified. To ensure this, infant baptism had to be rejected. All earlier and contemporary forms of Christianity were pushed aside since it was completely self-evident to the uncompromising Anabaptists that salvation was to be found in their community only. The fact that they were branded heretics, by both Reformers and Roman Catholics, at a very early stage—in Zurich as early as 1525—simply reinforced their conviction that they alone were the elect. The decision of the Zurich government, that they were to discontinue their meetings, accept infant baptism and that some of their number had to leave the city, was regarded as confirmation of the fact that the Reformation was copying Rome as regards religious coercion and the unity of Church and state. The true Christian's way is one of radical non-violence, separation of Church and state, and non-participation in the activities of government. These convictions were incorporated into the Schleitheim Confession as early as 1527. Lutherans and Calvinists, who believed that Christians could co-operate with the state or who argued in favour of the possibility of a Christian government with jurisdiction over the religious convictions of its subjects, were nothing but pagans.

This conviction fanned the missionary consciousness of the Anabaptists. The saved—so they argued—could not but experience a sacred obligation with regard to the unsaved. They felt themselves under a divine mandate to live in a manner radically different from unbelievers. Whoever hesitated to accept this responsibility was regarded as lost and therefore an object of mission. In this way every believer became a missionary and was allocated a specific missionary territory. Europe was once again a mission field. As in the time of the apostles, the gospel had to be introduced into a pagan world. Only in this way could the true Church be restored to what she had been before her 'fall' in the first centuries. This true Church had three exterior marks: she was pilgrim Church, missionary Church, and martyrs' Church. Beyond any doubt some genuine elements of a biblical understanding of the Church were recovered in this view. Luther's 'priesthood of all believers', which, according to Anabaptists, remained a mere theory in Luther's own case, became a reality here. Each believer was a missionary; as a missionary he was also a pilgrim and therefore *ipso facto* a martyr, for false Christianity would always persecute the true ambassadors of Christ. Anabaptists disregarded all existing borders; they crossed all frontiers, geographic, racial, cultural, economic and linguistic.

Like other groups of that period, Anabaptists believed that they were living in the last hour. Any strong eschatological expectation may find expression in one of three ways. It may lead to complete quietism, where God in his sovereignty inaugurates the end; this is what Lutheran orthodoxy believed, as did the Qumran community of the first century. It may, secondly, lead to people believing that they might precipitate the end by taking things into their own hands even to the extent of using violence; this is what the revolutionary groups in the Reformation era and the Zealots of the first century believed. It may however also lead to people putting themselves at God's disposal, in full surrender and commitment, so that he might use them in preparing for the end. This is how the Anabaptists understood their mission. They were 'captives in God's triumphal procession' (2 Cor. 2.14). They lived in the conviction that the antichristian persecution they experienced was a sign of the end as was their proclaiming God's last offer to a 'pagan' world before Christ's return. This third interpretation of the significance of the eschatological hour brings us closer to the New Testament than do the other two.

Anabaptism was first and foremost a *movement*, more so than Calvinism and Lutheranism, in which 'movement' and 'institution' existed in a mutual tension from the very beginning. The fact that Anabaptists were persecuted for their convictions and conduct, led to their being scattered across the face of Europe and Russia, and later also to North America. In the course of time, however, the movement became largely institutionalised. In the Netherlands today, for instance,. the Anabaptist movement has lost much of its original character; it has become both respectable and affluent. Elsewhere, for instance in the Mennonite colonies in Russia, formal orthodoxy and superficial moralism have supplanted earlier uncompromising Mennonite rigidities. Over the years Pietism has likewise made deep inroads into Mennonitism. On the surface Pietism and Anabaptism appear quite similar. In origin and essence, however, they greatly differ. Anabaptism is much more radical than Pietism. In recent decades certain Mennonite groups, especially in North America, have been spiritually renewed and have begun to emphasise what they call 'the recovery of the Anabaptist vision'.

PIETISTS AND MORAVIANS

Seventeenth-century Protestant orthodoxy, with its preoccupation with right doctrine and its absolutising of a particular theory of the word of God, contributed in no small measure to the eighteenth-century reaction, the Age of Enlightenment (*Aufklärung*). When theologians dogmatically elevated human reason to an organ of revelation, a popular deduction resulted: absolute truth could be arrived at by pure reason. This meant that divine revelation was no longer necessary. As a result supernatural religion became increasingly suspect. The Church was derided for her dogmatism, particularly her pessimism about man, and religious relativism carried the day.

In the course of time a new movement, Pietism, emerged as protest against the combined onslaught of Orthodoxy and Enlightenment. The formally correct, cold and cerebral faith of orthodoxy gave way to a warm and fervently pious union with the Lord Jesus, the emphasis being on emotion rather than reason. Confession of faith made room for experience. Concepts such as conversion, the new birth, and sanctification received new meaning. A disciplined life rather than right doctrine, subjective experience of the individual rather than ecclesiastical organisation, practice rather than theory: these were the hallmarks of the new movement.

What is of particular importance for our survey is the fact that Welz's proposals for a Protestant missionary enterprise, voiced in 1664, were to find an echo in the Pietists P. J. Spener and A. H. Francke more than a century later. They combined the joy of a personal experience of salvation with an eagerness to proclaim the gospel of a redemption to all. Undoubtedly Coccejus's theology of the Kingdom of God and the optimistic traits of early Enlightenment also exerted some influence on their thinking. Even so, we encounter here a radical departure from the melancholy view of history of late orthodoxy where the expectation of Christ's imminent return led to complete quietism. Early Pietism laid little emphasis on the *parousia*. This would only become an integral element in Pietism towards the end of the eighteenth century, as a result of the exegetical work of J. A. Bengel.[10]

Unlike orthodoxy, where the pure confession, whether Lutheran or Reformed, played a decisive role and led to mutual isolation, Pietism was ecumenical. Orthopraxis and personal experience of faith, rather than orthodoxy, were decisive. Pietists in all confessions felt drawn to one another, helped one another, prayed for one another: Lutherans in Germany and Scandinavia, Calvinists in Holland, Anglicans in England, Puritans in America. Missionary enthusiasm, above all, proved to be contagious and to unite all into a supra-confessional bond.

We find these same characteristics in Zinzendorf and the Moravian Brethren at Herrnhut, although their missionary practice differed markedly. Both the Pietists and the Moravians were primarily concerned about *conversio gentilium*, without clarity about what would happen to the people once they were converted. The 'planting of the Church' was not a goal of mission. Zinzendorf in fact stressed quite explicitly the conversion of *individuals*. Our task, he said, was merely to gather 'first-fruits'. To locate these, the Moravian Brethren, within a period of twenty-eight years, sent missionaries to twenty-eight countries and territories across the globe, including Greenland, North America, South Africa, Persia and India. The full harvest, Zinzendorf believed, would only begin after the conversion of the Jews and the end of disunity in Protestantism. In the meantime it was not the *ecclesia* (the formal, established Church) which was important, but the *ecclesiola* (the spontaneous, unorganised group of true believers). The entire emphasis fell on conversion. All missionary activities were merely aids serving this overriding primary goal.

This theological perspective explains why Moravians, and to a slightly lesser extent also Pietists, had precious little interest in any cultural mandate in mission. The concentration on the individual and his soul caused the cultural, national and social life to fall completely outside the purview of mission. The Kingdom of God was for all practical purposes limited to the sphere of converted souls.

In spite of everything, however, the young Moravian communities in the mission field developed into institutional
churches, just as the mother church in Herrnhut did.
Beyreuther remarks: 'For Zinzendorf it was the greatest
disappointment in his life when, during his absence in America,
the Moravian community in Herrnhut organised itself into a
confessional church, thus refusing to be what he intended it to
be, namely, a provisional guest-house'.[11]

In yet another respect Pietists and Moravians broke in
principle with contemporary Protestant and Roman Catholic
views on mission, namely, in their attitude to the role which
civil government was to play in mission. In this they were closer
to Anabaptism than to their own confessions, as was made clear
for example when Zinzendorf pointed out that mission under
the auspices of the state inevitably led to the Christian religion
becoming a 'civil matter' instead of a matter of heart and spirit.
'For this reason we should not necessarily attribute large-scale
conversions of entire nations to our dear Saviour.'[12] Precisely
because Zinzendorf broke with the *cuius regio eius religio*
principle, according to which only the missionary agencies of
state churches had access to the colonies of the states concerned,
he became one of the earliest ecumenical personalities, a man
who, before John Wesley did so, could say, 'The world is my
parish!' This is a consequence of his conviction that the Church
is pilgrim Church, a Church under the Cross, a Church of
martyrs.

FROM ECCLESIASTICAL MISSION TO CULTURAL PROPAGANDA

In the course of the nineteenth century, pietistic theology
underwent some changes and flowed into several different
channels, partly as a result of the growing influence of
Rationalism and the rise of historical criticism.

Friedrich Schleiermacher, who defined faith as 'a feeling of
absolute dependence', perpetuated pietistic theology of
experience, in more than one respect, not least because of the
relativistic attitude he adopted towards history. A. Tholuck, in
contrast, argued that the truth of the gospel could be communicated along three ways, namely, that of feeling or

experience (here he followed the Pietists and Schleiermacher), that of reflection 'based on the foundation of historical events', and that of speculation, 'by means of the scientific exposition of the dogma'. He thus offered a wider basis for mission than Pietism was able to do.

By and large, however, the continental pietistic missionary enthusiasm of the early eighteenth century had flagged by the nineteenth century. Something of it would be recovered in Karl Gützlaff's missionary venture in China. With this a new type of missionary enterprise was born, which was to serve as a model for many others, especially in England and USA, and which became known as 'faith missions'. Typical of such an enterprise is that it usually issues from the vision of a single man, that it works in isolation from and frequently directly over against the institutional Church, that many of these agencies (though certainly not all) in their earlier years tend to evangelise rather superficially, that they are spurred on by a strong apocalyptic consciousness, that their missionaries are often prepared to make extraordinary sacrifices, and that they, as their name indicate, labour 'in faith', dependent only on voluntary financial support. The most famous and largest of these agencies, and a direct fruit of Gützlaff's enthusiasm, is the China Inland Mission founded by Hudson Taylor in 1865.[13]

Towards the end of the eighteenth century, long before Gützlaff introduced the faith mission model, a new phenomenon had already emerged: the 'missionary society' model, which would dominate the nineteenth and early twentieth centuries. These societies were either the missionary organs of specific denominations, or confessional organisations without being tied to a specific denomination, or interdenominational societies which, for all practical purposes, were in course of time to become confessional societies. Thus the stage was set for the typical nineteenth-century missionary pattern where for Protestants as for others, mission came primarily to mean the planting of churches. This development was an important deviation from the pietistic view of mission as being first and foremost concerned with the saving of individual souls.

Three men, each a founder and long-time first director of a missionary society, played important roles in German missionary circles during the nineteenth century: Karl Graul,

Wilhelm Löhe and Ludwig Harms, respectively founders of the Leipzig, Neuendettelsau and Hermannsburg Missionary Societies.[14] All three men and their societies originated in Pietism, yet all were Lutherans to the marrow. Graul in particular had a formative influence on the missionary thought of his time; H.-W. Gensichen even calls him 'the founder of modern missiology'. At almost the same time (though perhaps even earlier) that Henry Venn in England and Rufus Anderson in America argued that the founding of autonomous, indigenous churches was the aim of mission, Graul shed his pietistic heritage and also put church planting in the centre of his missionary thinking. 'For Graul, mission was the apostolic road from Church to Church' (Hoekendijk). Löhe was more ecumenical than Graul, Harms more explicitly pietistic. Still, all three were deeply committed to the Lutheran confession.

Apart from this emphasis on the centrality of the confession, another element came to the fore in nineteenth-century German missionary thinking. Increasingly it was agreed that all young Lutheran churches on the 'mission field' had to become *national* churches. Hoekendijk has shown to what extent the ethnic element was to become *the* typical characteristic in German missiology. We have to go far back to find the roots of this, perhaps as far back as the century of the Reformation, but the development as such would come to full fruition only during the nineteenth century. The accent on autonomous *ethnic* churches would continue to accompany the stress on confessionally *Lutheran* churches; in some instances the former would even eclipse the latter, as may be observed in the missionary thinking of Bruno Gutmann.

Another unfolding of continental (especially German and Swiss) missionary understanding in the nineteenth century is to be found where mission was interpreted as *cultural propaganda.* This was actually an attempt to reconcile mission with the results of rationalism and historical criticism. In this view mission could not mean the proclamation of the Christian faith as the only salvific religion. Christianity was not unique as regards its contents, but indeed as regards its fruits. The *religious* superiority feeling of Western Christianity, attributed by the perpetrators of the new view to both pietistic and ecclesiastical missionary enterprises, gave way to a feeling of *cultural* superiority. Ernst Buss, author of *Die christliche Mission, ihre prinzipielle Berechtigung und praktische Durchführung* (1876) argued that conversion as the aim of mission was outdated; the aim of mission should now be 'christianisation', 'civilisation' or 'education', three concepts that were practically synonymous for Buss. The Church was interpreted in purely sociological categories, as an 'educational society'. Everything became inner-worldly; all missionary achievements were within reach through normal evolution and lay entirely within the capacity of man. We mention in passing that the culture-Protestant view of mission—just like the pietistic view, but unlike the ecclesiastical-confessional—was supra-confessional and supra-national. Like Pietism, it was also strongly influenced by Romanticism. It operated to a much lesser extent in religious categories, however. God's Kingdom was a utopian earthly kingdom in which brotherly love and peace reigned.

Buss and his associates evaluated the European colonisation of Africa and Asia very positively, a factor we have to understand against the background of the dominant Western ideas of the time. It was not noticeably different in the case of the advocates of a confessional missionary enterprise. There were, of course, all along missionaries who were highly critical of colonisation. There were, moreover, always missionaries who, with great devotion and often at the risk of personal danger, defended the rights of the indigenous population against colonial policies and the arbitrary actions of individual colonial officials. Nevertheless a fundamental challenge to the colonial system was for all practical purposes absent. Augustine's perspective gained new adherents. It would be to the benefit of pagan peoples if they were to be colonised by the Christian West!

Germany's joining in the race for colonies was to a considerable extent the result of pleas by German missionary leaders. Colonisation was a form of 'indirect missionary war'. Small wonder that Solf, German secretary of state in the latter part of the nineteenth century, could declare 'kolonisieren heisst missionieren' ('to colonise means to missionise'). In 1881 Gustav Warneck formulated the general 'law', 'missionary fervour among Western Protestant nations increases according to the increase in their overseas foreign trade'. It was not very different on the other side of the English Channel. In 1901, on the occasion of the second centenary of the Society for the Propagation of the Gospel in Foreign Parts, a commemoration volume was published under the title *The Spiritual Expansion of the Empire.*

The German theologian who put the seal of approval on this entire development was Ernst Troeltsch. In two contributions, published in 1903 and 1906, he discussed the Christian faith's claim to absoluteness and the significance of the Christian mission. As historian he came to the conclusion that Christianity, as far as its origins were concerned, could hardly lay claim to being unique. Its uniqueness, Troeltsch then argued, lay primarily in what it had to offer the world: spiritual values, civilisation, unity, and the highest form of culture. 'Mission today is the expansion of the European and American world of religious ideas, closely linked to the expansion of the European sphere of influence.' Mission aimed at 'cultural-spiritual uplifting'.[15] The missiologist Julius Richter concurs: 'The Protestant world mission is an integral part of the cultural expansion of the Euro-American peoples.'[16]

This whole development indicates, in reality, a foundation of mission on the events of history. The Pietists' supernatural foundation of mission had been turned into a natural foundation. In this respect nineteen century Protestant theology of mission proved itself to be closely related to its Roman Catholic counterpart. Josef Schmidlin rightly states, 'In the general foundation of mission, Catholic and Protestant views go hand in hand.'[17]

The foundation of mission on history is also evident from arguments for the proven superiority of Christianity. Because of its superiority Christianity deserves to be the world religion, just as the cultural and social achievements of the West give it the mandate to colonise. Schmidlin takes this superiority simply as a matter of course: 'The mission conquers the colonial territory spiritually and assimilates it internally, whereas the state can only colonise externally; it is the mission which, by virtue of its internal authority, subjects the natives spiritually and teaches them the required obedience and spirit of submission to the rightful government.'[18]

Gustav Warneck frequently appeals to the verdict of history.

It is hardly fortuitous, he says, that precisely the Christian nations became the bearers of culture and leaders in world history. 'What might still lack regarding power of proof for mission in biblical theological research, may be supplemented by history. The facts of history are also an exegesis of Scripture and they speak the final word if theological interpretations are called in question.'[19] As recently as 1929 Martin Schlunk could describe mission as 'proof of the reality of God'. In this way the practice of one's own missionary enterprise becomes the foundation of mission; the right and call to mission can be deduced from the achievements of mission.

GUSTAV WARNECK AND MARTIN KÄHLER

Gustav Warneck (1834-1910) has already been referred to several times. Since the eighteen-seventies he exercised an enormous influence on the entire continental theology of mission, Protestant as well as Roman Catholic. A quarter of a century after his death, Martin Schlunk in 1934 still claimed that 'everything that happens in Germany in the theory and practice of mission, lives on Warneck's legacy'.

It is difficult to reduce Warneck's theology of mission to only one denominator. Three large traditions converge in him, the confessional Lutheran, the pietistic, and the cultural Protestant. Elements of all three appear in his missiology, frequently without any proper integration. Hans Schärer, J. C. Hoekendijk and Johannes Dürr argue that there are, as it were, two 'storeys' in Warneck's theology of mission. In the upper storey the memory of the Kingdom remains alive and mission is allocated an eschatological role: the Church is God's people in the world. In the lower storey history exercises its 'holy right': mission becomes the christianisation of peoples.[20]

Martin Kähler (1835-1912), life-long friend and colleague of Warneck in Halle, interpreted mission in a way which differed in many respects from the interpretation of Warneck and almost the entire contemporary continental Protestant theology. Kähler was one of the first systematic theologians to occupy himself intensively with mission. Some years ago his most important writings on this subject were republished under the title *Schriften zu Christologie und Mission*.[21] Warneck wrote much more on mission and yet, in spite of his prolific contributions to the subject, mission remained for him theologically peripheral, an 'extra'. The reason for this—as Schärer has illustrated—lies in Warneck's 'double foundation' of mission.[22]

For Kähler, on the other hand, mission is founded on the central fact of the atonement. God's saving grace is the ground of mission and the inclusion of all mankind is God's goal (p. 145). The Christian is inescapably involved in witnessing; thereby he exchanges the terrible debt of sin with a new debt, that of gratitude (p. 457). Mission thus has its basic motivation in the necessity of witnessing, which is an essential aspect of faith (p. 80). The courage to witness issues from the faith that *has* conquered the world (p. 81). Because mission is an essential element in the Church's life it is not dependent upon circumstances. Both Church and theology are products of mission; indeed, mission is 'the mother of theology' (p. 190). Theology did not originate as a luxury in a world-dominating Church; it was, rather, the result of an emergency when the Church, engaged in mission, was by circumstances forced to theologise (p. 189).

Kähler distinguishes radically between 'mission' and 'propaganda'. The latter signifies the expansion of one's own ecclesiastical trademark. Whether we propagate a Christian Church, a moral system, or a specific theology, makes little difference—in each case we are merely publicising what is our own, in competition with other religions and views of life. We then merely produce proselytes, 'carbon copies of what we ourselves are' (p. 114). On 28th January 1910, on the threshold of the international missionary conference of Edinburgh, John Mott in a letter asked Kähler the following rather naïve question: 'Do you think that we now have on the home field a type of Christianity which should be propagated all over the world?' To this the seventy-five year old Kähler replied: 'We have no Christianity worthy of general and exclusive propagation. But we may and must spread the gospel ...' (p. 258). Propaganda, after all, is always the propagation of 'Christendom', that is of the gospel plus culture, the gospel plus a particular confession, the gospel plus a set of moral laws, the gospel plus a feeling of racial superiority (pp. 112-114).

Kähler nevertheless remained a child of this time. He could

refer to mission as 'a demonstration of power' and aver that Christianity's 'superiority' to Buddhism and Islam was 'incontestable' (p. 187).

In statements such as these he came close to a foundation of mission on the events of history. On the whole, however, he spoke of mission in an authentically theological manner. The 'absoluteness of Christianity', he said, was a category with which we could not co-operate. Our missionary duty was not to be derived from that but only from the 'definitive will of a personal God' (pp. 129-132). Following the footsteps of the Crucified in blind faith we relinquish of necessity all desires for visible success; in the ministry of the word, earthly calculations have no validity (p. 165). We have nothing to boast about, in fact, 'Christianity is an intractable thing which God alone can handle. It certainly causes him no less trouble than the Jewish people' (p. 427).

Kähler already stood on the threshold of the twentieth-century theological renewal. From the perspective of the theology of mission his contribution signified the end of one era and the beginning of another. Karl Barth, for instance, was to follow Kähler in more than one respect.

CHAPTER FIFTEEN

FROM JOHN ELIOT
TO JOHN MOTT

THE KINGDOM OF GOD

There is sufficient reason to treat Anglo-American developments in the theology of mission separately. The mere fact that,
in the course of the past two centuries, the English-speaking
world has produced no less than four-fifths of the Protestant
world's total missionary force[1] is in itself an indication that
theological, sociological and historical factors other than those of
the European continent have been working in this sphere. One
finds denominations in the Anglo-American world which differ
considerably from those in Europe in name, ethos and theology.
This statement applies to North America even more than to
Great Britain. In fact, even where continental European
ecclesiastical groups migrated to America—German and
Scandinavian Lutherans, Dutch Calvinists, Moravians, Mennonites and others—they soon differed in many ways from their
mother churches. The new country and environment proved
catalytic in bringing them closer to other denominations in
America than to those from which they originated. It was
especially the religious climate of the New England colonies
that put its stamp on the new arrivals. This applied even more
to developments in missionary thinking than to general theological development.

In his brilliant study *The Kingdom of God in America*,
H. Richard Niebuhr has shown that the motif of the Kingdom
dominated American theological thinking even where the
concept was absent. It has not, however, always borne the same
meaning. In the Puritan period the Kingdom of God signified
'God's sovereignty'; in the era of the Great Awakening it
referred to the 'Kingship' of Christ; during the nineteenth
century, the period of liberalism and 'social gospel', it meant
'God's Kingdom on earth'. To put it differently: in the first

period the emphasis was on God's omnipotence, in the second on his grace, in the third on hope. Naturally we shall not be able to divide the three understandings into watertight compartments, for they were in reality all present in all three periods and were closely interrelated. At most the accents differed from period to period.[2]

The Kingdom of God is a Calvinist rather than a Lutheran theological theme. During the early years of the North American colonies Calvinism exercised a significant influence. This was, in fact, the case in England as well, and, naturally, in Scotland. In England, however, partly because of political factors, Calvinism never became dominant, in spite of promising beginnings. The Calvinist substratum even in high-church Anglicanism can nevertheless not be denied. Scottish Calvinism, by comparison, existed in relative isolation and showed similarities with continental Calvinism rather than with the modified Calvinism of the rest of the English-speaking world.

In the New World Calvinism had a chronological advantage over other denominations, particularly in Massachusetts. This contributed to its powerful growth in the new soil. We shall here confine ourselves mainly to developments in the theology of mission in America, with occasional references to developments in the mother country.

PURITAN THEOLOGY OF MISSION: THE KINGDOM OF GOD'S SOVEREIGNTY

The first organised Protestant missionary efforts outside Europe were launched more or less simultaneously in the Far East and North America. The Dutch began mission work on Formosa in 1627.[3] Shortly before that date, Alexander Whitaker laid the foundation of mission work in Virginia. The real Protestant missionary pioneer, however, was John Eliot (1604-1690), who spent practically his whole ministry among the Indians of Massachusetts. Eliot was a Puritan, a member of a group who migrated from England to the Massachusetts Bay Colony in the years immediately after 1630. Originally, the vision of the immigrants was to establish a purified Anglican Church, but in time this faded. Breakaway movements led to the founding of several new denominations.

Eliot was a contemporary of Richard Sibbes and Richard Baxter. Together with them he laid the foundation of the Puritan theology of mission. Three elements stood in creative tension in their theology: God is the sovereign Lord of mission and holds everything in his hands; he uses means to accomplish man's redemption; and man is held responsible for accepting or rejecting the gospel. Where the sovereignty of God was one-sidedly emphasised, inactivity and a sterile belief in predestination took over and no mission work was possible. Where human responsibility was over-emphasised, everything was placed in man's hands and in the final analysis his salvation depended on his own activity.[4] Eliot sought to achieve a balance between these two extremes.

In order to attain this, the motif of God's sovereignty was deliberately retained. It is precisely for this reason that God's election was important to these Puritans. The motif of election did not however become a stumbling-block for mission, but, conversely, a stimulus. In this respect the Puritanism of the Colonies was remarkably close to the contemporary 'Second Reformation' movement in the Netherlands. The fact that all initiative lay with God did not mean that man should remain passive, just as God's wrath did not exclude his mercy. In fact, it is only against the background of God's initiative that man *can* do anything, only against the background of the divine wrath that he can experience God's mercy.

The Puritans' strong missionary consciousness flowed from this understanding. They were convinced that God had sent them to plant and cultivate his garden in a howling wilderness, just as he had sent the Israelites to establish themselves in untamed Canaan. 'Paradise' and 'wilderness' became eschatological concepts. God's election was not understood individualistically. The emphasis was on God's providential election of this nation and on its mission. The Puritans understood the Church as the assembly of believers, sent into the world under the Cross.[5]

The ultimate goal of mission was the Kingdom of God, the millennium. For the Puritans this meant the conversion of Jews and pagans, as well as the downfall of Rome and the dawn of a period in which the gospel would be the guiding principle for the conduct of all nations. Their vision was that the Kingdom of

God would span the globe.[6] They expected the realisation of the Kingdom to unfold itself in four stages. The first was the conversion of souls, or the rule of Christ in man's *heart.* Then would follow the gathering of believers into a community, or the rule of Christ in the *Church.* The third stage was Christ's rule in the *state* when the national government would proclaim God's will as the highest authority. Lastly, when a sufficient number of Christian governments had emerged throughout the world, Christ's *universal* rule would be established.[7]

Among the early Puritans these expectations were still undifferentiated; it was unclear whether the Kingdom would come about by way of evolution or by way of a radical revolution and divine intervention. The Puritans were 'millennialists', not in the modern, specialised sense of the word, but rather in the general sense of expecting a total cosmic improvement in the future. Cotton Mather (1663-1728), for instance, was a moderate pre-millennialist; he had a very pessimistic view of history, perhaps because of his contacts with A. H. Francke in Halle. The *parousia* would take place soon and unexpectedly, as a cataclysmic reversal of the entire existing order.

Jonathan Edwards (1703-1758) in whom, strictly speaking, we leave the Puritan era, represented another approach. He was, in fact, a transitional figure, between the first and second epochs of early American theological development. He was the spiritual father of the Great Awakening, a fact which would put him in the second epoch, but his contributions bore the hallmark of Puritan theology. In fact he reclaimed some elements of the optimistic view of history of early Puritanism. The millennium would arrive by way of progressive development. Revival and mission were signs of its coming. Edwards expected no catastrophic interruption of history, for 'such a spiritual estate as we have just described has a natural tendency to health and long life, ... to procure ease, quietness, pleasantness and cheerfulness of mind, also wealth and a great increase of children'; and he added, '... temporal prosperity will also be promoted by a remarkable blessing from heaven'.[8] In his *A Treatise on the Millennium* (1793), Samuel Hopkins (1721-1803) wrote in a similar vein, only much more elaborately. Chaney remarks:

This utopian minutia is almost completely concerned with the social, educational, and physical prosperity of man in the millennium. It will be a time of eminent holiness, which is disinterested benevolence, and all evils will be banished from the world. There will a great increase in knowledge. There will be universal peace and friendship. Sadness will vanish, and joy will prevail. Prosperity and plenty will reach into every home. The art of husbandry will be greatly advanced, and great improvements will be made in the mechanical arts. The world will be well populated, with full employment. One language will be used in every nation. Churches will be regulated in the 'most beautiful and pleasing order'.[9]

With his adapted Calvinism Hopkins is already far removed from early Puritanism. Nevertheless, with his emphasis on God's Kingdom on earth, he forms a bridge between the Puritans and the third period.

If we now summarise the contribution to the theology of mission of the Puritans and their successors, the following emerges. By and large they did not—as Hopkins was subsequently inclined to do—define the Kingdom in merely social categories. They were far too conscious of an interruption in history—an interruption which was experienced paradigmatically in each personal conversion. They could therefore not identify the present order with God's Kingdom, however enthusiastically and positively they evaluated it. In addition, they were too conscious of the sovereignty and initiative of God to attach any ultimate value to human achievements. Their missionary awareness was born of this creative tension between God's initiative and man's responsibility.

The Puritans' arrival in America was regarded as a mighty step towards the ultimate rule of Christ over the entire world. Referring to the Old Testament wars of extermination, some Puritans believed that God's Kingdom would come by way of the annihilation of the Indians; on one occasion they could even thank God for having sent an epidemic amongst the Indians 'which destroyed multitudes of them and made room for our fathers'. Yet, when John Eliot and others embarked upon mission, they soon found surprising support among the colonists. The idea of annihilating the heathen Indians gave way to the idea of converting them.[10] Their conviction of being called and chosen by God was thus guided into new avenues. Not only in Eliot's work did this find expression, but also in the founding of the New England Company, the first Protestant missionary society, in 1649—fifteen years before the Lutheran, Justinian Welz, unaware of the events of 1649, pleaded the case for a missionary society. Furthermore the founding of both the Society for Promoting Christian Knowledge (SPCK) in 1698-99 and the Society for the Propagation of the Gospel (SPG) in 1701 was stimulated by events in North America. Thomas Bray, spiritual father of both, was 'commissioner' for the Bishop of London in Maryland. He intended the SPG to be an organisation both to compete with the 'Dissenters' (in other words, various Protestant missionary enterprises) and to counteract the Roman Catholic mission. He expressly regarded the SPG as parallel to the *Sacra Congregatio de Propaganda Fide* (founded in 1622).

THE GREAT AWAKENING:
THE KINGDOM OF GOD'S GRACE

By the end of the first century of its existence on American soil Puritanism had lost much of its early sparkle. Cotton Mather (1663-1728) was typical of this period of decline. The past was to him more important than the present. The Kingdom of God was postponed to the future. As to the present, all emphasis was put on the heritage of the fathers, on institutions, laws, order, discipline and rigorous Sabbath regulations. The 'movement' turned into 'institution', a fact that was also reflected in the increasingly legalistic missionary programmes of the period. All this could not but generate an increasing sense of spiritual hunger among the people. God's gracious response was the Great Awakening of 1740-1743. Although at first largely confined to New England, it later spread to other parts of the thirteen colonies.

This awakening was largely due to the preaching of Jonathan Edwards and George Whitefield. Both were committed Calvinists. Indeed, Jonathan Edwards consciously drew on Puritan theology and strongly emphasised God's sovereignty in his preaching.[11] Both men discouraged emotionalism although they called for visible signs of the conversion experience. Gradually Calvinism was modified in significant ways by Arminian emphases. This meant that the initiative in redemption increasingly shifted from God alone to both God and man. This naturally led to great activism, in mission as well as in other spheres: if man's salvation was in the last analysis dependent upon his own decision, it was essential that all people should be given a chance to hear the gospel. These emphases produced considerable disruption in the Puritan churches and those that separated from the parent body in time became the nucleus of the Baptist movement in America.

The Great Awakening undoubtedly meant the end of the Puritan era. Influences from German Pietism also played their part, although this should not be interpreted as meaning that the Great Awakening was identical to Pietism. It was something quite distinctive: 'The Great Awakening, the American expression of the intercontinental spiritual renewal, ... was a mixture of Puritanism and Pietism ground together in the crucible of the American experience.'[12] It represented the shift of emphasis from the sovereignty of God to the Kingship of Christ, from predestination to grace, from the correctness of doctrine to the warmth of love.

In this period mission was specifically viewed as proclaiming individual conversion. The 'wilderness' that had to be tamed was no longer located in the physical and social world; the wilderness was in the hearts of men. Edwards still painted God's grand plan on the wide canvas of creation, providence and history; however, those associated with him in this revival movement increasingly concentrated on the conversion and sanctification of individuals. The personal experience of the truth taught by Scripture gained in importance. It should be noted that the evangelical movement which grew out of the Great Awakening and extended to England, Scotland and Wales under the influence of John Wesley and his associates gave little attention to political issues. Indeed, they prided themselves in the fact that politics were never mentioned in Methodist pulpits.

We are not suggesting that the preachers of this larger evangelical awakening throughout the English-speaking world were insensitive to social and political abuses. However, as they detected deficiencies in the body politic, 'they did not try to whip up their wills by admonitions, threats and promises. They sought to cleanse the fountains of life. In penitence and longing they turned to worship, to self-examination in the presence of God and to the contemplation of the Cross of Christ.'[13] New works of love in the form of social involvement flowed from this cleansed fountain, in both America and England. There certainly is truth in the thesis that it was the evangelical awakening that saved England and America from the woes of the French Revolution, *not* because the revival functioned as 'opiate of the people' but precisely because it spawned greater social consciousness and involvement. People such as William Wilberforce, Lord Shaftesbury, John Newton and many others whose names are associated with the abolition of slavery, the upliftment of the poor, and the war against vice, all hailed from the evangelical awakening.[14]

They did not, however, join hands with all abolitionists inspired by humanism, 'for the latter seemed at times to be more interested in condemning the sin of slaveholders than in promoting the interests of the slaves themselves'.[15] They trusted the gospel to do its work of renewal in themselves and through them in society. They did not as a rule at first proclaim as dogma that the relationship between conversion and social involvement was exactly the same as that between cause and effect. Only much later this would be elevated to an evangelical creed, by people such as Dwight L. Moody, Billy Sunday and A. C. Dixon.[16] Social involvement, in mission and elsewhere, was an integral part of their gospel.

Towards the end of the eighteenth century a new movement gathered great momentum on both sides of the Atlantic. In 1792 William Carey, a shoemaker and Baptist lay preacher, published his *An Enquiry into the Obligation of Christians to use Means for the Conversion of the Heathen*. As early as 1787, at a ministers' fraternal in Northampton, he had suggested as topic for discussion, 'whether the command given to the apostles to preach the Gospel to all nations was not binding on all succeeding ministers to the end of the world, seeing that the accompanying promise was of equal extent'. Dr Ryland, the chairman, frowned disapprovingly, jumped up and said: 'Young man, sit down, sit down. You're an enthusiast. When God pleases to convert the heathen, He'll do it without consulting you or me. Besides, sir, can you preach in Arabic, in Persian, in Hindustani, in Bengali? There must first be another pentecostal gift of tongues.'[17]

The view of John Ryland, a Calvinist Baptist, reflected the extreme predestinationism which held sway in some Calvinist circles of the period. Mission as human enterprise was unimaginable; it was a presumptuous interference in God's plan. In spite of this Ryland was elected one of the five first committee members of the 'Particular Baptist Society for Propagating the Gospel among the Heathen', which was founded in 1792 and of which Carey was the first missionary. As in the case of the Puritans, the belief in predestination was directed into missionary channels.

Outside the narrow circle of English Baptists the Baptist Missionary Society produced two results. It opened the eyes of many Christians, notably in England, to the world-wide dimension of mission, and it provided a new model of missionary organisation. In America, up to that time, mission among the Indians was usually undertaken denominationally, as 'church extension'. Yet precisely because of this, it often received only scant attention. Now that there were specific societies for mission, the situation changed. People who had a definite interest in mission, combined forces enthusiastically. A whole series of missionary societies came into being, in England, America, on the European continent and even in overseas colonies, such as the Cape of Good Hope.

The extraordinary range of Anglo-Saxon mission work dates back to this period. Where the societies on the European continent remained the concern of small, ecclesiastically peripheral groups, in England and America they became the concern of the whole Church. One of the reasons for this was that Carey and his colleagues in the English-speaking world could appeal to churches which had been touched by the evangelical awakening, whereas Pietism and other continental movements of renewal never influenced official Church life to any significant degree.

As regards the motive and goal of mission, it is noteworthy that Carey never referred to the glory of God—an element that was central in the 'Second Reformation' and Puritanism.

Similarly, 'sympathy with the poor heathen', a motive which emerged strongly in the subsequent period, was for all practical purposes completely absent in Carey. For him, the overriding missionary motive was the will of God. The word 'obligation' in the title of his 1792 publication already reveals that this was so from the outset. Carey's concern was always with 'obedience' to the missionary 'command'. Expressions such as 'we have to obey', 'it becomes us', 'it behoves us', 'it is incumbent upon us', occur frequently in his *Enquiry*. That this theological approach could lead to a certain rigidity hardly needs emphasising.

The extraordinary increase in missionary zeal associated with Carey's name was not the only accompaniment of the evangelical awakening. Other elements also played an important role. Three of these were the growing conviction of a manifest Anglo-Saxon destiny in the world, the almost apocalyptic events on the world front, especially the French Revolution and the Napoleonic wars, and burgeoning millennialistic expectations. These three elements were closely interrelated.

In America the belief spread that God had sifted the entire English people in order to select the best seeds for planting in New England. The Kingdom of God *in* America gradually became a specifically American Kingdom of God. Mission— including the global missionary enterprise that developed after the first foreign missions association was founded in America in 1810—increasingly tended to be regarded not merely as a Christian, but rather as a specifically American enterprise. The entire North American continent therefore had to be conquered, for both political and religious reasons. Jonathan Edwards had already taught that the millennium would in all probability be inaugurated in America. It was, after all, clear that salvation was constantly moving westward: from the Near East to continental Europe, then to England, to the American east coast, and from there westward, all the way to California. The immigrants arriving almost daily from Europe confirmed this conviction: they were leaving the old world, moving westward to the new. America was the land of opportunities and hope for the world. Between 1790 and 1860 the white American population increased eightfold, from less than four million to thirty-one million. The period from the inauguration of George Washington as president in 1789 up to 1829, when Andrew

Jackson, the hero of the masses, became president, was the most optimistic in American history. Who still dared to doubt that God had elected the American churches for a special destiny?

World events beyond the borders of America underscored this conviction. Protestant missions had, in their earliest days, wrestled with certain doubts and questions. Could the 'fullness of the Gentiles' be brought in before the Jews had been converted and antichrist destroyed? Was a new pentecost not needed *before* a world-wide mission could begin? Where were the terrible wars the Bible had predicted as the accompaniments of a global mission? Now, at long last, it appeared as though everything was fitting together perfectly. The French Revolution and the Napoleonic era led to wars on an unprecedented scale. The papacy, for many Protestants the embodiment of antichrist, shrank in power as never before. Indeed, the fact that the French Revolution broke out in a *Catholic* country, in itself spoke volumes. What is more, in 1798, the pope was forced by Napoleon's armies to abandon his throne. Jews in France were granted citizenship in 1790 and 1791, and everywhere in Europe emerged from the isolation of the ghettos, with many becoming Christians. These historic events, together with sensational revivals in America and burgeoning missionary zeal in all denominations, could not but cause waves of expectation to flood the land.[18]

A third element related to this intensification of religious fervour was a new emphasis on the millennium. We earlier mentioned that millennialism was a feature of the American ecclesiastical scene from the beginning. It now reached a new peak; it became the common possession of all American Christians and was especially connected with mission. Chaney remarks, with reference to this period: 'Not a single sermon or missionary report can be discovered that does not stress eschatological considerations.'[19] The events of the time brought the remote possibility of the millennium tantalisingly near. Social and cultural optimism, however, largely caused the expectation to be post-millennialist rather than pre-millennialist. The Kingdom of God would not invade history as catastrophe, but would rather grow gradually and mature in an organic way. Events about the year 1800 clearly indicated that the millennium had dawned. With admirable self-restraint preacher after preacher announced that the full unfolding of the millennium would take a scant two centuries. Man's negative and evil passions would gradually fade away. Licentiousness and injustice would disappear. Strife and dissension would be wiped out. There would be no more war, famine, oppression and slavery. Crime would cease. For the sake of the realisation of all this the American churches were inspired to embark on mission. The gospel was the panacea for the maladies of a sick world.

The attitude towards unbelief and non-believers changed considerably in the last decade of the eighteenth century. There was on all fronts a growing certainty that victory was imminent. Chaney remarks: 'Defense turned to offense. Optimism gripped Evangelicals. Infidelity was no longer the fearsome enemy against which bulwarks must be raised but rather a vulnerable enemy against which the churches could be rallied.'[20] The American missionary enterprise now became world-wide. The vast North American continent was too confined for the growing consciousness of imminent conquest. The 1811 annual report of the American Board of Commissioners for Foreign Missions expressed the conviction that the new open door for mission was 'to no nation ... more inviting than to the people of New England. ... No nation ever experienced the blessings of the Christian religion more evidently, and uniformly, than the inhabitants of New England'.

By the time of the third decade of the nineteenth century the earlier spiritual movements had lost much of their momentum, and this despite yet another revival period, this time in the eighteen-twenties, under the leadership of Charles G. Finney. Once again what began as a stirring movement soon became an institution, precisely when attempts were made to consolidate its gains. As had happened in the past, attack changed to defence. In Finney's era 'awakening' became 'revival', in other words, it ceased to be new conquests in the 'wilderness' and became instead an instrument for revivifying the existing order. 'Home missions' became a technique for maintaining Christian America. Mission now exclusively signified *foreign* mission and Matt. 28.19 was singled out to encourage that all emphasis be placed on 'Go ye therefore'. On the home front the chief concern was to check the spread of weeds. 'Home missions became the great divine hoe, for keeping the garden clean.'[21] Proselytising was therefore the order of the day in America—and it has been ever since.

We are not suggesting that the entire significance of these spiritual awakenings ended here. In a very special sense the overall Evangelical Awakening was for England, and even more for America, what the Reformation had been for the European continent. In many continental European circles there has always been nostalgia for the golden era of the Reformation; to a lesser degree, in some American Church circles, people still recall with a pang the glory of these awakenings. They liberated American Christianity from the mould of a rigidified Puritanism and brought a distinctly American form of dynamism to the Church.

THE KINGDOM OF HOPE

The American Civil War of the 1860s was, in many ways, catastrophic. It was followed by a period of spiritual leanness which is difficult to survey. The chief problem lies in the fact that different movements now either simply ignored one another or adopted diametrically opposed positions. The latter part of the nineteenth century brought to many churches the parting of the ways. It was a period of growing theological disarray. Although it would be simplistic to trace modern theological controversies directly back to divisions which developed at that time, the antecedents of the modern dilemma are undoubtedly there to be discerned.[22]

First, denominationalism thrived and affected the definition of mission. It was the age of Rufus Anderson (1796-1880) and Henry Venn (1796-1873), the general secretaries of the largest missionary societies in America (The American Board) and England (Church Missionary Society) and joint fathers of the three-selves formula: the aim of mission was seen as the founding of self-governing, self-supporting and self-propagating churches.

There has been a temptation to evaluate this development very positively, and doubtless it did constitute an improvement on the Pietistic understanding of mission where there was little concern about the organisational aspect of the groups of newly converted on the mission field. Venn and Anderson, like their counterparts in Germany, Karl Graul, Wilhelm Löhe and others, realised that the new Christians had to be incorporated into ecclesiastical structures and could not permanently be dependent upon Western missionary agencies. They nevertheless continued operating in pedagogical categories which revealed the West's superiority feelings. It was against these that Roland Allen protested so passionately at the beginning of the twentieth century, in for instance his *Missionary Methods: St. Paul's or Ours?*, and *The Spontaneous Expansion of the Church and the Causes which Hinder it.* In addition to questioning the pedagogic overtones in Venn and Anderson, we must also challenge their related preoccupation with the institutional character of the Church. Their definition of the aim of mission has for a long time been uncritically acclaimed. J. C. Hoekendijk was, in fact, the first to subject it to consistent criticism.

We need to evaluate Venn's, and especially Anderson's, missionary approach against the background of developments since 1830. The united evangelical front which dated back to the previous century collapsed after 1830. A fierce spirit of competition arose among the denominations. This was transferred to the mission fields as well, both at home and abroad. Each denomination tried to patent and export its own brand of the gospel. Interdenominational societies turned into denominational ones. This was even true of the largest of them all, the American Board. The churches emphasised their differing heritages rather than their common calling. H. R. Niebuhr goes as far as to say: '... that peculiar institution, the American denomination, may be described as a missionary order which has turned to the defensive and lost its consciousness of the invisible catholic church. These orders now confused themselves with their cause and began to promote themselves, identifying the Kingdom of Christ with the practices and doctrines prevalent in the group.'[23] For Lyman Beecher the institutional Church was 'the divine practical system for accomplishing the salvation of the world', an association for 'mutual defence and increased efficiency in the propagation of religion'. Niebuhr remarks, 'Here we have that very definition of the church of which dynamic Protestantism had been afraid;

the church has become a self-conscious representative of God which instead of pointing men to him points them first of all to itself.'[24] For all practical purposes God's Kingdom was here identified with one's own denomination. The Church in which people believed became the church to which they belonged.

A second development in this period, likewise with significant implications for the theology of mission, was the movement which was to become known as 'adventism'.[25] During the 'era of controversy' after 1830 and in the midst of mounting tension over matters such as slavery, denominationalism, and difficult economic conditions which followed in the wake of the 1837 financial depression, the popular mild post-millennialism in the churches gave way to a feverish pre-millennialism. In the eastern United States in particular, many dissident groups afforded fertile soil for preachers with heterodox ideas. Western New York State, for instance, became known as the 'Burnt-over District', as one revival fire after the other swept it. It became the cradle of Mormonism, Adventism and Spiritualism.

The movement with the widest influence was Adventism. William Miller (1782-1849) categorically predicted Christ's return and the beginning of the millennium for 1843 or 1844. Between 50,000 and 100,000 people joined the Millerite movement within a short period. The amazing aspect, for an outsider, is that the movement did not dissipate once the predictions turned out to be false. In fact, it grew from strength to strength. It is today a global movement with a typically adventist theology of mission.[26]

We do not find pre-millennialist mission theology in Seventh-Day Adventism only. Practically all denominations contain pre-millennialist groups, and frequently they are more active in mission than others, thus putting their stamp on the theology of mission. Gratton Guinness and Fredrik Franson are but two of many who in the nineteenth century emphasised the Second Coming in their missionary approach. Many missionary societies founded in those years—especially those of the faith missions type—appealed to Matt. 24.14 and regarded their activities as direct preparation for the *parousia*. It was calculated in 1887 that, if 20,000 new missionaries could immediately be sent into the field, the entire world would be evangelised by the end of the nineteenth century. The Second

Coming could therefore be expected in the year 1900. Even John Mott's slogan, 'The evangelisation of the world in this generation', had adventist overtones.

A third nineteenth-century movement of importance to our study is that which would eventually issue in the 'Social Gospel'. Whereas the first movement tended to locate the Kingdom of God in the Church and the second projected it into the future, this third movement described God's Kingdom almost exclusively in this-worldly categories. In several respects it was a more authentic continuation than the other two of the original Puritan heritage. It was Jonathan Edwards and Samuel Hopkins in a new dress.

In spite of this a decisive shift, away from Puritan origins, took place at the turn of the century. Man was increasingly divinised and God hominised. God became the sum total of man's most engaging characteristics. God's wrath and sovereignty could not be squared with his benevolence. Hence, it was jettisoned. This theology had little appreciation of crisis and judgment. The coming Kingdom did not involve the resurrection of the dead but the perfecting of the already existing order. This romantic thought-world had no room for discontinuity, sacrifice, the loss of everything, and the Cross. It had forgotten that the gospel was, in Whitehead's words, a 'transition from God the void to God the enemy and from God the enemy to God the companion'.[27] God was only the 'companion'. Continuity between God and man was attained by adapting God to man. Conversion, that radical revolution at the centre of life which was something indispensable to both the Puritans and the leaders of the Evangelical Awakening, now appeared to be redundant. Man was, after all, 'good'.

The coming Kingdom could therefore be painted in utopian colours without the dark shadows that remained even for Edwards and Hopkins. The original design was going into production and nothing would stop it! The slogan was 'progress' and there was no reason to dim the glowing enthusiasm it engendered. It was to be a kingdom of self-redemption.

We have mentioned that many elements in the 'Social Gospel' movement undoubtedly had their antecedents in Puritanism. The assumptions which lay behind those elements were, however, increasingly abandoned. For Edwards, God's wrath and omnipotence had remained 'a hard truth to which he had slowly learned to adjust his thought and life; for liberalism it was an untruth'.[28] Between Edwards and the last exponents of the 'Social Gospel' the capital of genuine, scriptural faith had gradually been squandered. Every new generation of liberal theologians had a smaller spiritual investment than the previous one. Walter Rauschenbusch still referred to the need for conversion and to the coming Kingdom as both judgment and promise. The following generation knew less about judgment, conversion and grace and their successors less still. Horace Bushnell (1802-1876) protested against the faith handed down to him and advocated a more liberal position. But, as Niebuhr points out, he had nevertheless received that faith, 'and his protest was significant in part because it arose out of an inner tension between the old and the new'.[29] Others no longer knew this tension. They ignored what they had never possessed and so their crusade became cheap. Nothing could disturb the idyll of their utopia. This tension-free optimism became the driving force behind their missionary engagement in the world. The password was evolution, not revolution, and it went without saying that this evolution would follow the pattern of the one and only normative model: North America. The gospel of social improvement became the panacea which the North American messiah would administer to the world's less privileged. The logical terminus of this entire development can hardly be characterised more aptly than in Niebuhr's classic description: 'A God without wrath brought men without sin into a Kingdom without judgment through the ministrations of a Christ without a cross.'[30]

It was to be expected that the 'Social Gospel' movement would not be allowed to dominate the ecclesiastical scene unchallenged. Reaction was not delayed, especially at the turn of the century. One form it took was the Pentecostal movement which appeared in 1901 as a fruit of the 'Holiness Movement', which in turn had sprung from the Methodist Church. Since then a specific Pentecostal dimension developed in the theology of mission of certain groups. For many years Pentecostals moved in an orbit of their own, away from other ecclesiastical groups and isolated from academic theology. During recent decades, however, this has changed dramatically.

Another form of protest against the 'Social Gospel' movement originated in the evangelical groups that began to muster their forces towards the end of the nineteenth and especially during the first decades of the twentieth century. Ostensibly they sought a return to the theological position of the first Great Awakening or even of Puritanism, but there were significant differences. One of the most important lay in the fact that, in their protest against the onesided ethical emphases of the 'Social Gospel', they abandoned the unity of word and deed, of conversion and social involvement, a unity which had been self-evident to most exponents of the Awakening. This important shift in the evangelical position has been epitomised as 'the Great Reversal' by Timothy L. Smith. People such as A. C. Dixon (editor of *The Fundamentals*, which earned him and his collaborators the epithet 'Fundamentalists'), Dwight Moody, and Billy Sunday increasingly identified a conservative political and social attitude with evangelical theology. In their proclamation they concentrated exclusively on the needs of the individual. David Moberg summarises this development as follows: 'A century ago evangelicals were in the forefront of social concern, but now we have become so identified with "the successful", in terms of this world's ideologies, that we put brakes on nearly every proposal for dealing with social problems. ... Instead of helping to alleviate the ills of the poor and underprivileged, we react against those who try to do so.'[31] Whereas among some 'Social Gospellers', the good news was merely social change, among some of these evangelicals it was the exact opposite.

Even before these evangelical groups and the Pentecostals appeared on the scene, another movement emerged, mainly from the American student world. The key figure here was John R. Mott (1865-1955). In the midst of the stagnant institutionalism of the churches, the superficialities of the Social Gospel Movement, and the inability of new evangelical groups really to speak a liberating word, a new spirit was at work among the students. Their restlessness, enthusiasm and initiative were eventually channelled into the founding of the Student Volunteer Movement in 1886. John Mott became its secretary in 1888. On his initiative, the World Student Christian Movement was founded in 1895. James Scherer describes the Volunteer

Movement as 'spontaneous and voluntary in character and charismatically organized. It was not a campaign of churches but a movement of men and women given to the discipline of prayer and Bible study and gripped by the Spirit. ... There was no uncertainty about the gospel as a power unto salvation. The *fact* of missionary obligation was more important than any attempt to state its theological basis. God's love for all, compassion for the lost, Christ's command to preach the gospel, pity for the dying, expectation of the Lord's return, a grateful sense of stewardship—these and other motives blended together.'[32]

It was this spirit that gave birth to the ecumenical movement. In some ways it embodied the best from Puritanism across the spectrum to the Social Gospel. The International Missionary Conference of Edinburgh (1910) was born of this movement and the vision and drive of John Mott. It was, among other things, to be the first real encounter between continental European and Anglo-American theologies of mission. At this point, however, we are already broaching the theme of our following chapter.

CHAPTER SIXTEEN

ECUMENICAL
MISSIONARY THEOLOGY

EDINBURGH 1910

If the nineteenth century was the great century of mission, the twentieth is the century of the ecumene. From the beginning of the present century it has become increasingly difficult for churches and missionary organisations to ignore one another. Even where specific groups, for reasons of principle, refused to participate in ecumenical gatherings, it was impossible simply to ignore—as they had previously done—what happened beyond the borders of their own group.

The man who, more than anybody else, became the architect of the ecumene was John R. Mott (1865-1955), a man who emerged from the student missionary movement, who was for a period of forty years the undisputed ecumenical leader, and who, in the course of his long public ministry, visited ninety countries and travelled about two million miles in the service of mission and ecumene.

Mott was the chairman of the first world missionary conference, held in Edinburgh in 1910. For the study of the development of missionary theology this means that, as from that date, it has not been as necessary as before to contrast Anglo-American and continental theologies of mission. The mutual isolation was transcended and since 1910 the interaction and mutual influencing which previously occurred only sporadically, was to assume a more permanent form.

The Edinburgh conference did not, however, succeed in integrating continental-European and Anglo-American theologies of mission. One of the problems, of course, lay in the fact that, as we have shown in the preceding chapters, neither of the two 'camps' represented a homogeneous theology of mission. Yet it remains true that both Edinburgh and Jerusalem (1928) revealed a predominantly American style, with a tendency to emphasise activism rather than the continental European appreciation of reflection. Heinrich Frick, for instance, maintained that Edinburgh indisputably inaugurated the triumph of Americanism in missionary theology.[1]

The Edinburgh conference represented the flood-tide of missionary enthusiasm and Western missionary consciousness. Mission stood under the banner of world conquest. In fact, 'world' was not primarily a theological concept, but a geographical-historical one: 'world' was divided into two components, a 'Christian' and a 'non-Christian'. The relationship between these two was basically that of apostolic imperialism: the 'Christian' world had to subdue the 'non-Christian'. This emerged for instance in Edinburgh's military terminology, which used concepts such as 'soldiers', 'powers', 'advance', 'army', 'crusade', 'marching order', 'council of war', 'strategy' and 'planning'.[2] It would nevertheless be wrong to suggest that Edinburgh reflected merely naïve optimism. Faith in God's all-sufficiency rather that a shallow optimism in man's ability formed the basis for the participants' cheerful view of the future.[3]

The delegates could clearly deduce God's all-sufficiency from the 'signs of the times'. The period in which they lived was exceptionally important. Words and expressions that were repeatedly employed, included 'opportunities', 'a decisive hour', '*this* generation', 'a critical time'. John Mott based his arguments for a world-wide mission on many proofs of 'the fullness of time': the accessibility of all countries, medical progress, the discovery of steam and electricity, the availability for mission of money and man-power, the existence of younger churches in virtually all countries, increased interest in mission on the 'home front', and so forth. All these 'convincing facts and providences', taken together, provided an 'irresistible mandate' for mission. Mission itself was not questioned. All that needed to be argued was that there had never been an hour as auspicious for mission as the present. The motivation for mission was not in itself to be found in these favourable circumstances; they did however provide the grounds for an immediate release of all energy for mission.

As to the aim of mission, Edinburgh made mention of extending God's Kingdom or Christianity, christianising the life of the nations, conversion, bringing people to Christ, evangelising the world, spreading Christian influence, etc. The central and all-embracing aim of mission, however, remained the extension of the Kingdom. This Kingdom was only to a limited degree interpreted in pre-millennialistic and apocalyptic categories. God was building his Kingdom by degrees, and was making use of man for this purpose.[4]

The explicitly theological harvest of Edinburgh was meagre. The fact that it had been agreed in advance not to permit any discussion of doctrinal issues was no doubt partly responsible for this. Nevertheless, Edinburgh represented a watershed, the end of an era and the birth of another. In the words of W. R. Hogg, 'Edinburgh may best be described as a *lens*—a lens catching diffused beams of light from a century's attempts at missionary co-operation, focusing them, and projecting them for the future.'[5]

JERUSALEM 1928 AND ITS AFTERMATH

Edinburgh 1910 was chronologically part of the twentieth century; from the perspective of world history, however, it still belonged to the nineteenth. Theologically it represented the culmination of Western (both American and European) messianic consciousness according to which the gospel, in its 'Western Christian' robes, was the solution to the problems of the entire world.

When the second world missionary conference gathered on the Mount of Olives, in 1928, the situation was fundamentally different. Between Edinburgh and Jerusalem lay the First World War (1914-18) and the Russian Revolution of 1917. Edinburgh's confidence of sure victory was shattered. Western civilisation proved itself to be bankrupt. The question was no longer: How do we let the 'non-Christian world' share in everything we Westerners have to offer? But rather: How do we salvage Jesus Christ from the ruins of Western civilisation? For the first time there was the realisation that Christianity was no Western religion and that the West was not Christian in its entirety. Its spiritual poverty was evident to all.

Jerusalem was therefore far less confident than Edinburgh, where, for instance, no mention was made of a 'theology of

religions'; the non-Christian religions were perfunctorily dis-
missed as 'perfect specimens of absolute error and masterful
pieces of hell's inventions which Christianity was simply called
upon to oppose, uproot and destroy'.[6] We need not try to
establish whether this view was primarily the result of theological reflection or of a Western superiority feeling. The fact is
that, when the latter began to crumble after World War I, one
of the consequences was a re-evaluation of non-Christian
religion.

The older liberalism was far from dead, however, and even
managed to emerge in a new form, as *the* authentic word for a
new world situation. It was particularly some American
delegates to Jerusalem, led by W. E. Hocking, who pleaded for
an imaginative alliance with non-Christian religions, an alliance
in which neither Christianity nor the other religions were to
lose anything. In subsequent publications Hocking employed
the idea of 'reconception' to identify his ideas.[7] Hocking was
also appointed chairman of the American Commission of
Appraisal of the Laymen's Foreign Missions Enquiry whose
report, *Re-Thinking Missions*, was published in 1932. The
report defined mission as the expression of the desire to
communicate the highest spiritual values to others, as a
'preparation for world unity in civilization', and as essential for
the inner growth of the Church. Two years after *Re-Thinking
Missions*, A. G. Baker's *Christian Missions and a New World
Culture* appeared, in which the author advocated a position
even more relativistic than the Laymen's Report. Religion was
for Baker 'a phase of cultural development, and missions one
aspect of a more general process of cultural impenetration'.
Sociologists had held similar positions for a long time; what was
new, was to hear a professor of missiology propagating such
views. Christianity had (at least for the time being, but the
situation could change) at most a head-start due to its 'accom-
plishment and inherent character'.

These extreme views, propounded at Jerusalem, did not
remain unchallenged. It was the continental European delegates
such as Karl Heim and Hendrik Kraemer in particular who
criticised the American approach. The draft report on 'The
Christian Message' was prepared by William Temple (later
archbishop of Canterbury) and Robert E. Speer. It was a

masterpiece,[8] and was accepted by a unanimous standing ovation of the conference, a gesture which can partly be explained by the fact that the report was compiled in such a way that every delegate could, to some extent, discover his own view in it!

Because of the relativistic attitude to religion of some delegates, it has become customary to write the Jerusalem conference off as the nadir of ecumenical missionary thinking. More recent research has however shown that this is an unfair judgment. As regards the motive of mission, Jerusalem actually surpassed Edinburgh in theological depth. In the earlier conference Christ's royal office was prominent, but then in close connection with the 'royal stature' which the Western Church had conferred upon herself. In Jerusalem it was rather Christ's priestly office that received emphasis. The continental theology of the Cross, as expressed by Karl Heim and others, found an echo in the hearts of many delegates. Edinburgh 1910 had also referred to the Cross, but it was the Cross as symbol of conquest, in Constantinian terms. In Jerusalem the Cross again became the symbol of service, responsibility, and sacrifice. In this Jerusalem reaffirmed a motif that had been operative in Zinzendorf, the Pietists, and even Warneck, but played a much more modest role in American theology of mission.[9] The conference could therefore say, without reserve, 'Our true and compelling motive lies in the very heart and nature of God to whom we have given our hearts. Since He is love, His very nature is to share ... Coming into fellowship with Christ, we find in ourselves an over-mastering impulse to share Him with others.'

As far as the purpose of mission was concerned, Jerusalem described this as the preliminary realisation of the Kingdom. Here, too, the point of departure was the priestly rather than the royal office of Christ. Mission was the Kingdom's servant in the world. Precisely for this reason Jerusalem, unlike Edinburgh and in spite of the protests of some delegates, explicitly concerned itself with the social dimension of the gospel, making it clear that this was not just a matter of a cheap 'social gospel' but an authentic consequence of God's revelation in Christ. It was not a mere supplement but an essential element in the theological understanding of mission. There was no such thing as an individual gospel over against a social gospel. The work done by mission agencies in the area of health, education and agriculture, was not just an 'auxiliary' to 'real' mission. A 'comprehensive approach' to man in all his relationships was called for. His spiritual life was inextricably intertwined with his psychological, economic, social, and political relationships. Christ was seen as Lord of man's entire life.

In no sense, however, did Jersualem criticise the overall structures of society; it expected social renewal to be achieved by the improvement of micro-structures.

The ultimate goal of mission was at Jerusalem still given only a vague or, rather, reserved expression: 'Since Christ is the motive, the end of Christian missions fits in with that motive. This end is nothing less than the production of Christ-like characters in individuals and societies and nations through faith in the fellowship with Christ the living Saviour, and through corporate sharing of life in a divine society.' The Church was therefore involved in this, but the relationship between Church and Kingdom remained unclear. The same applied to the ultimate shape of the Kingdom. Jerusalem did not go beyond a general 'hope and expectation of his glorious Kingdom'.[10]

KARL BARTH

We have argued that the theological contributions of Hocking and *Re-Thinking Missions* were in reality nothing but an adapted variety of the old nineteenth-century liberalism which Niebuhr has to devastatingly criticised. In a review of *Re-Thinking Missions*, J. A. Mackay pointed out that the report had completely ignored the fact 'that a revolution has broken out in the romantic theological playground of the nineteenth century'. What we found in the report was therefore nothing but 'the sunset glow of nineteenth-century romanticism caught and prolonged in the mirrors of Re-thinking Missions'.

The theological 'revolution' to which Mackay referred, had actually already started with Martin Kähler and had, as far as the study of the New Testament was concerned, been continued by Johannes Weiss and Albert Schweitzer. They showed that the prevailing liberal interpretation of God's Kingdom in the message of Jesus as an inner-worldly, evolutionary, progressive and ethical concept was an illusion and hermeneutically totally indefensible. Weiss and Schweitzer rediscovered the consistently eschatological elements in the message of Jesus—elements that at the time were only recognised by ecclesiastically peripheral groups and fanatics. The rediscovery, however, remained for some time the hobby of professional theologians who neglected to communicate the full implications of their find to Church and theology. The catastrophe of World War I was needed rudely to awaken the churches of Europe from their dream of the inner-worldly progress of mankind. It was as if people had suddenly been given organs to perceive a message they had previously been unable to grasp. In the field of the philosophy of history the first volume of Oswald Spengler's *The Decline of the West* was published in 1918. The title, with its apocalyptic allusion, alone was something never previously dreamed of.

Karl Barth's commentary on the Epistle to the Romans was published the same year. It was the beginning of a 'theology of crisis', of judgment, of the absolute transcendence of God. God was, for Barth, in heaven, man on earth. The only relation between us and him—no, between him and us!—was his judging and forgiving word. Barth therefore evaluated non-Christian religions in a way diametrically opposed to that of Hocking. In fact, he went further. He pronounced judgment on Christianity-as-religion. In this he agreed with Feuerbach. Religion was unbelief, it was a concern, indeed, we should say, it was *the* concern of godless man. Religion was self-redemption, it was the Fall of Gen. 3, where man set himself up against God and attempted to determine who God was and what he wanted. Christian religion, like all the others, belonged in the coffins of oblivion. Barth then contrasted religion with *faith*. The Christian religion, he added, might *become* faith, because of divine creation, election, justification and sanctification. God's revelation-in-Christ was no new religion but the abolition of all religion.

It was on this point that Barth's theology became relevant for mission, but then first and foremost for the Church on the *home* front, the sending Church, which believed that she 'had' the gospel and might now impart it to 'non-Christianity'. But, said Barth, we never 'have' the gospel; we perpetually 'receive' it, ever anew. The dividing line thus does not run between 'us' and 'them'; it also runs right through the sending, Christian Church herself. More than that: it runs through the heart of every Christian. We are all 'Christo-pagans'. For this reason there is no fundamental difference between preaching 'at home' and 'on the mission field'. The Church remains Church of pagans, sinners, tax-gatherers. The only difference is that, on the mission field, the Church ventures in the form of 'beginnings' what she ventures at home in the form of 'repetitions'.

Barth's accents sounded as strange in the ears of Pietists as they did in those of liberals. None of them could do anything with his theology. Karl Hartenstein, Basel Mission Secretary and delegate to Jerusalem, was the first to confront the pious missionary circles of his time with Barth's theology. He did this in a brochure entitled *Was hat die Theologie Karl Barths der Mission zu sagen?* (What has Karl Barth's theology to say to mission?), published in the year of the Jerusalem conference. He had learned from Barth that mission had to be undertaken in humility. We cannot accomplish it; only the Spirit can.

It was precisely this approach of Barth's which evoked criticism from missionary leaders who alleged that his theology had a paralysing effect on mission. In 1932 he was invited to address the Brandenburg Missionary Conference on 'Theology and Mission in the Present Time'.[11] He summarised his entire theological thinking on mission in a nutshell for the occasion. He questioned the traditional missionary motives and said that, however much we tried, we should never succeed in penetrating to the heart of the *one* true motive for mission, as it remained inaccessible to human research: it was the will of the Lord of the Church himself. He discussed the theological presuppositions of the pietists, the American 'social gospellers', and those Germans (such as Gutmann) who used ethnicity and indigenous culture as point of contact. He then proceeded to reject all three because they took man and (even more important) creation instead of redemption as the point of departure. He put a radical Christo-centric emphasis on redemption, over against any form of a 'theology of creation', especially in the form in which it was gaining popularity in the Germany of the nineteen-thirties.

Our missionary activities, Barth argued, remained mere human efforts, unless it pleased God to incorporate them into the service of his revelation. For this reason our missionary motives would never be adequate. In our missionary reporting we should rather say too little than too much. After all, we could never establish the real need of the pagan; only God could know that. Similarly, we should not be too garrulous about the *aim* of mission; what *we* regarded as the main purpose could not remotely express what *God's* purpose was.

With this paper Barth became the father of the modern theology of mission. The Danish missiologist, Johannes Aagaard, states categorically: 'The decisive Protestant missiologist in this generation is Karl Barth.'[12] The rediscovery of the eschatological dimension in mission, mission as *missio Dei*, the theology of the apostolate, the foundation of mission in the Trinity, and so forth, are all developments that would be difficult to imagine without the stimulus of Barth. In his Brandenburg paper Barth also responded to the accusation of missionary leaders that his theology had as a result a 'paralysing of the will to mission'. He referred to Jacob who was struck on his hip by the Angel of the Lord and limped ever after. Jacob thus became a man God could use. He received a new name, 'Israel', 'prince of God'. Perhaps, said Barth, only a similar paralysing blow would make mission a pliant instrument in God's hands.

Barth's influence was scarcely noticeable at the Jerusalem conference. In the ensuing years the situation would change considerably. This was one of the reasons why the Tambaram meeting would differ notably from that in Jerusalem.

TAMBARAM 1938

At Edinburgh, 1910, Christ's *royal* office was emphasised. Undoubtedly this had to do with the fact that the Western churches and missionary agencies were at the time riding the crest of the wave. Similarly there was a relationship between the time of crisis in 1928 and the emphasis on Christ's *priestly* ministry. At Tambaram (near Madras, India) the *prophetic* office of Christ would be prominent, something we have to understand against the background of the prevailing ideologies and dictatorships: National Socialism in Germany, Fascism in Italy, Marxism in Russia, State Shintoism in Japan.[13]

The central theme of Tambaram was *witness*, which was in line with the idea of the prophetic office. This theme, and in fact, the entire conference, showed the great influence of Barth's theology. He had published a booklet in 1934, entitled *Der Christ als Zeuge* (The Christian as witness). Many years later he would treat this theme more fully, in Volume IV/3 of his *Kirchliche Dogmatik* (1959), where mission is discussed under the over-arching heading, 'Jesus Christ, the true Witness'. The original and real Witness therefore is God himself, in Christ. Man becomes a witness on the basis of the atonement (the entire Volume IV of the *Church Dogmatics* deals with the doctrine of the atonement) and of the divine calling. The witness belongs to the calling, and the calling is a sign of grace. A withdrawal from mission thus signifies a withdrawal from grace rather than from duty. The true Christian cannot not-witness. Witness is the essence of the Christian's ministry to and involvement in the world.[14]

Tambaram did not understand 'witness' solely in the sense of oral proclamation. Witness was 'to present Christ to the world', and in the report on 'The Place of the Church in Evangelism' we read: 'The Gospel of Christ carries with it the vision and hope of social transformation and of the realization of such ends as justice, freedom and peace. A living Church cannot dissociate itself from prophetic and practical activities in regard to social questions.' This does not mean that for Tambaram, mission was absorbed in the 'social gospel'. After all, 'the Kingdom of God is within history and yet beyond history'. In this statement we already find an indication of the fruit of exegetical studies in eschatology which had recently defined the Kingdom as both 'already' and 'not yet', and this helped to liberate the theology of mission from the sterile alternatives of pre-millennialism, post-millennialism and a-millennialism.

It was for this reason that Tambaram could concern itself much more fundamentally than did Jerusalem with social issues. In 1928 the main concern had remained with the eradication of specific abuses and ethics were limited to the microstructures of society. Tambaram went further. God's goal is a new earth. We need not be thwarted by intractable creational patterns. Soteriology teaches us that everything is alterable. God's Kingdom 'acts both as a ferment and as dynamite in every social system'.

The influence of Barthian theology at Tambaram could best be seen in *Hendrik Kraemer's* contribution. In his theological evaluation on non-Christian religions Kraemer, in fact, stood closer to Emil Brunner than to Barth. Most English-speaking delegates did not differentiate between Brunner and Barth. In reality, however, Barth had mercilessly condemned Brunner's theology of religions as early as 1934, in a booklet which had the single word *Nein! (No!)* as title. In areas other than the theology of religions Kraemer nevertheless followed the general Barthian line. This found expression in his *The Christian Message in a Non-Christian World*, which he wrote at the request of the organisers of the Tambaram Conference and which was, in fact, part of the conference agenda. In this book Kraemer dissociated himself from both Pietism and 'Social Gospel'. Words such as 'sin', 'righteousness', 'alienation', 'judgment', 'lostness', 'forgiveness', 'conversion' and 'new birth', which were rare at Jerusalem and practically absent in Hocking's theology, were introduced as an integral part of the Tambaram vocabulary.

The fact that Tambaram defined the 'world' differently from Jerusalem and especially from Edinburgh was related to this change in emphasis. The differentiation between Christian and non-Christian countries, and with that the idea of 'Christian imperialism', was in principle abandoned. A delegate from China objected to Western speakers who still referred to 'unoccupied territories'; Europe and America also belonged within the missionary purview. Kraemer's book therefore referred to '*a* non-Christian world'—there was only *one* world, a world which needed Christ.

Yet another feature of Tambaram is important for an understanding of the development of the theology of mission: its statements on the relationship between Church and mission. A close connection between Church and mission was from the beginning absent in Protestant missionary thinking. The Reformation definitions of the Church were silent on its missionary dimension. Ecclesiological definitions were almost exclusively preoccupied with matters concerning the purity of doctrine, the sacraments, and Church discipline. Mission had to content itself with a position on the Church's periphery. During the nineteenth century the situation changed considerably, on both sides of the Atlantic. Graul, Löhe, Venn and Anderson regarded mission as the responsibility of the *Church* and the aim of mission as the planting of independent churches. This development was undoubtedly to be applauded but it also had a dark side. A rigid denominationalism developed and mission frequently deteriorated into proselytising and competition. The Church to which people belonged was equated with the Church in which they believed.

The 'Social Gospel' movement was a partial protest against this churchism. The student missionary movement from which John Mott emerged and which in several respects harked back to early Pietism was, like the 'Social Gospel' movement, ecumenical and anti-ecclesiocentric. The International Missionary Council, founded in 1921 as direct result of the Edinburgh conference, was for this reason explicitly a council of missionary agencies and not of churches. Theological developments after World War I, however, opened people's eyes to recognise that the faulty developments of the nineteenth century should not be regarded as a permanent hindrance to the emergence of correct relations between Church and mission. The fact that biblical and systematic theologians (such as Kähler) had begun to integrate mission into theology, helped ecclesiology to rediscover this forgotten dimension and opened the way for a new approach.

Tambaram reflected these developments. The concept 'Church' appeared in the themes of all five sections: 'the faith by which the Church lives'; 'the witness of the Church'; 'the life of the Church'; 'the Church and its environment'; 'the question of co-operation and the unity of the Church'. Did this not bring us back to the denominationalism of the nineteenth century? This is the way in which Hoekendijk subsequently interpreted Tambaram. It was, however, a one-sided interpretation. The nineteenth century use of 'denominational mission' developed in a context where churches and societies operated in isolation from one another. Tambaram however spoke of ecclesiastical mission within the context of an ecumenical meeting, a fact which militated against delegates thinking only of their own denominational missionary programmes. For Tambaram the

Church was 'The Divine Society founded by Christ and His apostles to accomplish His will in the world', and not exclusivistic denominations which because of their blinkers, ignored one another. The emphasis was on the witnessing Church which pointed towards the Kingdom and on the discovery of the younger churches which, together with the Church in the West, were en route to that Kingdom.

On the eve of the Second World War, with violence already the order of the day in China (a result of the Japanese invasion), Ethiopia, Spain, and elsewhere, this unity of the Church was an exhilarating discovery and precious treasure for many delegates. The German conference volume was published in June 1939, immediately before the outbreak of the war. It bore the significant title *Das Wunder der Kirche unter den Völkern der Erde* (The miracle of the Church among the peoples of the earth). In it Karl Hartenstein wrote (on p. 195, our translation); 'We no longer talked about churches in East and West, indeed, we did not at all concentrate on missionary societies and churches; we talked about the Church, God's community in the world. ... The magnificent vision of the Epistle to the Ephesians best describes the situation in Tambaram. ... Of decisive significance was the fact that the spiritual house of Jesus Christ was being built among the nations. ...' Such statements do not suggest that the Church was idealised at Tambaram. The conference could declare in plain words: 'No one so fully knows the failings, the pettiness, the faithlessness which infect the Church's life as we who are its members.' The empirical church was not identified with the Church of the Creed. Neither, however, was she detached from the Church of the Creed. There exists an indissoluble tie, a creative tension, between these two understandings of what the Church is.

THE ESCHATOLOGICAL DIMENSION

During the Tambaram Conference the German delegates prepared a document which became known as the 'German Eschatological Declaration'. This was prompted by the conviction that the eschatological dimension and context of mission was not sufficiently recognised by many delegates, especially those from English-speaking countries. Because of the exaggerated interest of certain groups in the 'signs of the times', in calculations of the date of the Second Coming, and an emphasis on the apocalyptic significance of practically every extraordinary event, 'respectable' Church circles in America and elsewhere had developed an aversion to the mere idea of eschatology. In this way not only apocalyptic, but practically the entire field of eschatology, gradually became the monopoly of enthusiastic groups and thus disappeared from orthodox theology and Church.

On the European continent, however, as we have indicated, eschatology had been rediscovered as an authentic dimension of the Christian message. The influence of this development on Protestant missiology was so pervasive that the Roman Catholic scholar, Ludwig Wiedenmann, identified the eschatological dimension as the characteristic par excellence of recent German theology of mission.[15] We do not suggest that everyone understood the same thing by 'eschatology'. There were at least four 'schools' of eschatology and each of them put its specific stamp on the understanding of mission.

In *dialectical theology* (Karl Barth) eschatology was understood as crisis, as radical divine intervention in and judgment of all human activities. Such human activities involved all forms of religion, including Christianity, and all ecclesiastical activities, including mission. Everything stands under the final, which means 'eschatological', judgment of God. In the theology of mission this approach was especially evident in the contributions of Paul Schütz and Hans Schärer—and, of course, in that of Barth himself.

The *existentialist eschatology* of Rudolf Bultmann received its classic missiological expression in Walter Holsten.[16] According to this interpretation mission means offering the individual the possibility of decision. This individual does not stand within the framework of historical development but is radically ahistorical and stands solely in a relationship to God. Man 'exists' only in so far as he is being addressed by God. There is no longer any 'future' in the sense of a further development of history. History has come to an end. In fact, in the existentialist missiology of Holsten practically everything is regarded as 'eschatological': the 'Christ event', revelation, the *kērygma*, justification, the Church.

Actualised eschatology (Paul Althaus and others) emphasised that the end was 'essentially' near. It was not the culmination of an extended historical process, but was always equally close. Each hour was seen as the last hour; the Christian lived in a time 'ripe for judgment'. Gerhard Rosenkranz concurred by saying that mission does not merely announce the end but was, in itself, an eschatological datum. Actualised eschatology is in several respects closely related to the realised eschatology propounded by C. H. Dodd and other British theologians.

Salvation-historical eschatology, which is especially associated with the name of Oscar Cullmann, regards *history* of greater importance than do the other three. Cullmann's influence is discernible notably in Karl Hartenstein and Walter Freytag. Hartenstein, who stemmed from Württemberg pietistic circles, gradually moved from Barth to Cullmann, at least as far as his views on eschatology were concerned. The same texts which Cullmann regarded as expressing a close relationship between mission and eschatology (Matt. 24.14; Mark 13.10; 2 Thess. 2.6-7; Rev. 6:1-8; Rom. 9-11, etc.) were also stressed by Hartenstein. The book of Revelation was of very special importance to him as can be evinced from the fact that he wrote a commentary on it, with the significant title *Der wiederkommende Herr* (The returning Lord). World history was for Hartenstein nothing but a battle between Christ and antichrist. Evil was maturing in the world. The world revealed itself all the more terribly as the desert into which God's Church was driven (Rev. 12). In the present all we can do is watch, wait, suffer, and hope—these verbs appear frequently in Hartenstein's writings.

In many respects Freytag concurred with Hartenstein. He was, however, more sober and reserved, and less apocalyptic. Yet, as in Hartenstein's case, he advocated a clearly pessimistic interpretation of history. All history was viewed as merely *human* history, the 'progress' of which was, at best, a multiplication of catastrophes. The Church was regarded as living between the 'already' of Christ's first coming and the 'not yet' of the Second Advent. Only one thing, Freytag said, gave meaning to this interim period: mission! In the 'salvation-historical pause' between the Ascension and the *parousia*, mission held the walls of history apart. Mission was therefore simultaneously preparation for and 'restrainer' of the end (cf. 2 Thess. 2.6-7). As soon as the missionary enterprise has been completed—in other words, as soon as the 'restrainer' has been removed—antichrist will come, and then the end. That the end has not yet come is a sign of God's patience.

This view implies an unbridgeable gulf between 'world history' and 'salvation history'. The one is, by its very nature, a product of man, the other an act of God. We can therefore not apply world-historical categories to mission, which is a salvation-historical event. 'Success' especially is no category with which mission can operate. Mission does not advance through the world as victor but, like its Lord, as servant and sufferer, without striving after success and results. It almost appears as if Freytag is worried that the ecumenical movement might be too successful, for then it would run the risk of not recognising its limitations and of attempting to consummate *now* what should be left to God's new creation.

In English-speaking missiological circles there was initially very little understanding of Hartenstein's and Freytag's positions. One of the few exceptions was Max Warren (1904-1977), for many years general secretary of the Church Missionary Society. In several publications, of which *The Truth of Vision* was basic and probably the most important, Warren paid attention to the relationship between mission and eschatology. He often acknowledged his indebtedness to Freytag. At the same time he rejected Freytag's views as dualistic. 'This world may indeed be enemy-occupied territory but the enemy has no property rights in it. He is a thief and a liar. Our responsibility as Christians is to be good stewards of the King's property.'[17] For this reason Christians may not be indifferent to the way in which the world is governed, nor to social and other malpractices. Salvation in Christ has to be realised *in* the world *now* already—this is a logical consequence of the Incarnation.

In this Warren concurred with several New Testament scholars among his contemporaries, of whom William Manson was one. Because of Christ's accomplished work and the coming of the Holy Spirit, said Manson, 'two orders of life, ... *two ages* have come to coexist in Christianity. The New Age has begun, the Old has not ended. The New dates from the Resurrection, the Old will last until the final manifestation of Jesus Christ in glory'.[18] Precisely for this reason, and on the basis of the New Era, we have the task and responsibility continually to challenge and change the Old. Nothing may remain as it is. At the same time we know that nothing will attain perfection here. In this tension we have to live.

When, after isolation on the continent during World War II, salvation-historical theology of mission entered the ecumene, it was gradually both deepened and broadened. The deepening manifested itself in the *missio Dei* motif to which we shall return. The broadening meant that, in the course of time, the conviction grew that God's salvific acts through the Church were flowing along a wider river-bed than the narrow salvation-historical definition of mission had allowed.

WHITBY 1947

In 1947, when the International Missionary Council met in Whitby, Canada, the shadow of the catastrophic war years still brooded over the world. The aims of the meeting included the rejoining of severed threads and lines of communication and the reaffirmation of the bonds of fellowship established at Tambaram. The delegates gathered in the awareness that one world was on its death-bed, while another was coming to birth.[19] Barthian theology was past its prime. Bultmann's existentialist approach would, for a time, offer some kind of escape route, notably in Germany, but could not provide a theological basis for the post-war period. Apocalypticism flared up for a while— there were, after all, 'signs of the times' in abundance for every would-be prophet!—but the experiences of the past made theologians careful and sceptical. In a sense an atmosphere of embarrassment characterised Whitby. Therefore, instead of referring to 'the desperate need of the world for Christ', in other words, instead of asking whether the preconditions for mission were present in the *world*, Whitby asked whether they were present in the *Church*. The correct attitude of the Church was more important than possible 'points of contact' or 'elements of truth' in the world or in other religions. The emphasis was on the Church as embodiment of mission, as *koinōnia*, rather than on mission as activity of the Church. The Church was the new community in which the fruit of the new life in Christ was experienced and enjoyed. Precisely in this way the Church was to become meaningful to the world. The authentic missionary event was the dynamic presence of this community in the world. Mission was not conquest of the world but solidarity with the world.

Whitby revealed the influence of Freytag and Hartenstein, an influence none the less already tempered by the contributions of Warren and others. Whitby thought in eschatological categories—how could it have been otherwise at that time? The eschatological vision took the form of 'expectant evangelism' (Warren). The future—including the period 'between the times'—was not empty but filled with the Kingdom, in all its incompleteness. Precisely the Kingdom, as already present yet still imperfect, implied that the Church-in-mission could not withdraw from the world. History and eschatology were inseparably intertwined. The Church's mission was moored to the Second Advent. In this way Whitby wanted to infuse the world with hope.

THEOLOGY OF THE APOSTOLATE

In German missiology Whitby's stimulus was channelled especially into a further development of the eschatological dimension; in Dutch missiology it led to the unfolding of the theology of the apostolate. This latter development meant that, in addition to Tambaram's distinction between a church-centric and a society-centric mission, there now emerged the concept of a mission-centric church. Mission—or the apostolate, as A. A. van Ruler, Hendrik Kraemer, J. C. Hoekendijk, E. Jansen Schoonhoven, and others preferred to call it during those years—was an essential characteristic of the Church.

The theology of the apostolate soon underwent a certain radicalisation, due to Hoekendijk's contribution.[20] He polemicised against the church-centric missionary thinking that had been especially in vogue since Tambaram 1938. The Church was an illegitimate centre. Not the Church but the world, the *oikoumenē*, stood in the centre of God's concern. Van Ruler's thesis that mission was a function of the Church, was inverted by Hoekendijk: the Church was a function of mission. There was no room here for a 'doctrine of the Church'. We should refer to the Church only in passing and without any emphasis. Ecclesiology should not be more than a single paragraph in Christology (the *messianic* involvement with the world) and a few sentences in eschatology (the messianic involvement with the *world*). A church-centric mission could not but miscarry for it had a false centre. The Church was, at most, an interlude, but she had designed a history for herself—Church history, salvation history—into which she could withdraw as into a 'reserve', or which she could use as a base from which to attack the world or exploit the world as training-ground, in an effort ultimately to fill the entire horizon.

Hoekendijk thus resolutely chose the 'event' above the 'institution'. He could never reconcile himself to the fact that the Church had time and again adjusted herself to the *status quo*. He was a spiritual child of Zinzendorf and John Wesley. He already wrestled with this problem in his doctoral thesis, *Kerk en Volk in de Duitse Zendingswetenschap* ('Church and Nation in German Missiology'): How *could* man bind the people of God, this 'sociological impossibility', this 'foreign body', to *one* category, in this instance the nation in the ethnic sense of the word? The Church-as-people-of-God may never accommodate herself to existing categories, whatever they may be. As a matter of fact, the Church does not as such 'exist', she 'happens'.

From the outset Hoekendijk could not accept a 'theology of mission'. If he did so it would imply that mission would once again be an extra. There would then also conceivably be other 'theologies of ...'. He therefore pleaded, not for 'theology of mission', but for 'missionary theology' as expression of *all* authentic theology. There was, for him, no theology save missionary theology. After all, theology comes into existence only when the Church is engaged in mission (Kähler!). The apostolate is therefore in this view not a result of apostolicity. Other theologians of the apostolate have put it thus: the Church has to engage in mission as her essential task because she is apostolic. Hoekendijk turned this round: apostolicity is a result of the apostolate; the Church is apostolic because she is mission.

In this way Hoekendijk's theology of the apostolate became a theology of the world. Theology is God inviting us to share the world with him. For precisely this reason it was a theology of the Kingdom. 'World' was for Hoekendijk a messianic concept and an eschatological correlate of the Kingdom. Mission was not the road from church to church; mission or Church was the interaction between Kingdom and world, involved in both. The form which this involvement took he called šālôm, Hebrew for 'peace', which he described as a 'social happening', and which was an ethical rather than a soteriological concept. Reconciliation became a universal humanisation process. In his earlier writings he did indeed characterise the task of the Church as kērygma, koinōnia and diakonia—proclamation, community, and service. In the course of time, however, his emphasis increasingly moved towards the last of the three.

Hoekendijk's influence on contemporary theology should not be underestimated. He even exercised an influence on Roman Catholic missionary thinking, although we have to admit that, as early as the 1930s, Yves Congar defined the Church as 'pilgrim', in this way beginning to prepare the ecclesiology of the Second Vatican Council. Catholic theologians such as Karl Rahner, J. Ratzinger, J. B. Metz and Ludwig Rütti, concur with Hoekendijk in many respects, consciously or unconsciously.

FROM WILLINGEN 1952 TO GHANA 1958

Hoekendijk was a member of the Dutch delegation to the second post-war meeting of the International Missionary Council (IMC) in Willingen, Germany, 1952. Between Whitby and Willingen, in the year 1949, Mao Tse Tung's forces finally became the masters of China. That vast country was the 'darling' of American missions in particular. During the first half of the twentieth century no country received as many Western missionaries as China. Now they were all dead, or gone, or jailed. When the Willingen meeting took place, several Western missionary agencies were still staggering from the blow delivered by events in China.[21] It was now even clearer than it was in 1947 (at Whitby) that a fundamental revolution had taken place in the world. In Asia the process of decolonisation was in full swing; in Africa it was just beginning. At the same time there were signs of an aggressive revival of Eastern religions. Willingen's atmosphere was one of widespread uncertainty. 'One does not any longer know what to say and how to say it. ... (This) has also made the discussion after Willingen very unclear and not at all convincing in any way.'[22]

The theme of Willingen was 'The Missionary Obligation of the Church'. In some sense it was a logical outcome of developments since Tambaram. It was against this that Hoekendijk polemicised so passionately. Apart from his 'high' missionary view there were, at Willingen, also advocates of a 'middle' missionary view exemplified by the Dutch theology of the apostolate, according to which mission was the 'heart' of the Church, as well as others who held a 'low' missionary view, which described mission, together with the pastorate, the diaconate and worship, as the essence of the Church. Discussions by representatives of these three views contributed considerably to greater clarity on several issues. Max Warren's paper, 'The Christian Mission and the Cross', acted as a catalyst. It had become increasingly clear that the starting point for a theology of mission was not to be found in the Church, but in God himself. To put it differently: mission should not be based on ecclesiology but on Christology. In fact, Willingen specifically referred to a trinitarian foundation of mission. This, however, was done in such a way that, in keeping with Barthian theology, the doctrine of the Trinity was interpreted on the basis of the doctrine of the atonement. Mission could be derived from the doctrine of the Trinity only indirectly. If soteriology, or more specifically the Cross, was taken as the starting point, it could however be derived directly. This explains why the Willingen report was not published under the original conference theme but with the title *Missions under the Cross* (1953).

The mooring of mission to the doctrine of the Trinity led to the introduction of the expression *missio Dei* (God's mission) at Willingen. The term was in all probability coined by Hartenstein. He intended it to give expression to the conviction that God, and God alone, was the Subject of mission. The initiative for our mission (*missio ecclesiae*, the Church's mission) lay with him alone. Only in God's hands *our* mission could be truly called *mission.* In the period after Willingen the concept *missio Dei* gradually changed its meaning.[23] It came to signify God's hidden activities in the world, independent of the Church, and our responsibility to discover and participate in these activities. This view was already discernible in embryo at Willingen, notably in the American report. In the nineteen-sixties it would be commonly accepted in ecumenical theology of mission. Rosin unhesitatingly calls the concept a Trojan horse 'through which the ... "American" vision was fetched into the well-guarded walls of the ecumenical theology of mission'. Whether Rosin's interpretation holds true or not, it cannot be denied that a problem was placed on the agenda of mission theology—a problem which Willingen did not solve and which, moreover, it has been impossible to ignore since then—that of the relationship between 'history' and 'salvation history'.

Six years after Willingen the last meeting of the IMC took place—in Achimota, Ghana, from 28th December 1957 till 8th January 1958. The explicit purpose of the conference was to prepare the IMC for integration into the World Council of Churches (WCC) which was founded in 1948. This integration was to be accomplished in New Delhi in 1961. Ralph Winter has recently published a very stimulating article on this proposed 'marriage'. What was probably the last contribution from the pen of Max Warren, before his death in August 1977, was likewise devoted to this theme.[24] Warren, who was present at the Ghana conference, discusses some of the reservations some delegates to the conference had on the advisability of integration at that stage and argues that now, many years after those meetings, several of the fears expressed then have indeed been realised. Winter clearly judges the integration to have been a mistake.

Both Warren and Winter argue that structural anomalies—such as the fact that the IMC was made up of Western *missionary* organisations and non-Western councils of *chur-ches*—cannot simply be solved by means of yet another structural magic formula. In addition, the integration of the IMC into the WCC (Winter jokingly asks: 'Why did the WCC not integrate into the IMC?') in some respects produced the very thing against which Hoekendijk fought so passionately: the institutionalisation of everything, the looking for solutions in structures, the imprisoning of the Holy Spirit. In the words of Warren: 'The Holy Spirit ... is as uncontrollable as the wind ... Unless the missionary movement can be responsive to the unpredictability of the Holy Spirit, it will soon cease to be a movement.' 'God does not appear to be as disturbed by differences in the forms taken by Christian obedience as many Christians are.'[25]

The WCC is a council of churches. Its organisational structure does not permit it to have other bodies as members— as the case was with the IMC. We refer especially to those missionary agencies that were members of the IMC but, because of structural considerations, were excluded at New Delhi. In 1957 only 42 per cent of all American missionaries were related to member churches of the American National Council of Churches and, through this council, to the WCC. By 1969 this percentage had dropped to 28, and by 1975 to only 14.[26] The contributions of the others were lost to the conciliar missionary movement, partly because of the disappearance of the IMC. Moreover, what was the primary concern of the IMC, namely the evangelisation of that two-thirds of the world's population which is not yet Christian, has at best become a secondary matter in the WCC setting. The Nairobi meeting of the WCC (1975) was the first to pay explicit attention to this aspect. In the meantime, however, a new movement would be launched: the 'evangelical ecumene'.

CHAPTER SEVENTEEN

DEVELOPMENTS SINCE 1960

ROMAN CATHOLIC MISSIONARY THINKING SINCE VATICAN II

The International Missionary Council was integrated into the World Council of Churches at the latter's New Delhi meeting in 1961. This was also the occasion on which the Eastern Orthodox churches joined the World Council. Meanwhile Pope John XXIII had already announced the Second Vatican Council which, with interruptions, would meet between 1962 and 1965. If we can state that Edinburgh 1910 had broken the isolation in which the various branches of Protestantism had lived for so long, we can with equal justice say that the early nineteen-sixties in many respects witnessed the establishment of links between Protestant, Orthodox and Roman Catholic churches. Mass-communication media also helped to demolish the walls of isolation and introduce neighbouring churches to one another.

World conditions, in addition, made it impossible for churches to continue living in isolation on little islands, ignoring one another. Each church today exists in a state of crisis; she is either still in a diaspora situation (in the Third World, for instance) or she is returning to such a situation (in the West, especially Europe). Since 1960 it has become ever clearer that the Second World War was a very important watershed in the history of mankind. The dream that the world would once again be 'put to order' after the feverish rebuilding in the years immediately following the war, has vanished like a mist. The tension between East and West has arrived to remain and everybody knows that the periodical signs of *détente* were not the promise of a new day but merely a false dawn.

The Third World presented itself in the council chambers of the world and demanded a share in everything. The West became increasingly aware—or was made aware—of its mistakes, blunders, and shortcomings. Western colonisation and civilisation were condemned often and together with them 'Western religion' as well. Western Christianity's guilt-feelings about its share in colonisation and its superiority feeling made it all the more timid and uncertain of itself. The non-Christian religions, by way of contrast, became emboldened and aggressive. Contrary to many expectations Marxism did not only maintain its position but, from 1960, managed to draw several new territories under its control, in addition to making its ideology a fashion on many campuses and among intellectuals and labourers in many non-Marxist countries.

It was against this background that the Second Vatican Council met. We want to highlight a few missiological implications of this historic event.

Vatican II is not conceivable without the stimulus of Protestant theology and Protestant missionary thinking in particular. Long before Vatican II Rome had already begun to adopt a milder attitude towards dissenting Christians. This tendency would reach a peak during the pontificate of 'good Pope John'. Protestants gradually changed from being 'sons of Satan', to 'heretics' and 'apostates', to 'dissenters', to 'separated brethren', to 'brethren in Christ'. Fine nuances were sometimes employed. *Lumen Gentium*, the Vatican Constitution on the Church, does not, for instance, simply refer to 'the separated brethren' but to 'the brethren separated *from us*'. Article 15 states that, because of baptism, Holy Scripture, faith in God and Christ, prayer, and the gifts of the Spirit, they are allied to the (Roman Catholic) Church. A Roman Catholic missiologist, Bernhard Willeke, described the new 'fraternal co-operation' as a 'gift of grace of God's Spirit'. This is not suggesting that all problems have been solved. As recently as 1970 another missiologist, André Seumois, could still argue that Protestants, including Anglicans, had no 'missionary mandate' because of their lack of apostolic succession.

Several Council documents have implications for the theology of mission, directly or indirectly. This applies especially to *Ad Gentes* (Decree on Mission), *Lumen Gentium, Unitatis Redintegratio* (Decree on Ecumenism), *Nostra Aetate* (on the non-Christian religions), *Gaudium et Spes* (on the Church in the modern world), and *Apostolicam Actuositatem* (on the lay apostolate).

For many centuries the conceptual picture of the Church as an institution dominated in Roman Catholicism. This concept of the Church is still discernible in the Vatican documents. It is, however, related to two other emphases that had begun to develop during the preceding decades, namely, a renewed understanding of the Church as the mystical Body of Christ and as God's pilgrim people in the world. In this way Rome's traditionally static ecclesiology gained an undeniably dynamic element. This also explains why—for the first time in history— a Council explicitly dealt with mission and even published a decree on it. It is, furthermore, of importance that missiology was not founded on ecclesiology, as would be expected on the basis of traditional Roman Catholic theology. A different course was pursued: ecclesiology was founded missiologically. It is not true that there is mission because there is Church; rather, there is Church because there is mission.

The new vision emerges in both *Lumen Gentium* and *Ad Gentes*. The Church is not an established entity nor a successful firm with high dividends; she is God's pilgrim people in the diaspora and for this reason essentially missionary, which means: sent into the world. The entire apostolic activity is Christ-centred rather than church-centred. The Church may be neither centre, nor point of departure, nor ultimate goal of mission. The Church's true task is to cross frontiers, not to fix them. The Christian message exists only 'in the form of being en route to the nations'. 'The being-under-way of the message to the nations, this we call Church.' 'Mission is the expression of the earthly homelessness of the word ...' (J. Ratzinger). The second paragraph of *Ad Gentes* begins with the words: 'The pilgrim Church is missionary by her very nature.' Several times the Church is referred to as *sacramentum mundi* (sacrament of the world). She is thus described essentially as not in relationship to herself, but to God and the world.

These theological assertions have some definite implications. They signify, for instance, that the Church can no longer be regarded merely as an institution centred on Rome. 'Local churches', everywhere in the world, develop a missionary significance in their own environs. *Ad Gentes*, however, breaks less with the traditional partition of the world into 'Christian' and 'non-Christian' blocks and with church planting as the most important missionary aim, than does *Lumen Gentium.*

Developments after Vatican II reaffirm the tendencies which had developed during the Council. As in Protestant ecumenical theology, there is a growing emphasis on the Church's involvement in the world, so much so that it sometimes appears as if the Church as worshipping community has faded away. In this respect we refer to Johannes B. Metz, W. B. Frazier, J. Schmitz, and especially Ludwig Rütti. The latter defines the Church almost exclusively in world-political categories. The abstract distinctions between Church and world are for him, in the last analysis, meaningless. According to Scripture, he says, the Church is a second-order reality. Rütti thus, in several respects, follows in the 'ultra-Protestant' footsteps of Hoekendijk.

The Vatican document *Nostra Aetate* has a special significance for the theology of mission, in that it broaches a new interpretation of non-Christian religions. Few subjects have been dealt with more frequently than this one since Vatican II. In these publications the non-Christian religions are described alternatively as 'ordinary ways of salvation', 'anonymous Christianity', or 'the latent Church'.

Theological developments during and since Vatican II in many respects led to a crisis in the Roman Catholic missionary enterprise. Questions were being asked. If the Church is involved in mission everywhere, why do missionaries still have to go to distant, foreign countries? If non-Christian religions also provide ways of salvation, why do we have to convert their adherents? If Protestants are our 'brethren in Christ', why do we still have to compete with them on the mission field? If, according to *Dignitatis Humanae,* Christianity should not be foisted upon anyone, does mission still have any right of existence?

The Fourth Synod of Bishops (October 1974) and the apostolic exhortation, *Evangelii Nuntiandi,* which issued from the Synod, contributed considerably to clarifying some of these issues. The exhortation is one of the most valuable documents of recent years. In unambiguous language it subscribes to the Church's involvement in the socio-political issues of the world;

but her call to world evangelisation, in which every believer is involved, is endorsed equally unequivocally. Of additional importance is the fact that leaders from the Third World played a far more crucial role at the Fourth Synod of Bishops (and thus also in the deliberations that led to the compilation of *Evangelii Nuntiandi*) than they did at Vatican II, which reflected the discussions of predominantly Western theologians.

EASTERN ORTHODOX THEOLOGY OF MISSION

The Eastern Orthodox churches joined the World Council of Churches in 1961. In this way they, too, stepped out of isolation and began to participate in discussions of the theology of mission.

The Orthodox understanding of mission differs in many respects from that of Western Christianity, both Protestant and Roman Catholic.[1] Partly because of the political situation in the countries of the Orthodox churches, mission was, with a few exceptions (for instance, in Russia) far less aggressive than in the West. Pagans should not be steamrollered with the gospel but rather attracted by it. Mission is therefore centripetal rather than centrifugal. The liturgy is the key to the Orthodox understanding of the Church; this implies that mission, too, is moored to liturgy. The light of grace which shines in the liturgy should, like a magnet, draw those who live in the darkness of paganism. The novice is led into the mysteries of the liturgy by the priest.

In Orthodox missionary thinking the Church is central. Missionary societies, even missionary orders as we have them in Roman Catholicism, are inconceivable here. The Church as Body is fulfilment rather than instrument of mission; she is herself part of the missionary message. Church renewal is therefore in itself already mission. For the individual witness this implies that he has to sanctify himself, as Jesus, the sent One, did (John 17.18-19).

Mission and unity coincide in Orthodox theology. Because of this, the fragmentation of Protestant missionary bodies and their mutual proselytising are criticised relentlessly. Unity takes pride of place. This partly explains why, after the breach with Rome in AD 1054, active Orthodox mission work practically ceased.

The restoration of the unity had to be given priority. The missionary who was not a representative of the *one* Church could not go to pagans. Those who, like many Protestants, regarded unity as secondary or projected it to the distant future, simply increased the existing confusion.

The purpose of mission in the Orthodox view is theosis, the deification of man, the restoration of the divine image. In this process of deification, this divine economy, there is also room for adherents of non-Christian religions. In this respect Orthodox theology comes fairly close to Roman Catholic interpretations, in spite of their different points of departure. The fact that, according to Orthodox theology, the Holy Spirit does not proceed from the Son, but only from the Father, also facilitates the view that the Holy Spirit is regarded as active in non-Christian religions, outside of the revelation in Christ.

During recent years, even before they joined the World Council of Churches, the Orthodox Churches have experienced certain shifts of emphasis in their understanding of mission. One of the leading figures in this regard is Anastasios Yannoulatos, at present Bishop of Androussa. Since 1959 there has existed a movement in Greece called *Porefthendes* ('As you go ...', Matt. 28.19) which applies itself to the awakening of missionary interest and a more explicitly 'centrifugal' missionary understanding. Yannoulatos argues that this actually flows from the essence of the Orthodox understanding of the Church; it represents, in other words, a rediscovery of a long neglected dimension. Coupled with this, there has recently been a growing interest in the social dimension of Christian mission as an outcome of the traditional Orthodox cosmic understanding of salvation.

FROM NEW DELHI 1961 TO NAIROBI 1975

During the third plenary meeting of the World Council of Churches (WCC), at New Delhi in 1961, the International Missionary Council was integrated into the WCC and transformed into one of its divisions, the Commission on World Mission and Evangelism. On that occasion the aim of mission was described as 'the proclamation to the whole world of the gospel of Jesus Christ to the end that all men may believe in him and be saved'—a statement that still reflected the theological influences of Barth and Kraemer. At the same time, however, new voices were heard which would—at least partially—cause mission to embark upon a new course during the ensuing years.

In an important paper at New Delhi Joseph Sittler introduced the concept of 'the cosmic Christ' into the ecumenical discussion. On the basis of Col. 1.15-20 he pleaded for a much closer relationship between creation and redemption: we should regard the latter as being as inclusive as the former. The outcome of this interpretation was that God was regarded as being active in every facet of world history. The contrast between Church and world was in principle abandoned. In a way M. M. Thomas concurred with this interpretation at the New Delhi meeting itself. This provoked Lesslie Newbigin to protest that, according to such an approach, God was for all practical purposes identified with the historical process of development.

Sittler's paper held special significance for the theology of religions. 'Dialogue' would soon be a key word in the theology of mission. It is interesting to follow the changing fashions in this regard. In 1963 reference was still being made to 'The *witness* of Christians to men of other faiths'. A year later it became 'Christian *encounter* with men of other beliefs'. After three more years, it was 'Christians in *dialogue* with men of other faiths'. In all these instances the point of departure remained the *Christian's* witness, encounter, or dialogue. In 1970, however, it became 'Dialogue *between* men of living faiths'. The earliest sign of a reversal of this trend was discernible at the Nairobi meeting (1975). That there was indeed a change in approach became more apparent at the consultation on dialogue at Chiang Mai in Thailand (April 1977). The theme was 'Dialogue in community'. Some of the statements at this gathering were even reminiscent of Kraemer and Tambaram. Michael Mildenberger calls the Chiang Mai meeting 'a pause for reflection on dialogue'.[2]

Two years after New Delhi, the newly established Commission on World Mission and Evangelism held its first meeting in Mexico City. The consequences of the integration of the Missionary Council into the WCC were now becoming apparent. If mission belongs to the essence of the Church, this applies everywhere, including the West. The Church is then always a missionary Church, even in its own environment. Mexico City gave expression to this with the slogan, 'Mission in Six Continents'. Mission could no longer be a flight to 'far away' paganism, whereas the paganism close by, for instance in the West, was ignored. This, after all, would imply that the missionary Church was giving up the very soil upon which she stood. The new emphasis has at least five advantages: it makes the Church conscious of her missionary calling in her own environment; it stresses the global extent of the missionary dimension; it helps to combat antiquated paternalistic structures; it questions the traditional one-way traffic in mission as well as Western pride of possession; it makes room for reciprocity.[3]

The idea of 'mission in six continents' is, however, not without its problems. The (correct) observation that the Church is always in a missionary situation, may in specific circumstances lead to myopia, so that the Church remains busy only with her immediate neighbourhood and, as Ralph Winter puts it, forget 'that 84 per cent of all non-Christians are beyond the normal evangelistic range because (they are) outside of the cultural traditions of any national church anywhere in the world' and that the Mexico City slogan helps little to 'cut through the massive cocoon within which the churches of the world ... now live.'[4]

The value of the Mexico City deliberations was further limited by the vague and generalised way in which the concept 'mission' was discussed, by the very positive evaluation of the secularisation process, by the prevailing spirit of optimism, and by the lack of appreciation of the fact that the world adopts an essentially negative stance towards mission. Only W. A. Visser 't Hooft's paper on 'Missions as a Test of Faith' dealt adequately with these issues.

Mexico City in fact marked the beginning of the broadening of the concept 'mission', at the expense of the depth contained in the expression *missio Dei* when first introduced. The slogan 'Mission in Six Continents' put the emphasis onesidedly on the geographical and socio-political dimensions.

The optimism of Mexico City continued in the fourth assembly of the WCC (Uppsala 1968). However paradoxical it may sound, the spirit of Uppsala in many respects resembled that of Edinburgh 1910. Uppsala represented the apex of the ecumenical theology of secularisation. The key word was 'development', and Uppsala was confident that its plans for this and other socio-political enterprises would succeed.

Uppsala regarded mission largely as *humanisation*. A study project on the 'missionary structure of the congregation', which was launched seven years earlier at New Delhi and which owed its birth chiefly to the church-centred missiological thinking then still in vogue, was presented to the assembly. In the reports all attention was focused on God's work in the secular world; the Church was relativised to such an extent that it could be said that 'the church does not have a separate mission of its own'. Mission was still described—as happened in Willingen— as *missio Dei*, but this now meant 'entering into partnership with God in history', 'understand(ing) the changes in history in the perspective of the mission of God', 'point(ing) to God at work in world history', 'point(ing) to the humanity in Christ as the goal of mission'. Everything became mission at Uppsala: health and welfare services, youth projects, work with political interest groups, constructive use of violence, the protection of human rights. H. Berkhof is correct when he observes that the apostolic commitment to the world of the nineteen-fifties changed during the subsequent decade into a diaconal commitment to the world;[5] to which we might add that, for many people, 'diaconal' gradually became the equivalent of 'revolutionary'.

The influence of Hoekendijk's *šālôm* theology—he was member of the American working group and consultant to the European group—is clearly evident in the preparatory documents. In the final report, 'Renewal in Mission', many of the views just referred to were moderated to some extent, due to the influence of John Stott and others. The almost entirely positive evaluation of the world and world events (after all, 'the world provides the agenda', as the European document had it) was, however, maintained in essence.

The Commission for World Mission and Evangelism had its second meeting in Bangkok, in January 1973. The theme was 'Salvation Today'. The lines of force from New Delhi, Mexico City and Uppsala now emerged more clearly. The opening address by M. M. Thomas, chairman of the Central Committee of the WCC, already revealed the theological trend which would dominate the conference. The conference was in fact occasioned by the question whether or not salvation was more than individual liberation from sin and eternal death. What was at issue was the social and temporal dimensions of salvation and, consequently, of mission. After Bangkok (and, of course, in many quarters even before that) these dimensions of salvation were accepted as axiomatic and never contested. The new question was rather whether salvation could possibly have *more* than a social and temporal dimension!

Thomas made a fleeting reference to 'the eschatological hope of final salvation'; for the rest he seemed interested only in the 'infinite possibilities ... of the eschatological becoming historical, even political'. He could therefore declare as something self-evident: 'Herein lies the mission of the Church: to participate in the movements of human liberation ...' Concern for bodily health, material wealth and social justice were described as '*an expression of* a certain spiritual relation between the people and God' (italics added). In view of this, Klaus Bockmühl argues that, where it used to be taken for granted that the Christian faith ought to stimulate social involvement, Thomas had reversed the sequence: social involvement required a certain spirituality.[6]

Related to this is Thomas's contention that mission could no longer imply 'a choice between Christianity and other religions'. In language reminiscent of Kaj Baago and Georges Khodr,[7] he queried the validity of conversion and baptism in India today and suggested that the task of the Church should be one of forming 'new sects in the sense of groups with a prophetic and evangelistic vocation, within the movements of cultural creativity and social liberation, rather than to try to bring about one organized Church of India, which may only mean several small ghettos joining forces to form one large ghetto'.

The reports of the various sections of the Bangkok Conference endorsed Thomas's views in several respects. The Bible Studies by Christoph Barth, Ulrich Wilckens, and Paul Minear, together with the contributions of Arthur Glasser and others helped, however, to some extent to tone down some of the recommendations. In this respect we refer to the document, 'An

Affirmation on Salvation Today', which had its origin in one of the Bible Study groups and was subsequently referred to the member churches by the plenary.

The fifth meeting of the WCC took place in Nairobi, late in 1975. Indications are that here, for the first time since 1961, a turn of the tide in ecumenical missionary thinking could be detected[8] (despite the fact that P. Beyerhaus has in several critiques argued that Nairobi was in no way different from the preceding WCC meetings). In Nairobi the euphoria of Uppsala gave way to more sober realism. The tone was more subdued. Too few of Uppsala's grand schemes had been realised. The dream of a 'theology of development' as key to the solution of the world's problems was shattered. The years since Uppsala produced more failures than successes, both for the WCC and its member churches. The 'theology of history', that is, the idea that God's will can be deduced directly from world events and that we are expected to join in these events, which had become the fashion since New Delhi, had proved to be more ambiguous than many had at first expected. The programme of dialogue with other religions had in many respects run into a blind alley. The one-sided idea of salvation as humanisation or shalomisation had proved to be too restricted a base for the Church's involvement in the world.

The address that roused the most attention at Nairobi was Mortimer Arias's, 'That the World may Believe'. He distinguished between 'mission' and 'evangelisation' and judged that the WCC had lately done very little about the latter. He called the Council back to this 'essential priority' and to the fact that evangelisation was the Church's primary and permanent responsibility. He rejected all dichotomy between vertical and horizontal, between evangelism and social action, and pleaded for a 'holistic' approach. Arias's paper found an echo in the discussions and especially in the final report of Section One, 'Confessing Christ Today'. We quote a few sentences from this document which abounds in theological insights:

> The gospel always includes the announcement of God's Kingdom and love through Jesus Christ, the offer of grace and forgiveness of sins, the invitation to repentance and faith in Him, the summons to fellowship in God's Church, the

command to witness to God's saving words and deeds, the responsibility to participate in the struggle for justice and human dignity, the obligation to denounce all that hinders human wholeness, and a commitment to risk life itself ...

The world is not only God's creation; it is also the arena of God's mission. Because God loved the whole world, the church cannot neglect any part of it—neither those who have heard the saving Name nor the vast majority who have not yet heard it. Our obedience to God and our solidarity with the human family demands that we obey Christ's command to proclaim and demonstrate God's love to every person, of every class and race, on every continent, in every culture, in every setting and historical context ...

THE NEW 'EVANGELICAL' THEOLOGY OF MISSION

In our section on the Ghana meeting of the International Missionary Council we drew attention to the fact that the integration of the Council into the WCC left a great many missionary organisations without any mutual bond. Some of these, together with others who had never had any connection with the Missionary Council, established contact with one another during the nineteen-sixties and also attempted to involve evangelical churches in the West and in the Third World. The resulting congress on 'The Church's Worldwide Mission', held in Wheaton, Illinois, in April 1966, was an attempt to consolidate evangelical forces.

Wheaton was a predominantly North American meeting. It was followed, later the same year, by a ten-day congress in Berlin, attended by 1,200 delegates from a hundred countries. The theme was 'One Race, one Gospel, one Task'. In both Wheaton and Berlin attempts were made to draw all evangelicals under one umbrella. Evangelicals also attempted to influence the WCC meeting in Uppsala (1968). Donald McGavran and John Stott may be mentioned in this regard.

After Uppsala it was Peter Beyerhaus in particular who emerged as champion of the evangelical cause. He was, for instance, the main architect of the Frankfurt Declaration (1970) on 'The fundamental crisis in mission'. Seven 'indispensable basic elements of mission' are tabulated in this declaration: the ground of mission is to be found solely in the command of the risen Lord; the main purpose of mission is the glorification of God, not humanisation; there is no salvation except in Jesus Christ; eternal redemption can be attained through proclamation, conversion, and baptism; the concrete and visible task of mission is to establish a church as the new people of God; the offer of salvation is for all men, but the adherents of non-Christian religions can share in that salvation only through faith, conversion, and baptism; the Church is engaged in mission until Christ's return.

One of the problems about the compilers of the Frankfurt Declaration was their tendency to brand all those who did not entirely agree with them as enemies of the cause of Christ. In 1973, after Bangkok, the 'Missionary Convention of the Conference of Confessing Communities in the Evangelical Churches of Germany', under Beyerhaus's leadership, prepared another declaration in which Bangkok was rejected in its entirety and accused of 'treason' and an 'anti-gospel character'. On Ascension Day 1974, yet another declaration followed, the 'Berlin Declaration on true and false Ecumenicity', under three headings: the sifting time for world Christianity; the gospel and false ecumenism; the conflict between true and false ecumenism.

Meanwhile a group of evangelicals from all quarters of the globe had begun preparations for a new congress. This resulted in the 'International Congress on World Evangelization' which met in Lausanne during July 1974. Here the concept 'evangelical' was interpreted more broadly than it had been by the German action groups. We have already pointed out that 'evangelical' does not mean the same for all and that Beyerhaus identifies no less than six different evangelical groups. Representatives of all six were present in Lausanne. This had the advantage that speakers complemented one another and that Lausanne was less polemical than a meeting of supporters of any one 'evangelical' category would have been. This explains why the Lausanne Covenant reflected not only one school of thought but, rather, a dynamic interaction between many different approaches. This emerges most clearly in paragraphs 4 and 5 of the Covenant which deal, respectively, with 'the nature of evangelism' and 'Christian social responsibility'.

We have mentioned that the Nairobi meeting of the WCC (1975) reveals a slight change of tone when compared with earlier WCC meetings. It cannot be disputed that this change was due, in part at least, to the influence of the Fourth Roman Catholic Synod of Bishops (1974) and especially of Lausanne. The similarities between the documents of these three ecumenical gatherings are indeed remarkable, although the important differences should not be underestimated.[9] Whereas, until the early nineteen-seventies, the tendency used to be to polarise, there now appears a degree of convergence. This naturally applies to only some elements in the evangelical and ecumenical 'camps'. Some fundamentalists and confessionalists in the first group, and certain champions of the theology of liberation and revolution in the second, manifest little interest in a possible convergence.

In the last part of this book we shall venture to evaluate the various contemporary currents in the theology of mission. Meanwhile we simply emphasise that the debate on what mission is continues in the different groups. The WCC Commission on World Mission and Evangelism is planning its third meeting (that is, after Mexico City 1963 and Bangkok 1973) for 1980 in Melbourne. The theme will be, 'Your Kingdom Come!' The Lausanne Continuation Committee is planning a second conference on world evangelisation, also for 1980, in Pattaya, Thailand. Both these meetings regard themselves as legitimate continuations of the first world missionary conference in Edinburgh, seventy years earlier. In more than one respect they will determine whether the road ahead during the next decade will bear the stamp of polarisation or convergence.

This entire issue is certainly of more than merely academic interest. It has crucial implications for the practice of mission and the role of the Church in the world.

PART IV

TOWARDS A THEOLOGY
OF MISSION

CHAPTER EIGHTEEN

THE CENTRALITY OF MISSION

MISSION AS ESSENTIAL TASK

In this final section we intend attempting to indicate a road ahead for the theology of mission. After attending, in the first part, to the contemporary confusion in this field, and identifying, in the second part, four elements of a biblical theology of mission, we have, in the third section, studied the definition of mission in the various periods of Church history. This produced a mosaic, some parts and colours of which stood in glaring contrast to others. It is therefore essential to proceed now to indicate some guidelines for a responsible theology of mission.

It goes without saying that we should not endeavour to force such a theology of mission into a precise, unalterable pattern. Yet it is, after all, no more than human to attempt this. It affords a sense of security to have hard-and-fast forms for our convictions; yet, this type of security is not without problems. Any systematisation is in itself already an impediment to truth. God is more concerned about authenticity than content. His freedom is greater than our theological formulations. Naturally this does not mean that the way we formulate our convictions of faith is of no consequence. For our own sake and because of our human limitations we *need* guidelines. In that way we obtain greater clarity about what is expected of us—as long as we remember that such guidelines are, and remain, relative.

When discussing a responsible theology of mission it has to be said in advance that mission is an essential aspect of the life of the Church and of the individual Christian. We have seen that this has not always been the case. Both Roman Catholic and Protestant ecclesiologies developed in a period when Christianity for all practical purposes ceased to be a missionary religion. This explains the total absence of any missionary dimension in the definitions of the Church during the sixteenth and seventeenth centuries. Stephen Neill says the Reformation definitions of the Church 'call up a vision of a typical English village of not more than 400 inhabitants, where all are baptized Christians, compelled to live more or less Christian lives under the brooding eye of parson and squire. In such a context "evangelization" has hardly any meaning, since all are in some sense already Christian, and need no more than to be safeguarded against error in religion and viciousness in life.'[1]

It was only gradually, in fits and starts, that the missionary aspect of the Church's existence was rediscovered. This development reached its zenith between the nineteen-thirties and fifties. We refer especially to the Dutch theology of the apostolate. Despite all criticism we may level against Hoekendijk, his crucial contribution in this regard should not be overlooked. He could for instance say: We shall never understand what the apostles taught unless we do what the apostles did, namely, mission. Apostolicity without apostolate is not apostolicity but apostasy. As early as 1933 Gerardus van der Leeuw, famous historian of religion, said: Mission is a vital expression of the Holy Spirit whom we may never hem in. For this very reason every constricting of the activities of the Holy Spirit to the individual or the Church or orthodox doctrine drains the vital force of mission.

Mission as an essential aspect of the Church's existence is also related to the fact that God's grace—in Barth's words—is never 'brutal grace'.[2] God does not want to appropriate man to himself against man's will. He wants to offer man the opportunity to refuse God in liberty. And this opportunity which God offers man is called mission.

'DIMENSION' AND 'INTENTION'

Simply to designate mission in general an 'essential aspect' of the Church does not yet clarify all ambiguities. It is in this context that H.-W. Gensichen's distinction between 'dimension' and 'intention' comes to our aid.[3] Everything the Church is and does, says Gensichen, must have a missionary *dimension*, but not everything has a missionary *intention.* To put it differently: the Church's entire nature is missionary but she is not, in all her activities, explicitly aimed at the world. The Church must in all circumstances be 'missionary', but she is not in every moment 'missionising'. The Church is 'missionary' when she is able to welcome outsiders, when she is no mere object of pastoral care, when lay members are involved in congregational activities, when the congregation is structurally pliable, and when she is not defending the privileges of a select group. Only a Church that manifests this missionary dimension can also be deliberately 'missionising', moving actively into the world.

Hoekendijk tends to subsume the Church entirely in 'intention': she is only Church if and while she is actively en route to the world. 'Intention' can, however, exist only on the basis of 'dimension'. The congregation should, in her existence as such, have a missionary dimension, or else she simply cannot become involved in mission. This is an aspect which D. van Swigchem has especially highlighted.[4] What is happening and being experienced in the bosom of the Church—kindness, unity, love of neighbour and brother, obedience, joy, good works (cf. Phil. 2.14-16; Col. 4.5; 1 Thess. 4.9-12; 1 Pet. 2.12; 3.15)—contains a missionary dimension; it is already proclamation to those outside (cf. Col. 4.5; 1 Thess. 4.12; 1 Cor. 5.12-13). By their mere existence and even before they have crossed any frontiers to the world, the believers are 'a letter that has come from Christ ... any man can see it for what it is and read it for himself' (2 Cor. 3.2-3).

The Eastern Orthodox Church, as we have already indicated, defines mission in 'dimensional' categories: the congregation's sacramental life is the centre of mission. This is certainly a valid point of view. Where, however, Hoekendijk runs the risk of absolutising the 'intention', the opposite danger confronts us here: that 'dimension' might be regarded as adequate. Dimension and intention should be dynamically interrelated. The one nurtures and stimulates the other. The Church is, to use an expression of Zinzendorf, both *'Asyl'* and *'Pfeilschmiede'*—both 'asylum' and 'forger of arrows'. She is fulfilment, foretaste, first-fruits, realisation of salvation, and precisely *as such* sent into the world. A witnessing, serving, missionising Church is conceivable only on the basis of a very strong inspiration. The purely apostolic approach to the Church is, on close scrutiny, indefensible. Without the dimension, the intention quickly dissipates. In his broadly planned treatment of soteriology, Karl

Barth therefore rightly discusses the Church under three aspects. Volume IV/1, §62, deals with 'The Holy Spirit and the *Gathering* of the Christian Community' (pp. 643-739); here the institutional aspect of the Church's life also receives attention. Volume IV/2, §67, deals with 'The Holy Spirit and the *Upbuilding* of the Christian Community (pp. 614-726); the communal aspect, the *koinōnia*, is here emphasised. In Volume IV/3, §72, a discussion on 'The Holy Spirit and the *Sending* of the Christian Community' is presented (pp. 681-901). None of these three aspects may ever be considered in isolation from the other two.

All this does not imply that any finality has been reached as to what the content of the 'missionary intention' and the goal of mission ought to be. We shall address ourselves to these issues in the following chapters. It goes without saying that our 'solutions' make no claim to infallibility. We all suffer from the limitations of what might be called 'theological optics'. The theological views and judgments of each person are, at least in part, the result of a specific background and context. The best we can hope to achieve is to undertake—as far as such human limitations permit—to open our ears and hearts to all opinions, to weigh each carefully, and then, in the light of the wide framework of God speaking to us through his word, to arrive at our own positions, fully conscious of the fact that others may come to conclusions which differ from ours on crucial points.

There are today, as we have indicated in Chapter 4, essentially two missiological models contending for supremacy. The evangelical model accentuates the discontinuity between God's activities and ours, between salvation history and world history, between eternal and temporal salvation. The ecumenical model emphasises the continuity between Church and world, God's salvation and socio-political liberation, redemption and humanisation. Can it be that both are right? Or perhaps that both are wrong?

CHAPTER NINETEEN

AN EMACIATED GOSPEL

SHADES OF DUALISM

In this chapter we intend focusing on what, in our view, are the typical shortcomings in the evangelical theology of mission.

There is a tendency among evangelicals to regard Christ as Lord only of the Church and not of the cosmos as well. Since the birth of the Church there have been Christians who have been inclined to despise the world. They have interpreted the gospel in terms of a religion of redemption along the lines of the Greek mystery religions. Concern has been for salvation *from* the world rather than for the world's renewal. The burning conviction, the passionate hope, the 'eager expectation', and the groans 'as if in the pains of childbirth' (Rom. 8.19, 22), that the entire creation should surrender to Christ, have been lost.

Sanctification among some evangelicals is defined by those who share this perspective as withdrawal from everything that is 'worldly'. The forgiveness of personal sins is equated with redemption. As Augustine put it: 'Our hearts are restless in us until they find rest in Thee'; when that rest has been found, the believer has arrived at his destination. Mission thus means the communication of a message that will bring about that 'rest'. The preacher concentrates on 'eternal healing' rather than the merely temporary amelioration of conditions in this world— apparently a matter for which ecumenicals campaign. The changing of social structures is thus of secondary importance because they are in the last analysis irrelevant.

The attitude towards social and political involvement can take several forms. The most extreme view is to regard any form of social involvement as a *betrayal of the gospel*. Such involvement, so the argument goes, represents an unwarranted shift from the legitimate to the illegitimate. Where it does occur—simply as result of the fact that the Christian has no choice but to be *in* this world—it is often with a bad conscience, a feeling that the gospel birthright has been bartered for a mess of pottage. The believer however feels most happy when he is building dykes against the threatening flood of social involvement. He has to watch against any satanic tactics of diversion and any adulteration of his faith. After all, 'the whole frame of this world is passing away' (1 Cor. 7.31). In this view the dualism between spirit and body, eternal and temporal, personal and social, sacred and profane, is total.

It is also possible to regard social involvement *as the means to an end.* This has been one of the arguments advanced in favour of educational and medical missions. These activities were not in themselves mission, but they could serve a useful purpose by 'softening up' missionary objects for the gospel. They functioned as baits and forerunners for 'real' mission. 'Service is a means to an end. As long as service makes it possible to confront men with the Gospel, it is useful.'[1]

A third alternative is to regard social activities *as optional.* In itself there is nothing wrong with getting involved in social action, but it is simply not a priority. If there is time and if opportunities present themselves, it may even be good to engage in social action.

Perhaps the most popular approach among evangelicals is to describe the relationship between personal redemption and social involvement as that of *seed and fruit,* or as primary and secondary. 'The *mission* comes first, and the *ministry* follows as the harvest follows the sowing.'[2] Elton Trueblood puts it as follows: 'If we do not start with what is primary, we are not likely to achieve what is secondary, for this is a resultant. ... The call to become fishers of men precedes the call to wash one another's feet.'[3] The Lausanne Covenant employs a similar phrase: 'In the church's mission of sacrificial service evangelism is primary.' Evangelicals frequently call attention to what they do in the area of charity, of relief after natural catastrophes, and so forth. This is undoubtedly praiseworthy; the question remains, however, what function these activities have in their overall theological approach.

A variation of the primary-secondary approach is found in the widespread view that, if people are truly converted, they will become socially involved simply as a matter of course. Martin Luther adopted this attitude with regard to the state.

He believed that, if only God's word was allowed to take its course unhampered, it would change rulers and rich men and would produce a fatherly, benevolent system of government.

In recent years a strong conviction has been developing among evangelicals that none of these four approaches is adequate. Efforts have recently been made to link witness and service more closely. Frequently, however, there has been little success, with the result that service remains a secondary element. Both the Wheaton Declaration (1966) and the Lausanne Covenant (1974) reveal this. The problem is that the solution is usually found in that the social dimension and the believer's involvement in the world are added on to evangelism. Despite the best intentions, they therefore remain a supplement.

DOCTRINE AND LIFE

It is frequently said by evangelicals that purity of doctrine is of incomparable importance. The 'acceptance in faith' of the salvific facts concerning the death and resurrection of Jesus Christ guarantees redemption. The salvation events are located in the remote past (biblical history), or in the future (the coming of the millennium) or they are internalised (redemption takes place in man's heart). The present age as such, however, remains empty. It is the task of the Church to preserve the traditions of the past as a treasure and safeguard them against adulteration.

In this process 'sound doctrine' is usually very narrowly defined. Distinctions are carefully drawn between the doctrine itself and its 'ethical application'. We have, however, urgently to ask whether heresy has to do only with the first. W. A. Visser 't Hooft put it plainly to the Uppsala assembly (1968): 'It must become clear that Church members who deny in fact their responsibility for the needy in any part of the world are just as guilty of heresy as those who deny this or that article of faith.' When an unchristian practice hides behind orthodox theological formulas, we have to do not only with hypocrisy but also with apostasy. The doctrine of redemption may never content itself with the pious recitation of salvation-historical facts, but has equally to do with the living up to that confession here and now. Evangelicals sometimes tend to defend rather than practise the gospel. This leads to the view that the Church's most important and almost exclusive activity is public worship, and everything connected with it: baptism, catechesis, prayer meetings, funerals, and the like. The concern is thus with sacred ceremonies, *away* from daily life, at special places and on special days. Reformation and Church renewal essentially mean fortifying one's own ecclesiastical institution and improving one's own programmes. The Church is a fort, a bulwark, a sanctuary, separated from the world; she is the possessor of truth, the source and distributor of the means of salvation.

Because of these views, some evangelicals tend to identify their own convictions with God's will and without hesitation to label their own enterprises as 'the Lord's work'. This tendency reveals itself in an open letter of Donald McGavran to the Nairobi meeting of the WCC in which he, adopting a clear-cut, black and white approach, identifies his own view with the mind of God. He writes, for instance:

> We have come to the conclusion that two radically different systems of doctrine are battling for acceptance. The one believes that the Bible is the inspired, authoritative, infallible Word of God. The other believes that the Bible is the words of men through which God speaks on occasion. ... The one believes that the church is the Bride of Christ. The other that the church is one of God's many instrumentalities to bring about a juster human social order.

Peter Beyerhaus's tendency to brand everybody who co-operates with the WCC as an 'enemy of the gospel', is another example of this thinking. The implications are clear: those who agree with him are on the Lord's side. But the others ... ?

Such an approach has, of course, far-reaching ramifications, as is shown by an article by A. J. R. McQuilkin in *Crucial Dimensions in World Evangelization.*[4] The identification of one's own enterprise with God's work here reaches new heights. If others do not engage in evangelism (as defined by the author), God will raise up 'fresh, dynamic movements' that will ignore the old ones (p. 301). Unity is important but may never be regarded as a decisive factor (p. 302). Only too frequently our preoccupation with unity and the fact that we take into consideration the views of others, such as the younger churches, lead to a restricting of 'the freedom of the Holy Spirit to move where he will' (p. 303, quoting Herbert Jackson). Competition with others and even proselytising are therefore in order. All that counts is 'effective evangelism', and if others do not see it the way we do, they have to be opposed or thrust aside.

The problem becomes more acute when evangelicals with such high claims on divine sanction for all their ventures reveal themselves to be as self-centred as the 'world' they are opposing. When Christians, with the aid of an either-or scheme, contrast themselves with other Christians, they are in fact inviting the world—and those other believers—to subject their claims to careful scrutiny. They are saying, in so many words, 'With us, it is different'; but then they should also be able to substantiate their claim. The test is not simply whether they resist the temptation of 'pot, pubs and pornography'[5], but much rather how they view and treat their fellow men. At least nine of the sixteen 'works of the flesh' mentioned in Gal. 5.19-21 have to do with man's attitude to his neighbour; of the nine 'fruits of the Spirit' at least six have important social dimensions.

If we communicate only that part of the gospel which corresponds to people's 'felt needs' and 'personal problems' ('Are you lonely? Do you feel that you have failed? Do you need a friend? Then come to Jesus!'), while remaining silent on their relationship to their fellow men, on racism, exploitation and blatant injustice, we do *not* proclaim the gospel. This is the quintessence of what Bonhoeffer has called 'cheap grace'. After all, '(God) is especially moved to wrath when his own people engage in such practices. It makes them disgusting in His sight, an offence to His nostrils; and in the face of *this* evil-doing He cannot stand their religious posturing. He cannot bear to hear their prayers; hates their festivals; is weary of their hypocritical sacrificings; views their faithful attendance at His house with loathing, as nothing more than an uncouth trampling of its precincts: "I cannot endure iniquity *and* solemn assembly"'.[6]

Some years ago an American, Dean Kelley, created a stir when he stated that the phenomenal numerical growth of conservative churches in America was due to their strictness, whereas the statistical decline in 'liberal' churches was a direct result of their laxity. Kelley's thesis has been challenged from several sides. The growth in evangelical denominations, so some say, should be ascribed to the fact that orthodoxy and social conservatism go hand in hand in these churches: people get the opportunity to hear the old, familiar and comforting message without having to introduce any changes in their pattern of life as regards social involvement. Many evangelists, despite their spine-chilling sermons about sin, Satan and hell, do not constitute any real threat to their listeners' life-style. They are not challenging people to reorientate their lives socially; they merely try to make them into good Christians who are expecting the Second Advent. The fact that, since the beginning of the nineteen-seventies, an unparalleled pessimism has been developing in many Western countries, and that this pessimism has given rise to a kind of spurious transcendentalism in which other-worldly religiosity flourishes, contributes to the creation of a sounding-board for this type of preaching.

SELECTIVE CONSERVATISM

At this point, however, we have to unmask a peculiar inconsistency. Whereas evangelicals emphasise that everything in this world is temporary, relative, and therefore unimportant, it is precisely in these circles that we find an almost fanatical clinging to existing structures and patterns of life. The confession that the frame of this world is passing away, in a paradoxical manner leads to an absolutising of the existing order. The Church's task, it appears, is to help maintain the status quo. The more the gospel is proclaimed as an other-worldly reality, the more the existing order is uncritically upheld. Perhaps this phenomenon can be explained with reference to the dualism that is typical of pietistic evangelicals. Man lives on two 'levels'. On the one, the personal, everything belongs to Christ; he is obeyed without reserve. On the level of man's corporate relationships, however, *other* constituent factors are operative. This becomes especially evident in some extreme manifestations of the Lutheran doctrine of the Two Kingdoms. A Nazi officer in the Third Reich could, for instance, be the ideal family man and piously go to Church on Sunday, but for the rest participate, without any pangs of conscience, in the extermination of the Jews.

This kind of selective conservatism also reveals itself where evangelicals, on the one hand, lament the increasing secularisation of all areas of life and, on the other hand, accept all the technical products and achievements of secularisation as proofs of 'divine providence'. In a remarkably perceptive contribution to the volume *American Missions in Bicentennial Perspective*, Stephen C. Knapp has drawn attention to this phenomenon.[7] A classic example in this respect, he says, was John R. Mott. God provided us, said Mott, with many wonderful facilities, doubtless 'to further some mighty and beneficient purpose'. Each of these was 'primarily' intended to serve as 'handmaid' of mission. God has opened 'door after door among the nations of mankind', 'unlocking the secrets of mankind' and 'bringing to light invention after invention', such as steam and electricity. 'The Church of God is in the ascendent. She has well within her control the power, the wealth, and the learning of the world.'

Many modern evangelists, says Knapp, argue exactly like Mott used to, while at the same time they lament the secularisation process. They seem to accept that there are, within this process, certain neutral elements which the missionary can isolate from the rest and utilise. Apparently it does not dawn upon the missionary that he is in this way made a victim of the capitalistic mentality and frequently operates in neo-colonialistic categories. Church and missionary society are run like secular corporations. In this way Western thought-patterns, which in themselves have nothing to do with the gospel as such, remain dominant, even if in a very subtle way. Success must be demonstrable. Therefore the emphasis on growth in numbers. An example of this approach is to be found in Donald McGavran. He believes that a church grows more quickly if her members all belong to the same cultural background. If it should happen—for instance in the USA—that racial integration in a specific church causes a decline in church membership, he recommends racially segregated churches because, so he believes, it has been proved that such homogeneous churches grow more quickly than those with a heterogeneous composition. This is only one of the ways in which evangelical churches tend to perpetuate traditional social patterns in American society. What is more, it leads to the 'American way of life' becoming identified with what God wills. Criticism of this sacralised culture is frequently branded an antichristian conspiracy.

CHRIST AS HEAD OF CHURCH AND COSMOS

When a man's personal piety positions itself between him and his fellow man, when his religious commitment closes his heart to his neighbour, when the ministry of the Holy Spirit is confined to the area of personal ethics, when Christianity is defined solely in terms of sacred activities at appointed times, when biblical statements concerning people's concrete needs are spiritualised, when redemption is confined to man's personal relationship to God, when somebody is saved but all his relationships remain unaffected, when structural and institutionalised sins are not exposed, we are involved with an unbiblical one-sidedness and a spurious Christianity.

Christ is, after all, not only the Head of individual believers and of the Church, but also of the cosmos.[8] It is here that the concept of the 'cosmic Christ' safeguards an element of truth. 'Full authority in heaven and on earth' has been committed to him (Matt. 28.18). God 'put everything in subjection beneath his feet, and appointed him as supreme Head of the Church' (Eph. 1.22). *Therefore* we may boldly pray, 'Thy Kingdom come, thy will be done, *on earth* as in heaven' (Matt. 6.10). The Kingdom comes wherever Jesus overcomes the evil one. This happens (or ought to happen) in fullest measure in the Church. But it also happens in society. Christ refuses to be our Redeemer if we continually reject him as Lord of our entire life. The tendency to interpret his 'sitting to the right hand of God' in the Creed as non-activity, is based on a misunderstanding (cf. Acts 7.55). The intention of this article of the creed is, on the contrary, to speak of intense activity, of Christ's purposeful rule over and involvement in the world. After all, on the Cross 'he discarded the cosmic powers and authorities like a garment; he made a public spectacle of them and led them as captives in his triumphal procession' (Col. 2.15).

The 'authorities and cosmic powers' in the Pauline letters allude to the way in which supernatural beings, as it were, incarnate themselves in structures—political, religious and intellectual structures (-ologies and -isms)—which hold man in bondage but over which Christ has triumphed and which he now wants to employ in his service on earth.[9] They were created by God but have rebelled against him. This rebellion still flares up from time to time and the Church has to remain vigilant in this respect. This is, for instance, what happened during the Third Reich. The eyes of Christians began to open to the fact that the 'authorities and cosmic powers' did not reside in the heavenly regions only; they became flesh and blood in this world and they demonised society. Not only had the kingship of Christ to be confessed over against such demonic structures; it also had to be maintained and lived out actively. Where Christianity loses its ability to recreate the world, other powers will take its place—science and technology, but also atheistic revolution. The old docetism which denied Christ's existence in the flesh has its modern analogy in the tendency to place the Church and the believer outside the turbulent events of the world; the consequences are equally disastrous.

The implications are that the Christian faith may never regard world events with gloomy pessimism and fatalism, merely looking for survivors in an area hit by a disaster. If we do not maintain that the same God who acted in biblical times is still active today, we are deists.

The new age has arrived with the coming of Christ; it has invaded the old. And we share in this. Eschatology is the doctrine about things already in the process of fulfilment. And if it appears that the Church is shying away from too much realised eschatology, retreating into other-worldliness, then this is so because she has not understood the message and ministry of Jesus Christ, and because the tension in which she lives has proved to be too much for her.

We draw attention to one final aspect. In the Church's social involvement her credibility too is at stake. Of course, this does *not* imply that she has to concern herself with the social implications of the gospel with the explicit purpose of improving her image. This would just be another, more subtle form of other-worldliness. Rather, whenever she communicates the entire gospel, she herself begins to change in the process. No church which is involved in true mission ever remains unchanged. She discovers new dimensions of truth, new depths of discipleship. This happens *not* when the Church is powerful and is going from strength to strength, but precisely when she is weak, in distress, questioned on all sides. It is then that the Holy Spirit accomplishes his powerful work of witness through her. Witness, *martyria*, means the way of the Cross.

CHAPTER TWENTY

A DILUTED GOSPEL

THE RELEVANCE OF THE ECUMENICAL
THEOLOGY OF MISSION

Does what we have said in the previous chapter suggest that the ecumenical theology of mission is to be preferred to the evangelical?

There can be little doubt that the ecumenical theology of mission is indeed, at decisive points, a corrective to its evangelical counterpart. The gospel is not intended for man's soul only but for man as a whole, not for the individual only but for society. To argue that the Church should have nothing to do with politics is self-deception, not to get involved in politics means, in fact, to support the political status quo publicly or implicitly. Did Jesus concern himself with politics? Evangelicals might answer 'no'. And yet his activities were regarded as politically dangerous, by both Jews and Romans. He was condemned by public bodies on the basis of political accusations. We are not suggesting that Jesus was a Zealot or a revolutionary, as was often contended during the nineteen-sixties. It is undeniable, however, that not only his words but also his deeds questioned the existing social and religious order in practically every respect.[1]

What is more, we have to uphold the criticism voiced by ecumenicals concerning the preoccupation of some evangelicals with the quantitative growth of the Church. God's arithmetic differs from ours.[2] Orlando Costas asks whether, when we talk about 'church growth', we do not in fact frequently have to do with churches which just grow 'fatter'. The key question is not whether churches grow in numbers, but whether they grow in grace. In addition to an emphasis on numerical growth, Costas therefore pleads for a stress on 'organic' expansion (the internal relationship between members), 'conceptual' expansion (regarding her nature and mission to the world), and 'incarnational' growth (referring to the degree of the Church's involvement in her social environment).[3]

FROM CHARITY TO REVOLUTION

It is very illuminating to study the changes in the views of the Church's involvement in society, which gave rise to the present ecumenical position.

At the beginning of this century the missionary diaconate was by and large regarded as an auxiliary service. It took the form of care of the poor, expressed in orphanages and hospitals and of relief after natural or man-made disasters. The changing of structures was hardly ever contemplated.

In the nineteen-twenties, and especially at the time of the Jerusalem Conference (1928), the idea of a 'comprehensive approach' in mission became the vogue. Medical services (including preventive medicine), education, and agriculture were emphasised. It was better—so the argument went—to erect a protecting wall on a dangerous cliff than to introduce an excellent ambulance service at the foot of the cliff. Structures indeed have to be changed, but in a way which places the emphasis on gradualness and evolution. In the nineteen-sixties this approach broadened, with the rise of the 'theology of development'. Hoekendijk's *šālôm* theology, as well as the idea of humanisation as the aim of mission, converged to some extent in this approach. Both the Second Vatican Council and the WCC Assembly at Uppsala (1968) stood under the banner of development. A. Th. van Leeuwen's monumental work, *Christianity in World History*, in which he assessed very positively the technological and secularising influences of the Christian West upon the Third World, may in a sense be regarded as symptomatic of this trend.

Before Uppsala, however, other voices were already being raised. During the Church and Society Conference in particular (Geneva, 1966) a definite alternative to the theology of development was advocated. The solution was to be found in revolution, not in evolution. The relationship between the West and the Third World was not one of development versus under-development, but one of dominance versus dependence, or, more specifically, of oppressors versus oppressed. The gap between rich and poor countries was not narrowing but widening, despite (or perhaps precisely because of) colossal development projects. As Gustavo Guttierez puts it: there is poverty because there is wealth. The colonising West has built up a head-start which no evolutionary or development project can ever overtake. This insight gave rise to the theology of liberation. A termination of the existing order and a completely new beginning were demanded.

The opinion is frequently expressed that the theology of liberation, in its various manifestations, is a direct descendant of the older liberalism. This is, however, not at all the case. In classical liberalism, salvation was described as liberation from superstition and as the gradual improvement of mankind. God's Kingdom was described in immanent, progressivistic, and evolutionary categories. It would come by means of education, cultural diffusion, and social and political instruction. There were no doubts about man's abilities. The emphasis was on continuity.

The theology of liberation however confesses, together with many evangelicals, that the world is evil, and that the required change can only come by means of a catastrophe. On this side of the catastrophe everything is misery and anguish, on the other side all is glory. The dualism between the two ages is absolute. Liberation theology is therefore a form of apocalypticism and a child of pre-millennialism. It differs from classical pre-millennialism in that it believes that the levers of change are within man's reach and that he need not sit and wait passively for God's intervention.

It is, however, precisely in respect of this aspect that liberation theology does indeed become an heir of classical liberalism. It harbours the same unquenchable optimism: man *can* do it; he is the architect of his own future and will make a success of it. The more extreme forms of liberation theology can therefore also approve of violence. The end justifies the means. In some circumstances a plea can even be made for an atheistic, secularistic Christianity.

Although the documents of the Nairobi Assembly (1975) betray a certain ambivalence at this point—it is not entirely clear whether political and inner-worldly liberation is in itself identified with salvation—such an identification takes place without any reserve elsewhere. What is more, in some circles salvation is completely absorbed in socio-political liberation. Sin is defined without qualification in categories of oppression and exploitation. Salvation occurs nowhere but in the battle for liberation. A document prepared for Uppsala (1968) states: 'We have lifted up humanization as the goal of mission'; and Gibson Winter argues: 'The categories of biblical faith are freed from their miraculous and supernatural garments. ... Why are men not simply called to be human in their historical obligations, for this is man's true end and salvation?'[4]

Here evangelisation is absorbed in political action; salvation is social justice.

REDUCTION OF THE GOSPEL

We cannot accept these and related views of the ecumenical theology of mission. Why not?

There is a danger in ecumenical missionary theology of jettisoning conversion understood as a decision which man takes before God's countenance. In a preparatory document for Uppsala we read: 'Through the resurrection of the New Man, Christ Jesus, every human being has become a member of the new humanity'—that is, without any decision on his part. This is what Barth would have called 'brutal grace', where man is simply bulldozed, where all men are doomed to salvation. P. G. Aring writes: 'A church which regards the world as world that still has to be reconciled and in which mission work still has to be undertaken, excludes herself from the already reconciled world of God, because she makes the world about which God has already taken a decision an object of her own activities'.[5] According to this view the Church has, at most, the task of telling the world that it is already saved. The flood-gates of universalism are thus thrown wide open.[6]

It must, secondly, be asked whether ecumenical missionary theology is not running the risk of abandoning what may be called the 'eschatological reservation'. This is undoubtedly what happened at Uppsala and, to a lesser extent also at Nairobi.[7] The tension which is peculiar to biblical eschatology, the tension between the 'already' and the transcendent, ultimate 'not yet', is not maintained. Over against the evangelical

message of individualistic piety and other-worldly hope we
encounter here the temptation of historically immanent humanism. Man, impatient with a God who 'is a long time coming',
redefines the Kingdom, takes matters into his own hands and
tries to build the future with his own means. There is a danger,
notably in liberation theology, of a monistic view of history
where salvation history is fully absorbed in world history and
disappears as such. However, where the lighthouse of
eschatology has ceased to shed its beam, man cannot but drift
about chartless on the sea or perish in the waves or on the
rocks.[8]

We add a third remark, closely related to the foregoing two.
It happens far too easily in ecumenical circles that man and his
judgment become normative. A new theology of experience
surfaces here, this time not in the pietistic sense where man's
personal experience becomes a mine or quarry, but in such a
manner that society, history, and world events become the mine
out of which man extracts whatever experiences suit him. So it
is that the Giver and the gift are separated. God's Kingdom is
domesticated on earth—a mere variation of the old heresy which
locates the Kingdom either in the Church or in man's heart. At
the deepest level we have here a return to Constantinianism and
the idea of Christendom: the inhabited world is synonymous
with the Kingdom of God. The finiteness of man's judicative
faculty is, however, overlooked here and the ambivalence of
historical reality not appreciated. It is—to say the least—naïve
to hail all revolutionary movements as harbingers of the
Kingdom. 'After the revolution the new status quo sometimes
enshrines more injustice and oppression than the one it has
displaced.'[9]

The logical outcome of many elements in the contemporary
ecumenical theology of mission is, fourthly, nothing short of the
liquidation of the Church. Gensichen points out that the
documents on the 'missionary structure of the congregation'
which were prepared for Uppsala, betrayed an 'almost
monomaniac opposition' to the traditional local church.[10] The
problem here is once again the human tendency to think in
mutually exclusive categories, as if we have simply to choose
between the Church asserting herself or liquidating herself. And
where Christians have (re-)discovered that the Church ought

never to assert herself, they almost masochistically demand her deletion. The Church becomes entirely a part of the world, indistinguishable from any other element in it. 'The abstract distinction between Church and world is, in the final analysis, meaningless.'[11] The earlier ghetto existence in isolation gives way to an unqualified absorption by the world. People are summoned to a new exodus, this time out of the 'Egypt' of the Church.

The four aspects here discussed may be summarised. In ecumenical missionary theology we encounter a serious *reduction of the gospel*. It frequently lacks a powerful biblical stress on the reality of sin in every man. As a consequence it also lacks a resolute summons to repentance and conversion, that radical revolution in the centre of life which dynamic Christianity has always emphasised. Liberation theology's one-dimensional interpretation of history leaves precious little room for divine justification and sanctification. After all, the gospel does not only proclaim the Incarnation but also the Cross, Resurrection, and the indwelling of the Holy Spirit. One of the heresies repudiated by the early Church was Monophysitism, according to which Christ had only one nature, a divine one. In liberation theology we encounter an inverted Monophysitism where the 'new man in Christ' also has only one nature, this time a human one. The gospel is here reduced to an approved political theory and practice. When this happens, the gospel is changed into law, as Braaten correctly points out. The gospel is no longer a gift but only a demand. Eschatology and soteriology are reduced to ethics.[12]

Evangelicals are often inclined to interpret the 'poor' in the Gospels as referring to those who are 'spiritually' poor. This is a convenient heresy, the fruit of centuries-old docetism and Monophysitism, and a mutilation of the gospel.[13] It is a message of cheap grace, where the materially rich join the ranks of the spiritually poor with the greatest of ease, thus eluding the summons to conversion in respect of possessions and life-style.

To combat one heresy with another is the same as driving out the devils by Beelzebub (cf. Luke 11.19). This is what happens where the 'poor' in the Gospels are regarded *exclusively* as the materially poor and deprived. Then the gospel is intended for them only. For the wealthy there is no message and no longer any hope. Their way to *metanoia*, to repentance and conversion, is barred. God himself is then limited in the exercise of his grace: he can and may only save the materially poor. The radius of his activities is prescribed by man, his agenda is prepared by human planners. Human beings thus degrade him to a God without mercy.[14]

THE LIMITS OF SALVATION

We do not have the mandate to change the biblical idea of salvation to suit our own taste. If we still accept the Bible as normative (and where this no longer applies, the basis for common reflection in any case falls away), we have to be guided by the Bible. Salvation in biblical terms is more than the relief of physical misery. *šālôm* is more than a 'social happening' (Hoekendijk). Redemption is more than a political programme. When Jesus preaches in Nazareth (cf. Luke 4.18-19), he indeed alludes to political events such as the exodus from Egypt and the return from exile, but he does this within the context of 'more than the exodus is here'. His statement: 'Today, in your very hearing, this text has come true' (Luke 4.21), has to do with *his* presence and actions, and is a summons to *metanoia*, to a conversion to *him*.

It is true that the Gospels frequently use the word *sōzein* (save) for 'heal', but it has to be noted that *sōzein* is always related to the idea of 'believing', something that does not apply to the other two words which the Gospels also use for 'heal' (*iaomai* and *therapeuein*). The primary use of *sōzein* in the New Testament, in the Gospels and elsewhere, is moreover not that of 'heal'; it refers rather to man's total change in all his relationships, his adoption into a new community, the forgiveness of his sins, and deliverance from eternal judgment. We cannot get around it: *sōtēria*, salvation, is primarily something that takes place in the *Church*, here and now.

Paul uses the related concept *apolytrōsis* more or less as a synonym of *sōtēria*, but in such a way that *apolytrōsis* stresses the eschatological character of salvation. In a concise but illuminating survey of these concepts, Ronald Sider says:

It is important that the only time Paul used language about

salvation and redemption, for anything other than the justification and regeneration occurring now in the church, is when he discussed the *eschatological* restoration at our Lord's return. Sin is far too rampant to justify the use of this language in connection with the tragically imperfect human attempts to introduce social justice in the interim between Calvary and the Eschaton.[15]

The implications are clear. Church and world do not coincide. To deduce from Amos 9.7 that God did not have a special relationship with his covenant people different from his relationships with other nations, is a misinterpretation of Scripture. These words are, on the contrary, an appeal to Israel, a summons to return to the covenant relationship. Naturally, if Israel attempts to monopolise Yahweh as a tribal deity, the continued existence of the covenant is at stake. Israel then turns itself into a people like others, a pagan nation. This danger is constantly at the heels of the Christian Church also, both when she wants to monopolise God and when she disparages her special relationship with him.

For the very sake of her service to the world the Church has to be distinguishable from the world. She can only be meaningfully apostolic if her being-in-the-world is as the same time a being-*different*-in-the world. The New Testament upholds a boundary, a separation between Church and world, between the 'outsiders' and 'those within the fellowship' (1 Cor. 5.12-13). The summons to an antithesis between Church and world features at least as prominently as the demand to turn to the world. We have Eph. 4.17-24 in addition to Eph. 3.1-10, Col. 2.20-3.11 in addition to Col. 1.15-29.[16]

One of the most crucial responsibilities of the Church towards the world is that of intercession. That presupposes once again the essential difference between Church and world. In her prayer the Church vicariously does for the world what the world neither does nor can do for itself. The world cannot pray. Only believers, the Church, can. The Willingen conference stated: 'The closer we come to Christ, the closer we come to the world.' The converse does not hold. If, in our experimenting with renewal, we turn our backs upon the Church or let her be absorbed in the world, we are running the risk of losing not only the Church but Christ as well. 'Frustrated renewal may end up as a serious exodus—not only from the houses of Egypt, but from the House of God.'[17]

CHAPTER TWENTY-ONE

THE CHURCH AND
THE WORLD

CREATIVE TENSION

Evangelicals are inclined to subdivide mankind in the 'saved' and the 'lost', while exponents of liberation theology draw a functionally similar distinction between the 'oppressed' and the 'oppressors'. Both groups are naïve in their classifications because they do not maintain the relationship of tension between Church and world. The one group stands over against the world, the other regards itself as wholly in solidarity with the world. It is indeed difficult to be *for* and *in* the world without being *of* the world. Dualism runs in our blood; it is human and natural to gravitate to either one side or the other.

We cannot circumvent this problem. We have to navigate it. The overwhelming majority of Christians spend the largest part of their time in the world, not in the Church as institution. Many try to maintain a pendulum existence between Church and world. They oscillate, simply because they do not know how to apply their convictions of faith to life in the world, nor do they manage to relate the world of Monday to Saturday to their lives as Christians. The Church thus tends to fill the role of a social agency for the relief of painful disappointments; she is the place where uncomprehended fears are suppressed, where uncomfortable memories and embarrassing expectations are covered up. She becomes a cosy ghetto of kindred souls, a cave into which man flees when day to day problems overwhelm him.

Others, again, have stopped 'journeying' between Church and world. The dividing wall between the two has been demolished. The world has flowed into the Church.

The correct relationship between Church and world is a matter of the greatest importance. Christ is Head of both Church and cosmos, yet only in the Church is his headship acknowledged and confessed. The world has no faith to confess. It can neither pray nor believe. It cannot enter into a personal relationship with God. The Church is that segment of the world which submits consciously to Christ, obeys and serves him, albeit haltingly and with a stammer. The Church is not the world, for the Kingdom has already begun to manifest itself in her. And yet she is not the Kingdom, as the Kingdom is acknowledged and realised in her only partially and imperfectly.

This means that the Church is a foreign body in the world. She fits nowhere. The old and the new overlap in her. She is 'too early for heaven and too late for the earth' (O. Noordmans). She lives in a double relationship: to the *world*, for she is part of this world and of secular history; to *God*, as expression of his saving love reaching towards a perishing world. These two relationships are interdependent. Without a faithful and sustained contact with God the Church loses her transcendence. Without a true solidarity with the world she loses her relevance.

There is indeed sin in the world; the reality of this should never be underestimated. But 'world' and 'sin' are not synonymous. In fact, while it is true that there is sin in the world, it is equally true that there is sin in the Church, for the Church is herself a fragment of world.[1] And yet the Church is different, for she is God's chosen agent. We cannot exclude this 'particularism'. It 'is an inherent aspect of the scandal of the gospel, the offence of the cross. Theological speculation has tried to build wider bridges for God to attain the goal of universality, but it is a blow to the Christian mission when speculation soars into lofty universalism at the expense of the particularity of the historical media of salvation'.[2] We encounter here an element of dualism—if that is what we want to call it—which is not to be denied. Christ is indeed the Head of both Church and world, but the world is not his Body. Only the Church is that.

THE NEW COMMUNITY

Only as community which is simultaneously distinguishable from and in solidarity with the world, can the Church be missionary.

The Church is the community of believers, gathered by

divine election, calling, new birth, and conversion, which lives in communion with the Triune God, is granted the forgiveness of sins, and sent to serve the world in solidarity with all mankind (cf. both the Heidelberg Catechism, Questions 54-56, and the Belgic Confession, Art. 27). Being the Church thus implies conscious decisions, a new life under a new Lord, a being under way towards a new future. Conversion is not primarily an emotional experience or an exchange of sentiments, but a new way of life (cf. Luke 3.10-14). Conversion is also not simply the acceptance of a new doctrine or religion; it is following Christ, it is discipleship (cf. Matt. 16.24).

The Church is, however, discipleship-in-community. She is God's new creation, the messianic community, the 'single new humanity' in Christ, who has broken down the dividing wall and has reconciled Jew and Gentile 'in a single body to God through the cross' (Eph. 2.14-16). The mutual solidarity within this community is not prescribed by the loyalties and prejudices of kinship, race, people, language, culture, class, political convictions, religious affinities, common interests, or profession. It transcends all these differences. There was room in the early Church for simple fishermen from Galilee, for erstwhile Zealots such as Simon and one-time tax-collectors of whom Matthew was typical, for the likes of Paul, an erudite Pharisee, for members of the nobility such as Manaen who grew up with Herod, for Jews and Greeks, for blacks from Africa, among them the eunuch from Ethiopia and Simon caller Niger who served with Paul as an elder in Antioch, for the slave Onesimus but also for his master Philemon, for prisoners no less than members of the imperial guard, and for a captain in the Roman army.

For the early Christians this new community was frequently the occasion of amazement. Genuinely surprised, Peter said to the group assembled in the house of Cornelius: 'I now see how true it is that God has no favourites ...!' (Acts 10.34). Paul writes to the Ephesians about the mystery revealed to him, namely that 'the Gentiles are joint heirs with the Jews, part of the same body, sharers together in the promise made in Jesus Christ' (Eph. 3.6). As we have already pointed out in Chapter 6, Jesus has removed the divine vengeance that hung like a threatening cloud over the nations and has made believers drawn out of each of them into members of his Body. They are no longer strangers, living in a world without hope and without God (Eph. 2.12), but fellow-citizens with God's people and members of God's household (2.19). There is, in this new community, no such thing as Jew and Greek, slave and freeman, male and female; all are one in Christ Jesus (Gal. 3.28). Paul can therefore exclaim, 'Circumcision is nothing; uncircumcision is nothing; the only thing that counts is new creation!' (Gal. 6.15).

The new community is not only a product, but also an agent of mission. Time and again, in the early Church, it was amazement provoked by the new life in community which attracted Gentiles to the Church. Paul and Barnabas had spent only three weeks in Thessalonica and already there was a firmly established brotherhood between newly converted Jews and Greeks. This was too much for the other Jews. They recruited some loafers and attacked the house of Jason, the host of the apostles. Their accusation? 'The men who have made trouble all over the world have now come here ...', or, as the King James' Version has it: 'These that have turned the world upside down are come hither also' (Acts 17.6). If Jews and Greeks accept one another as brothers, it indeed means that the world is turned upside down. People notice it and are won for Christ through this astonishing event.

The course of events in Thessalonica proves that this is not all that happens. On the day of Pentecost the Holy Spirit threw the doors of the Church open and allowed the powers of the coming age to stream in. But the counter-forces are also streaming in. The Church is reminded of the fact that she is a stranger in this world, that she fits nowhere and is accepted nowhere. Evangelicals have always known this, but they frequently draw the wrong conclusions from it. They define the Church as a ghetto community. Everything is spiritualised. Material, social and political issues are taboo to the Church. Exactly the opposite happens in ecumenical circles. The difference between Church and world is relativised. The Church is secularised and abandons her identity. However, a secularised Church has little to offer the world. What the Kingdom of God means to the world should become evident in the Church, but if Church and world are no longer distinguishable, the Kingdom loses its profile. The Church-as-community must be sufficiently distinguishable to resist and challenge the homogenising power of the world. Only as prophetic minority in the secularised society of today can the Church remain faithful to her role of being a stranger in the world.[3]

It is precisely as stranger that the Church is God's experimental garden in the world. She is a sign of the coming age and at the same time a guarantee of its coming. She lives on the border-line between the 'already' and the 'not yet'. She is a fragment of the Kingdom, God's colony in man's world, his outpost and bridgehead. The Church alone has the 'firstfruits of the Spirit', as 'pledge of what is to come' (cf. Rom. 8.23; 2 Cor. 1.22; 5.5; Eph. 1.14). The Church 'exists as exemplar' in the world (Karl Barth).

Moreover: precisely as stranger and as God's experimental garden on earth, the Church is Church-for-others. On 3rd August 1944 Bonhoeffer wrote to Eberhard Bethge from prison: 'The church is the church only when it exists for others ... The church must share in the secular problems of ordinary human life, not dominating, but helping and serving. It must tell men of every calling what it means to live in Christ, to exist for others'. In Volume IV/3 of his *Church Dogmatics*, Barth takes up the same theme under the heading 'The Community for the World'. The Western European and North American study documents issued in preparation for the WCC Assembly in Uppsala (1968) were published respectively as *The Church for Others* and *The Church for the World*.[4]

The Lund meeting of Faith and Order (1952) put it as follows: 'The Church is always and at the same time called out of the world and sent into the world.' The two elements of this 'double movement' never exclude but always include one another—life as new community, with one another and Christ, *and* life for others, in which the proclamation of the gospel is related to mankind's total need. Community and worship lead to mission, mission leads to community and worship.

Karl Barth points out[5] that the Christian's personal enjoyment of salvation nowhere becomes the theme of biblical stories of conversion—not in the case of those who listened to John the Baptist's preaching (Luke 3.10-14), nor of Zacchaeus or Paul or

the Philippian gaoler. Enjoying salvation is indeed a truly
biblical element (cf. Col. 3.15; 1 Tim. 6.12; Hebr. 9.15;
1 Pet. 5.10; Rev. 19.9) and therefore not unimportant. However,
the Bible refers to it as something almost incidental; people
receive it, as it were, without expecting or seeking it. What
makes one a Christian, is *not* his personal experience of grace
and redemption, but his ministry. Conversion and vocation in
the Bible mean being given a task in the world.

Newbigin says essentially the same thing, referring to
baptism: 'The baptism which the Church gives is the act by
which we are incorporated into that baptism of Christ with its
focus in the cross. It is not baptism just for our own salvation ... Rather, it is our incorporation into the one baptism
which is for the salvation of the world. To accept baptism,
therefore, is to be committed to be with Christ in his ministry
for all men'.[6]

The Church is an 'alternative community'. This does *not*
mean that she—like some radical evangelical groups, following
the example of sixteenth-century Anabaptists—admits the
necessity of worldly government but refuses to participate in it.
It also does not mean the creation of an alternative Christian
society as an expression of the conviction that Christians cannot
improve the existing secular and sinful society. 'For Christians
to opt out of civil society and set up evangelical islands ... is to
confess to a truncated and disjunctive understanding of God's
working. It is to arrogate God to the Church much more than
God himself has chosen to do. It is the newest form of
triumphalism.'[7]

A. A. van Ruler elucidates the Church's role in the world by
making use of Abraham Kuyper's distinction between 'particular' and 'common grace'. The stream of particular grace
breaks all dykes and spills out over all the world. Common
grace is being 'fertilised' by particular grace, says van Ruler.
There is thus an essential difference in the 'density of grace'
between Church and world but both partake of grace.[8] The
Church has therefore to be upheld as a distinctive community.
What makes the Church into a ghetto, says Stephen Knapp, is
not the idea of a separate community as such, 'but the tendency
of communities to slip over into spiritualism, into a *de-
materialization* and *de-politicization* of the Gospel'.[9] Knapp

argues that this tendency manifests itself precisely where the true distinctiveness of the Church grows dim and the Church becomes a captive of culture and politics. To solve the problem by deliberately relinquishing the distinctiveness of the Church and integrating her into the world, is likewise self-defeating.

THE SCOPE OF MISSION

We have to determine the Church's missionary involvement in the world more accurately. What is the nature and scope of mission? Since the nineteen-twenties, when the concept of the 'comprehensive approach' in mission began to develop, there has been a recognition that mission is more than proclamation. This awareness is expressed in various ways. The most adequate formulation subsumes the total *missio* of the Church under the biblical concept *martyria* (witness)[10] which can be subdivided into *kērygma* (proclamation), *koinōnia* (fellowship) and *diakonia* (service). This is how the Willingen Conference (1952) put it: 'This *witness* is given by *proclamation, fellowship* and *service.*' We should in fact add a fifth aspect, that of *leitourgia*, liturgy, that is the encounter of the Church with her Lord. This is, in the last analysis, the fountain of the entire mission of the Church and the guarantee for her distinctiveness.

How are the three elements of the Church's witness, the *kērygma, koinōnia* and *diakonia*, related to each other? There is tendency to contrast—or, at the very least, juxtapose—the first and the third as witness by word over against witness by deed. This however attenuates the gospel. God's word is a ringing deed and his deed a visible and tangible word. If we study the images used for the Christian community in Matt. 5.13-16— salt, light, a city—it is impossible to establish which of these refer to the Church's *kērygma* and which to her *diakonia*. Sider rightly argues that it makes little sense to subsume the 'Great Commission' (Matt. 28.18-20) in *kērygma* and the 'Great Commandment' (Matt. 22.39) in *diakonia*.[11] Rather, they resemble the two blades of a pair of scissors which operate in unison, held together by the *koinōnia*, the fellowship, which likewise is not a separate 'part' of the Church's task, but rather the 'cement' which keeps *kērygma* and *diakonia* together, the 'axle' on which the two blades operate. 'Word', 'service' and 'fellowship' are not three separate missionary activities but the three colours cast in spectrum by a single prism. All forms of service to the world 'only get their right missionary foundation and perspective if they belong as intrinsically to the category of witness as preaching or evangelization'.[12]

This is not saying that *kērygma* and *diakonia* are the same thing. Neither does it mean that *martyria*, witness, is merely the sum of evangelism and social involvement. It is not true that if we already have any one of the pair, we have merely to add the other to achieve a fine 'balance'. Mission is not the aggregate of evangelism plus service. Authentic *kērygma* has an inherent social dimension, genuine *diakonia* an inherent proclamation dimension. Sider rightly says: 'The time has come for all biblical Christians to refuse to use the sentence: "The primary task of the Church is ..." I do not care if you complete the sentence with evangelism or social action. Either way it is unbiblical and misleading.'[13] Both dimensions are indissolubly bound together. If you lose the one, you lose the other.

Naturally this does not imply that we should have to check that every fragment of witness contains all the necessary elements. Then we would be with the 'theology of balance' we have already rejected. The New Testament mentions a variety of gifts: healing, prophecy, knowledge, service, and so forth. Consequently different Christians play different roles. Even more important: situations vary and demand a diversification of forms of Christian witness. The good Samaritan did not preach to the victim of the robbers. He poured oil on his wounds. This is what the situation demanded. Somebody who is hungry, needs food, a thirsty person needs water (cf. Matt. 25.35).

A WCC document of 1959 put it in the following words: 'There is no single way to witness to Jesus Christ. The Church has borne witness in different times and places in different ways. This is important. There are occasions when dynamic action in society is called for; there are others when a word must be spoken; others when the behaviour of Christians one to another is the telling witness. On still other occasions the simple presence of a worshipping community or man is the witness. These different dimensions of witness to the one Lord are always a matter of concrete obedience. To take them in isolation from one another is to distort the Gospel.'[14] Emilio Castro concurs: 'In carrying out God's mission, we *cannot opt per-manently* for one aspect of mission or another, be it liberation, development, humanization, or evangelization. These are all essential, integral parts of the mission entrusted to us and cannot be set against one another without becoming, simply, caricatures of what they really are.'[15]

The *context* therefore indicates where our emphasis ought to be and the *circumstances* dictate the way in which our witness has to be communicated. A missionary and evangelism model used in the USA is most likely not only inappropriate but completely impossible in countries under Marxist regimes or where Islam is dominant. In *all* instances, however, the witness must be communicated on the basis of solidarity with the people for whom it is intended. A *silent* presence may, in some circumstances, signify authentic solidarity, as when Ezekiel came to the exiles at the river Kebar and sat with them for seven days, dumbfounded (cf. Ezek. 3.15).

Only genuine solidarity gives credibility to our *martyria*. People will never believe what they hear—however attractive it may sound—if it is blatantly contradicted by what they see and experience. All our efforts at renewal in the area of evangelism, catechesis, liturgy, and so forth, are futile unless something is done about the credibility of the quality of our lives. In fact, the more attractive our verbal proclamation sounds, the more flagrant may be the glaring contrast between this message and the lamentable quality of our lives. The Church is frequently an obstacle rather than an aid to the gospel because she allows her life and conduct to obscure her witness and make it impotent. Ronald Sider, himself an evangelical, expresses his concern in this regard to his fellow evangelicals: 'Only if we biblical Christians throw ourselves into the struggle for social justice for the wretched of the earth so unequivocally that the poor and the oppressed know beyond all question that we will risk all in the struggle against economic and political oppression—only then will Third World theologians be willing to hear our critique of unbiblical definitions of salvation. And only then will the oppressed of the earth be able to hear our Good News about the risen Lord Jesus.'[16]

CHAPTER TWENTY-TWO

MISSION, HISTORY
AND ESCHATOLOGY

THEOLOGY OF HISTORY?

Our preceding chapters have broached the question of the theological evaluation of history and of historical events. It is important to reflect on this from the perspective of the theology of mission.

We have already argued that evangelicals tend to regard salvation history as something quarantined from world history. The logical consequences of this frequently are that God is regarded as being active only in salvation history. Secular history is under the sway of evil powers and always threatens to extinguish salvation history.

Salvation history is, moreover, usually pictured as a very detailed programme in which God planned everything minutely, even before the world was founded. He knows in advance the moves of the evil one and allows for them. His plan unfolds according to his blueprint and will be unveiled at a pre-determined moment. In this blueprint the Church's global mission occupies a key position, so much so that we can, as it were, deduce from the geographical progress of mission what time it is on God's watch and how close we are to the final unfolding of salvation history. All we need to do is to discern the 'signs of the times'. As a matter of fact, the activities of some religious groups consist practically exclusively in speculating about the signs of the times. The theological hobby horse of such a group usually provides their hermeneutical key to everything. God is regarded as active only where it suits them. All other events are ascribed to the machinations of the evil one which, fortunately, have been allowed for in God's carefully prepared plan.

In ecumenical circles there has been a reaction to this narrow salvation-historical interpretation. Here, however, salvation history has been desacralised completely, a procedure which is equally naïve and unacceptable. It is, after all, also a signs-of-the-times theology, the difference being that God is here regarded as being operative in areas precisely the opposite to those in which, according to evangelicals, he is at work, namely, in the secular world. The desacralisation of salvation history is counterbalanced by the sacralisation of world history.[1] World history *is* salvation history.

Both evangelicals and ecumenicals thus operate with the same model, though they arrive at opposite conclusions. Both are subjectivistic. There was a time, for instance, when the colonial expansion programme of European countries was regarded as divine providence, as 'salvation history'. Today, on the contrary, decolonisation is regarded as proof of God's direct intervention. In the past, capitalism was labelled 'Christian'; today the same is said of socialism. Time and again the tendency thus is to ascribe to divine providence the sociological forces dominant in a particular period. Behind this lies historical positivism. Warneck could state flatly: 'What has come about historically also has a divine right.'

A 'theology of history' thus presents itself in different forms. Emmanuel Hirsch hailed the 'German turning-point' of 1933 unreservedly as divine intervention. Bruno Gutmann exalted ethnicity and the so-called *'urtümliche Bindungen'* (primordial ties) of any specific people as inviolable data of creation and declared everything that serves and upholds the people, to be in accordance with God's will. Elsewhere adventists incorporate national disasters and all manner of world events into an apocalyptic understanding of history. Or, violent revolutions are interpreted by liberation theologians as direct extension of the biblical exodus event.

When we reject these and similar interpretations, we are not suggesting that God is not active anywhere in history. If we did, we should have to regard history as a stringing together of accidents, or as the playground of fate. We should then, with J.-P. Sartre, be peering into the abyss of nothingness, and have to judge past, present and future to be completely empty and meaningless. All things would be nothing save *hominum confusio* (men's confusion), without the perspective of *providentia Dei* (God's providence). Then God—where we still make reference to him—would be the abdicated God of deism. Our criticism therefore is not levelled at the notion of God as being active in history—far from it—but at the one-dimensional interpretation of history which is so frequently presented by both evangelicals and ecumenicals.

We confess that God acts in history. The pages of the Old and New Testaments reveal a God who takes action in the events of the world. Salvation history is not something divorced and segregated from world history. We should not look for God's involvement only in men's hearts, but also in their daily lives. Jesus was born under Augustus and crucified under Pontius Pilate. Religion is no private affair but the acknowledgment that God is actively present in this world. The New Testament confession about Jesus as *Kyrios* (Lord) had sociological and political overtones because this confession relativised the concrete lordship of other rulers. The Church does not have to withdraw from the world in order to become the Body of Christ; she is his Body, rather, by being in the midst of the world. The Church is, as we have suggested, simultaneously a theological and a sociological entity. This means that she does not have to become less and less 'sociological' in order to become more and more 'theological'. All things considered, the sociological dimension does not endanger the theological. On the contrary. The Church is 'a phenomenon of world history which can be grasped in historical and psychological and sociological terms like any other'.[2]

The focal point of God's involvement in world history is called mission. Christian consciousness of history is a missionary consciousness that recognises a divine commission; it is therefore a consciousness of the contradiction inherent in this unredeemed world, and of the sign of the Cross under which the Christian mission and hope stand.[3] Therefore, even if there did exist strong apocalyptic tendencies in the early Church, it was mission that prevented apocalypticism from detaching the Christian community from world history, something that happened to the Qumran community. Even the Holy Spirit, as A A. van Ruler has often pointed out, does not confine his activities to the hearts of men or to religious revivals; he is active in daily life as well, in the world of history and culture.

That God acts in the world is something discernible only by

the eye of faith. Because of Christ's death and resurrection and the gift of the Spirit the believer can perceive something of God's providence in the midst of human confusion.

The believer's interpretation of God's acts in history nevertheless remains an ambivalent matter. God's activities cannot be derived directly from history. History is full of contradictions, gaps, discontinuities, puzzles, surprises, mysteries, temptations, and confusions. After all, not only God, but the counter-forces too, are at work in it. God's activities in history are therefore for the eye of faith simultaneously revealed and hidden.

We therefore have to be extremely wary of a signs-of-the-times theology. The Roman Catholic apostolic exhortation, *Evangelii Nuntiandi,* which was released after the Fourth Synod of Bishops (October 1974), rightly points out that the signs of the times have different meanings for different believers in various countries and contexts.

That this is so, immediately becomes apparent if we ask individual Christians what they regard as 'signs of the times' in contemporary world history. In a recent article on mission and the signs of the times, B. H. Willeke tabulated four such signs: 1. The coming of age of the peoples of the world (a fact which has consequences for the coming of age of younger churches). 2. The struggle for freedom and development (which has implications for the Church's role). 3. World-wide secularisation. 4. The yearning for new spiritual values.[4] In his *I Believe in the Great Commission,* Max Warren discusses seven 'signs of the times' which correspond only in part to those of Willeke.[5] The 'signs' Willeke and Warren identify, however, differ completely from those which John Mott recognised in the world of 1910. These so-called 'signs' are therefore certainly ambiguous.

Should we then, rather, refrain from interpreting 'signs'? In his *Christ the Meaning of History,* H. Berkhof judges that we may not try to evade this responsibility.[6] We should indeed be very modest in our efforts since we can never completely fathom history. We may never simplistically distinguish between light and dark—especially since our interpretation is easily determined by our own prejudices and predilections; we see God at work only where and when it suits us.

The parables of Matt. 24 and 25, especially those that summon us to vigilance, should caution us here. People who stay alert are people who do not know what course events will take. They continue to wait for the unveiling and do not anticipate the final judgment. They must interpret the reality in which they live, yet not so much by judging it as by keeping their lanterns burning and making the most of their talents. While doing this, they develop an 'instinct' which enables them to discern, however imperfectly, who their fellow servants are and who are in need of their help (cf. Matt. 25.31-46). The one who watches, thus interprets the facts of history, albeit fallibly. Such a person has the courage to take decisions, even if they are relative. He knows, however, that the best way of interpreting history is to allow God to send him into the world. Mission is an exegesis of history.

MISSION AS ESCHATOLOGICAL EVENT

We have now, in fact, reintroduced the theme 'eschatology', even if we have not mentioned it explicitly. In our third part we have discussed the role and meaning of eschatology for the understanding of mission through the ages, highlighting especially, in this respect, the enrichment that the rediscovery of the eschatological dimension during the nineteen-thirties yielded. Its special contribution was to relate eschatology and history in a dynamic way.

Before the late nineteen-fifties this eschatological dimension was, however, partly obscured by the radically transcendental eschatology of Barth on the one hand and the existentialist eschatology of Bultmann on the other. It was only during the nineteen-sixties that W. Pannenberg's theological contributions and especially J. Moltmann's theology of hope opened the way to a more historical understanding of eschatology in which the future held the primacy. The Latin American theology of Liberation in some respects corresponds with this, as does Cullmann's salvation historical approach. José Miguez-Bonino, for instance, is a student of Cullmann and in 1967 contributed to his Festschrift.[7]

In this development taken as a whole, eschatology ceased to be 'the doctrine of the last things'. It has to do with the here and now as well. This, again, relates to the rediscovery of the intimate connection between eschatology and Christology. Only too often this indissoluble bond was not recognised. Eschatology then became either *archaism,* where people dreamed about restoring a golden era of the distant past, or *futurism,* where people turned their backs upon the past and in a utopian spirit invaded the future, or *escapism,* where they attempted to flee from this world into another.[8]

The rediscovery of the eschatological dimension of the Christian faith, the close relationship between eschatology and Christology, and the awareness of a dynamic tension between eschatology and history, necessitate a brief discussion of the way in which mission may be understood as eschatological event.

First, we want to emphasise that mission may never be regarded as pre-condition or prerequisite for the coming of the end, neither may the Church hasten the end through her missionary fervour. Mission is no hand on the clock of the world. The high eschatological fever in some Christian circles, the fanatical missionary enthusiasm that flows from it, and the bizarre calculations and grotesque speculations that accompany it, change eschatology into apocalypticism and ascribe to it a weight of its own, isolated from Christology.

Almost a century ago Martin Kähler had already rejected the view that Matt. 24.14 prompts us to do mission work so as to hasten Christ's return. Missionaries who hold these views, Kähler said, do not really aim at christianising the nations; they rather want to preach the gospel 'as a witness' to them so that they might have no excuse. They have no compassion for the multitudes and do not mind whether they perish, as long as the elect may be saved and Christ's return precipitated. How little, said Kähler, do they think of our Saviour that they want to interfere with his time-table for the world! And how highly do they regard themselves![9]

Mission as eschatological event moreover does not mean that, in reaction to what we have just said, the Church should develop a ghetto mentality and simply turn in upon herself. The Old Testament references to the 'remnant' and Jesus' reference to the 'little flock' (Luke 12.32) have often been interpreted in this way. Some Jewish communities of the early centuries shared this mentality of the little group congregating around the temple, fearful lest the world should swallow them. The Christian Church has frequently betrayed the same mentality.

Mission, eschatologically understood, wishes on the contrary to place the Church's calling and responsibility in the widest context imaginable: to the ends of the earth and the end of time. The mission of the Church replaces apocalyptic self-preservation in view of the end.[10]

Thirdly, mission as eschatological event reminds the Church that her task is never finished. 'Mission eschatologically understood is a constant stimulus for the Church.'[11] God's plan for the salvation of the world is only disclosed in the Church's missionary involvement in the world. While believers carry the message across all frontiers, the mystery unfolds itself to them.[12] The Church's mission into the world is Jesus' only reply to the question about the date of the coming of the Kingdom (Acts 1.6-8). To wait for the end never implies passivity but rather intense activity in the here and now. Involvement in the world is one of the chief ways of preparing ourselves for the *parousia.*

Even more important, in many respects, than the three elements already mentioned, is a fourth. Mission as eschatological event proceeds from the certainty that the Kingdom of God is not only a future reality but is already present in our midst. New Testament eschatology manifests itself in three divisions of time: past, present, and future. Israel expected salvation exclusively from the future. Christ cleft that future in two. Where Christians project salvation entirely into the future they are maintaining a pre-Christian position. In Christ the forces of the coming age have flowed into the present.

The future, including the future *before* the end, is not empty but filled with the Kingdom. Admittedly the Kingdom is still hidden and can be perceived only by the eyes of faith; admittedly the form the Kingdom takes is still inchoate; yet this does not imply that the presence of the Kingdom is illusory. We live on the basis of the 'already' en route to the 'not yet', but in such a way that the challenge of the 'already' outweighs the vision of the 'not yet', that the 'already' strives towards gaining possession of the 'not yet'.[13] Eschatology does not refer only to a future divine answer which we have to accept blindly or on authority; it also refers to anticipations in human experiences now. The meaning of history can be ascertained, since the goal of history has been revealed.

At present the 'already' and the 'not yet' still exist in mutual tension. We cannot escape this tension; what is more, we should not be able to. The believer is already a naturalised citizen of the New Age and yet he still lives fully in this world. There is, in other words, an admittedly dualistic element here. 'A person with an eschatology in the midst of this world is willy nilly a citizen of two worlds'[14] and the only reason why he can endure this almost unbearable tension is to be found in the fact that these two worlds overlap in Christ, that the new has arrived while the old has not yet passed away.

Mission as eschatological event means, fifthly, that in our missionising, we approach the *fulfilment.* The Kingdom is already present, as we have indicated, but we can talk about the present Kingdom only if we see it in the perspective of the coming Kingdom. One of the gravest dangers facing the Church today is that all expectations of a future prepared by God may disappear from our field of vision, that future expectations may be entirely subsumed in this-worldly categories. As Aagaard puts it: '... the social challenge to-day is so strong that hope in things not seen seems rather frustrating and useless, when so many things, which can be seen, are worth hoping for.'[15] We are so easily misled into believing that salvation is at our disposal.

It is precisely mission which should keep alive the hope for a divine fulfilment of the Kingdom. Where the expectation of God's intervention withers, mission loses its true character and eschatology is reduced to ethics. It then becomes either merely humanitarian improvement without a transcendent dimension or a private affair where the concern is not with the renewal of the entire creation but simply with individual salvation, a living on after death.

Mission as eschatological event, furthermore, means infusing the world with hope. Mission is faithful hope-in-action and therefore manifests itself in the patient impatience of hope.

Hope discloses itself in the taking of the next step. Hope is action and only as such authentic.[16] It does not mean hoping only for a new heaven, but also for a new earth—the first Christians expected both!

In her mission the Church fulfils her obligations to the world. Precisely because of his hope-ful confidence in the 'ultimate' the Christian attends to the 'penultimate'. The Church thus exerts herself for changes in the area of the penultimate as well—not because she has abandoned her hope for the ultimate, but for the very reason of that hope. The penultimate may be neither despised nor neglected for the sake of the ultimate. The idea that things may stay the way they are, is the absolute antithesis to the gospel. The Christian who concerns himself only with 'ultimate things', arguing that the present things are no more than provisional and passing away, does not understand the Christian hope.

Lastly, mission as eschatological event arms the Church-in-mission against despondency. The eschatological motif, as we have seen, impels us to involve ourselves in the matters of this world, to exert ourselves for the erection of signs of the Kingdom here and now, yet at the same time it fortifies us against the danger of disappointment, disillusionment and frustration. The message of the transcendent Kingdom and the knowledge that, in the final analysis, everything is in God's hands, gives us the necessary distance and austerity towards everything in the world.[17] God is the One who prepares the feast; we are but the servants who distribute the invitations. The awareness of this determines the horizon of our expectations. If we lose this perspective, the gospel ceases to be a gift and becomes law. A restiveness and nervousness then appears in our activities because everything seems to be dependent on us. This danger is not an imaginary one. Only a healthy eschatological perspective can fortify us against it.

CHAPTER TWENTY-THREE

MISSIO DEI

MISSION IN TRINITARIAN PERSPECTIVE

In the preceding chapters we concerned ourselves with the theology of mission—the foundation, motive, aim and nature of the Church's commission to the world. We traced the course of mission through the centuries and established that, in many periods, mission had forfeited its essential nature and become little more than an expression of the prevailing spirit of the age or a convenient mechanism to serve group interests. We saw how the foundation, motive, aim and nature of mission were perverted and are still being distorted today. We drew attention to elements of short-sightedness and one-sidedness, to the inability of people to discover authentic insights in others, and to the universal tendency to absolutise one's own opinion.

In this last chapter we intend to concern ourselves once again, from a somewhat different perspective, with this entire problem and shall attempt to penetrate to the centre of a genuine theological reflection on mission. We shall do this, in the first place, by describing mission as *missio Dei,* God's mission.

Mission has its origin neither in the official Church nor in special groups within the Church. It has its origin in God. God is a missionary God, a God who crosses frontiers towards the world. In creation God was already the God of mission, with his Word and Spirit as 'Missionaries' (cf. Gen. 1.2-3). God likewise sent his incarnate Word, his Son, into the world. And he sent his Spirit at Pentecost. Mission is God giving up himself, his becoming man, his laying aside of his divine prerogatives and taking our humanity, his moving into the world, in his Son and Spirit.

From this it is clear that it is the *Triune God* who is the subject of mission.[1] For many centuries in the Christian Church the word *missio* was a concept used in connection with the doctrine of the Trinity, a reference to the mission of the Son by the Father, and of the Holy Spirit by the Father and the Son. It is only since the sixteenth century that the concept *missio* has begun to develop its modern connotation of the Church's being sent into the world. Unfortunately the relationship between the original and the modern meaning of *missio* has for a long time not been recognised. Abraham Kuyper was one of the first theologians to point this out explicitly. Warneck likewise alluded to a trinitarian foundation of mission in his *Evangelische Missionslehre.* Karl Hartenstein saw the implications of this and worked them out more fully, first in 1933 and then particularly in his contribution to the Willingen conference (1952) where the concept *missio Dei* was introduced. Mission is not, as Karl Graul put it more than a century ago, 'the apostolic road from Church to Church', but the Triune God moving into the world.

Roman Catholics and Protestants alike subscribe today to this view. We have moved from an ecclesiological to a trinitarian missiology. There is now a danger, however, that the doctrine of the Trinity might function only vaguely and abstractly in Church, theology and mission. It is therefore necessary to elaborate in more detail what we mean by a trinitarian foundation of mission.

Mission has its origin in the *fatherly heart of God.* He is the fountain of sending love. This is the deepest source of mission. It is not possible to penetrate any deeper: there is mission because God loves man. Forty-six times in the Gospel of John alone Jesus says that the Father has sent him, often adding that it is for the sake of the salvation of the world. Several parables have the same theme. The ground of mission is God's *agapē* (love) or his *charis* (mercy-love). 'For God is love; and his love was disclosed to us in this, that he sent his only Son into the world to bring us life' (1 John 4.9; cf. Rom. 8.32). 'God loved the world so much that he gave his only Son ... ' (John 3.16).

In what we have just said, we have in fact already touched upon the role and significance of the second Person in the Trinity. It was Karl Barth in particular who based mission not only on the doctrine of the Trinity, but much more specifically on Christology. With this, he intended severing at the root the possibility of a speculative interpretation of a foundation of mission on the Trinity. The Incarnation, Cross and Resurrec-

tion compel us to take *history* seriously and thus also mission as
historical involvement in this world. On the Cross God revealed
that he took the world seriously, in that he judged the world. He
not only *judged* the world, however; on the Cross, as well as in
the Incarnation and Resurrection, he claimed the world for his
Kingdom, he reconciled the world to himself. In the sign of the
Cross, symbol of both judgment and reconciliation, the Church
is sent into the world. Mission thus indeed has a trinitarian
basis, but in such a way that it has a christological concentration, because it is precisely Christology that accentuates
God's entrance (his mission) into the world.

Mission signifies a new dimension of God's concern for the
world. What is more, it is God's final and definitive concern.
Since Christ came we can no longer expect a salvation other
than that which he inaugurated. Neither can we expect another
Saviour. Jesus as Missionary is, at the same time, the model for
our mission (the Incarnation) and its foundation.

The trinitarian foundation of mission is further manifested in
Pneumatology. The Spirit does not replace Christ; his presence
is the presence of Christ. The mission of the Son is continued in
the mission of the Spirit and made concrete by the mission of
the disciples into the world: ' "As the Father sent me, so I send
you." Then he breathed on them, saying, "Receive the Holy
Spirit" ' (John 20.21-22).

Christology, Pneumatology and missiology are thus brought
into the closest possible relationship. In Jesus' baptism in the
river Jordan the Spirit immediately revealed the missionary
character of Jesus' ministry. At the end of his earthly life Jesus
promised his disciples his Spirit within the framework of his
missionary commission (cf. Luke 24.49; Acts 1.8).

The New Testament reveals, particularly in the Pauline
epistles, the Spirit not only as outward-directed but also as
inward-directed in his concern with the sanctification of the
believer and the Church. At first, these two aspects were
understood to be in a dynamic relationship. Subsequently the
former aspect was, for all practical purposes, disregarded. From
the second century onwards the emphasis was almost exclusively
on the Spirit as 'possession' of the believer and the Church. His
task was to purify and enlighten the believers. In the liturgy of
the Eastern churches in particular, he became the Spirit of

truth, light, and life. The Reformation introduced a limited degree of change in this respect. Because fanatics claimed that they enjoyed special revelations by the Spirit, the Reformers tended to regard the Holy Spirit almost exclusively as the One who interprets Scripture, the Exegete who would guide the Church into all truth.[2]

Although the missionary dimension of Pneumatology was rediscovered at the time of the birth of the Protestant missionary movement in the eighteenth century, it played no significant role in Protestant theology. Pneumatology continued along more or less traditional avenues. Roland Allen was one of the first to protest against this. Subsequently Harry Boer made a thorough study of the close relationship between the Holy Spirit and mission.[3] As far as systematic theology is concerned, it was particularly Karl Barth who, in the fourth volume of his *Church Dogmatics,* in which he treated Soteriology, discussed the missionary dimension of Pneumatology. Berkhof rightly points out that, according to the New Testament, the Holy Spirit is not primarily an institutionary or inward, but an historical force. We ought to realise, he says, that this third person in the divine Trinity 'expresses God's being-a-person in his outward directed activity'. 'The name for God-in-action towards the world is: Spirit'.[4]

THE COMPROMISE THAT DESTROYS THE DREAM

Because of its trinitarian foundation, Christian mission is always *missio Dei.* This means—as we have indicated in our previous chapter—that mission is God's work from first to last. In the course of time the *missio Dei* concept underwent a metamorphosis. It was abridged to a mere theological preface to an anthropological text. God became an anaemic deistic figure, the great discoverer and initiator of mission who, however, gradually withdrew, leaving the execution of his mission to his ground staff.[5] In this way mission became *our* enterprise, dependent on us, and we were supposed to goad on ourselves to ever greater exertion and sacrifices. It was then however that mission moved from the area of gospel to that of law.

Faithful to Hartenstein's original intention we have to

maintain that mission is concerned with God's Kingdom, that it exists on the basis of an expectation of that Kingdom, and that the salvation belonging to that Kingdom is wrought by God himself.

This implies that our missionary successes may never be the criterion by which we assess the *missio Dei*. If that were the case, and because of the slowness with which the Kingdom takes shape, we might be tempted to develop instant techniques to hasten the Kingdom. This is a real danger where we regard the Kingdom as purely transcendental, but also where it is understood as something this-worldly. It is, however, a greater danger in the latter instance.

Wherever we lose sight of the merely relative and variable nature of this world and act as though it is perfectable, we are in fact turning our backs on the divine Kingdom and our faces towards the passing world. We then operate with blueprints we have ourselves drawn up, with plans we are ourselves going to execute. We then easily exclaim in euphoria: *'Eureka!'*, in the belief that our blueprint is finally being translated into reality. This blinds us to the pock-marks of sin which disfigure even the most perfect human community. It becomes an easy boast that what we do is nothing but God's work. Our crusader mentality demands that the whole of society be re-created in *our* image. Our religion becomes a mechanism to control God. Salvation is made dependent upon the right kind of religious, moral and political activity and we forget that the 'authorities and powers' will not be finally dethroned before Christ returns. We are unable to recognise the tragic imperfection of even the best of our human attempts.

All this in no way suggests—and we say it with the greatest possible emphasis—that we may now just as well sit back, arguing that in the final analysis everything comes from God and there is nothing that we can alter. The escape to quietism is in principle excluded for us. Activism and quietism after all suffer from the same presupposition: that if God works, man is pushed into the background, and if man works, God's activity is being interfered with. Both approaches see God and man as competitors.

Our description of the *missio Dei* thus in no sense implies that we may look on passively while 'God alone' does it. We

cannot base a refusal to combat social injustice on an appeal to
Jesus' words in Mark 14.7 ('You have the poor among you
always'), since this would be nothing but a distortion of the
gospel. Precisely because the Kingdom has already dawned, we
may not resign to things as they are. Precisely because we
believe that everything comes from God, we ought to dedicate
ourselves unreservedly to his mission in the world.

There is a tendency among Christians to content themselves
with limited goals and moderate expectations. Such a sober and
realistic approach has much to commend itself. Our missionary
enterprises will, after all, be only partly successful. Not all
people will accept the gospel. Not all evil, injustice and
exploitation will be removed. We should therefore—so the
argument goes—not be aiming at the stars or dream of utopias
but rather settle for compromises.

Krass tells us that he, too, was tempted to subscribe to this
approach. But, he continues, he listened once again to van Ruler
and others, and looking more closely at that 'realistic' view, he
knew '... it represents the compromise that will kill the dream.
As soon as our hope is compromised—as soon as we stop
expecting the "wholesale transformations" the Bible tells us to
hope for— ... that soon do we confess our doubt that Christ
really is King, ... that soon do we begin to assign the
transformation to the far future, the eschatological wedding
feast to the time of the second coming'.[6] But then we also can no
longer pray the Lord's Prayer—'thy Kingdom come, thy will be
done, *on earth* as in heaven'. To offer that prayer, implies
believing that Christians make a difference to this world, that
things need not remain the way they are. It implies having a
vision of a new society and working for it as though it is
attainable. It means, in other words, getting involved in God's
mission in the world, and calling people to faith in Christ not
only so that they may come to sing hymns in the Church but
much rather that they—the community of those who have
enjoyed a foretaste of perfection—should share in the mission of
transforming the world.

FAITH, HOPE, LOVE

It is a misconception that missiology is a theological minor, a dispensable extra, a special field of study exclusively for those who plan to do mission work in Third World countries. After many centuries it has gradually begun to dawn on us that the Church is essentially missionary, or she is not the Church of Jesus Christ.

This 'discovery' is not only the fruit of deepened theological insight. It is, partly at least, also due to the fact that the Church in the West has lost her dominant position and began to see herself as Church-for-others. Feitse Boerwinkel mentions various important shifts in the image and role of the Church in the West, especially as these have manifested themselves since 1945. The powerful Church of the past has now become a small community. Instead of persecuting the 'sects', there is now dialogue with them. Events such as those in Nazi Germany have prepared us for dialogue and joint study projects with Jews. A critical distance has developed between Church and state. It is no longer assumed that all Westerners are church members. A new theology of hope and expectation has developed. Pentecostal gifts and charismatic offices have revived. The material wealth of the Church is increasingly criticised. And Jesus of Nazareth has once again become the focal point of interest, even in extra-ecclesiastical and non-Christian circles.[7]

These developments signify several shifts in mission and missiology. In the past mission was almost exclusively interested in 'religious man', in the sense that he was regarded as adherent of a non-Christian religion. Today the emphasis is moving increasingly towards secularised man. The missionary front is everywhere today, no longer only on the lonely missionary outpost in a pagan territory. Our entire life in the world is life-in-mission. The Church in the world is only Church insofar as she has a missionary dimension. 'The pilgrim Church is missionary by her very nature' (Vatican II: Decree *Ad Gentes*).

The Church owes the world faith. In her mission she calls people to faith in Christ, 'that men, while still in life, should cease to live for themselves, and should live for him who for their sake died and was raised to life' (2 Cor. 5.15). As members of the Church we know that God has reconciled us to himself through Christ, has enlisted us in the 'service of reconciliation' (5.18) and has entrusted us with the 'message of recon-ciliation' ꞏ (5.19). As Christ's ambassadors we turn to people as if God were appealing to them through us, and we implore them: 'Be reconciled to God!' (5.20). We do this because the love of Christ leaves us no choice (5.14).

This summons to faith does not issue from the heights of superiority but from the depths of solidarity. We are, in this, merely beggars who tell other beggars where to find bread. Where the missionary enterprise is not undertaken in this spirit, it fails, even if it records many demonstrable successes. In fact, the Church's first missionary responsibility is not to change the world but to change herself.

The Church has no 'rights' to which she may lay claim. It is God who, through her, lays claim to the world for his Kingdom. Her mission in the world therefore has nothing to do with arrogance, condescension or self-complacency. It is possible to be unaggressive and missionary at the same time; it is, in fact, the only way of being truly missionary. The Church therefore has no guarantee that her witness will be acceptable or accepted. On the contrary, she will encounter the same reactions as those experienced by her Master: either allegiance or opposition, frequently a mixture of both.

This in no way implies vagueness and hesitancy in the Church. She has a unique commission and message, and she has the right to a continued existence only if what she offers remains unique.

The Church owes the world hope—for both this and the ultimate, new world. Because the Church knows that she is a commissioned witness of the coming new order, she has to erect signs of the Kingdom already. Because she knows that the gates of hell cannot prevail against her, she can risk the impossible. Because she heard God saying: 'Behold! I am making all things new!' (Rev. 21.5), she can already begin something new. Nothing may remain unaffected. Satan achieves a tremendous victory when it becomes apparent that those who believe in Christ so frequently identify themselves with sinful structures in society and with vested interests of the mighty. Hannah's song of praise (1 Sam. 2.1-10) and Mary's *Magnificat* (Luke 1.46-55) should long ago have convinced us of the opposite. The suggestion that things might stay as they are, is the very antithesis of the gospel. It is nothing less than a denial of Christ's resurrection and of the inauguration of the New Age.

Someone who knows that God will one day wipe away all tears, cannot with resignation accept the tears of those who suffer and are oppressed now. If we believe that one day all disease will vanish, we cannot but begin to anticipate here and now the victory over disease in individuals and communities. If we accept that the enemy of God and man, the devil, will ultimately be completely conquered, we cannot but begin at once to unmask his stratagems in the individual, family and society. We believe in God not because we despair of the present and future; rather, we believe in the present and future of both man and the world because we believe in God. Precisely because we hope for the eternal and ultimate things, we also hope for the temporary and the provisional.

However, if the Church wants to impart a message of hope to the world, something of that hope and of the new dispensation should take shape in the Church herself. She is the 'single new humanity' (Eph. 2.15) out of Jews and Gentiles;[8] and the process which gives birth to the new humanity we call mission. The barriers between people are here torn down in principle and the 'dividing wall' demolished (Eph. 2.14). A new people has come into being, where all who believe in Christ, are 'the "issue" of Abraham' (Gal. 3.29), where nobody is any longer judged according to 'worldly standards' (2 Cor. 5.16), where all are 'one person in Christ Jesus' (Gal. 3.28), where 'the old order has gone, and a new order has already begun' (2 Cor. 5.17), where there are no more 'aliens in a foreign land' (Eph. 2.19).

The Church owes the world love. The love she has experienced ought to be passed on to others. The love of Christ constitutes the model and the measure of the Church's love to the world. Christ's love revealed its deepest dimension on the Cross. It will not be different with the Church.

The Cross is the hall-mark of the Church, as it was of Jesus. The proofs of Jesus' identity were his scars. Because of them, the disciples believed (John 20.20). Likewise, because of the scars of the Church the world will believe.

Too often precious little of this was apparent in the past. The Cross was the symbol of the power and victory of the Church, not of her weakness, wounds and defeats. For precisely this reason the Church in many respects stands judged before the world. She has forgotten that she is called to live according to the example of One who said, 'Here am I among you like a servant' (Luke 22.27).

Christendom, the *corpus Christianum,* has collapsed. Many have lamented this; many still lament it today. In reality, however, it is a liberation. The Church can now once again truly be the Church. Out of the ruins of the *corpus Christianum* the *corpus Christi,* the Body of Christ, arises, stripped of her earlier self-assurance, of her self-confidence and megalomania. Precisely in her mission the Church confesses her guilt about the way in which she has always attempted to dominate the world. 'Mission is ... the penance of the church, which is ashamed before God and man.'[9] Mission is the Church-crossing-frontiers-in-the-form-of-a-servant.

NOTES

CHAPTER 1 (pp. 2-10)

1. J. Dürr, 'Die Reinigung der Missionsmotive', *Evangelisches Missions-Magazin*, vol. 95, no. 1 (1951), p. 3.
2. Cf. Feitse Boerwinkel, *Einde of Nieuw Begin?* (Ambo, Bilthoven, 1974), pp. 54-64.
3. Cf. Eugene A. Nida, *Religion across Cultures* (Harper & Row, New York, 1968), pp. 48-57.
4. Hans Küng, *Christenheit als Minderheit* (1966), pp. 9-11.
5. Cf. M. Mildenberger, *Heil aus Asien?* (Quell Verlag, Stuttgart, 1974).
6. Cf. G. F. Vicedom, *The Challenge of the World Religions* (Fortress Press, Philadelphia, 1963).
7. Quoted in *IAMS Newsletter*, no. 11 (Nov. 1977), p. 13.
8. *Salvation Tomorrow*, p. 135.
9. Quoted in *Reformed Ecumenical Synod News Exchange*, 22nd Feb. 1972.
10. Cf. D. J. Bosch, 'The Question of Mission Today', *Journal of Theology for Southern Africa*, no. 1 (Dec. 1972), pp. 5-15.
11. *The Coming of the Third Church* (Orbis Books, Maryknoll, 1977), p. 98.
12. Cf. R. D. Haight, S.J., 'Mission: The Symbol for Understanding the Church Today', *Theological Studies*, vol. 37, no. 4 (Dec. 1976), pp. 620-49.
13. *Occasional Bulletin of Missionary Research*, Vol. 2, no. 3 (July 1978), p. 87.

CHAPTER 2 (pp. 11-20)

1. Cf. A. A. van Ruler, 'Theologie des Apostolats', *Evangelische Missionszeitschrift*, vol. 11, no. 1 (1954), pp. 1-11.
2. Cf. M. Geijbels, 'Evangelization, its meaning and practice', *Al-Mushir*, vol. 20, no. 2 (Summer 1978), pp. 73-82. Geijbels, to a large extent, relies for his views on R. M. C. Jeffery, art. 'Mission, Theology of', in Alan Richardson, *A Dictionary of Christian Theology* (SCM, London, 1969).
3. Cf. J. Moltmann, *Gott kommt und der Mensch wird frei* (Kaiser, Munich, 1975), pp. 21-35.
4. We shall return to this in Chapter 21.
5. Hans Bürki, *The Christian Life in the World* (Reprint IFES Journal, 1969), p. 26.
6. Cf. in this connection Walter J. Hollenweger, *Evangelisation gestern und heute* (Steinkopf, Stuttgart, 1973), pp. 25-48.
7. Cf. Mortimer Arias, 'Evangelization: Incarnational Style', *The Other Side*, no. 84 (Sept. 1978), pp. 30-43.

8. 'The Confessing Community', *International Review of Missions,* no. 264 (Oct. 1977), p. 341.

9. *Occasional Bulletin of Missionary Research,* vol. 2, no. 3 (July 1978), p. 88.

10. Cf. also Klauspeter Blaser: *Gottes Heil in heutiger Wirklichkeit* (Otto Lembeck, Frankfurt, 1978), pp. 104-13.

CHAPTER 3 (pp. 21-29)

1. *Concise Dictionary of the Christian World Mission* (Lutterworth, London, 1970), p. 594.

2. Cf. Thomas Ohm, *Machet zu Jüngern alle Völker* (Wevel, Freiburg, 1962), pp. 139-220.

3. See also Karl Barth, 'Die Theologie und die Mission in der Gegenwart', originally published in *Zwischen den Zeiten,* 1932, republished in *Theologische Fragen und Antworten.* Vorträge, 3. Band (Evangelischer Verlag, Zollikon, 1957), pp. 100-26.

4. *Occasional Bulletin from the Missionary Research Library,* vol. 14, no. 1 (1964).

5. *Variaties op het Thema Zending* (Kok, Kampen, 1974), p. 14 (our translation).

6. Cf. Jean-Louis Leuba, *New Testament Pattern* (Lutterworth, London, 1953). This is the English translation of his French book, *L'Institution et l'Evénement,* published in 1950.

7. Cf. F. Boerwinkel, *Einde of Nieuw Begin?* (Ambo, Bilthoven, 1974), pp. 64-5.

8. Cf. H. R. Niebuhr, *The Kingdom of God in America* (Harper & Row, New York, 1959), p. 167.

CHAPTER 4 (pp. 28-40)

1. *Christ to the World,* vol. 19, no. 4 (1974), pp. 310-18.

2. Cf. P. Beyerhaus, in W. Künneth and P. Beyerhaus (eds.), *Reich Gottes oder Weltgemeinschaft?* (Bad Liebenzell, 1975), pp. 307-8.

3. Cf. John W. de Gruchy, 'The Great Evangelical Reversal: South African Reflections', *Journal of Theology for Southern Africa,* no. 24 (Sept. 1978), pp. 45-57.

4. Arthur P. Johnston, *The Battle for World Evangelism* (Tyndale House, Wheaton, 1978), pp. 18, 302-3.

5. Cf. Harvey T. Hoekstra, *The World Council of Churches and the Demise of Evangelism* (Tyndale House, Wheaton, 1979).

6. Cf. Stott's response to Johnston in *Christianity Today* 5th Jan. 1979, pp. 34-5.

7. Johnston, op. cit., p. 50.

8. *Ibid.,* p. 59.

9. C. E. Braaten, *The Flaming Center* (Fortress Press, Philadelphia, 1977), p. 112.

10. John Stott, *Christian Mission in the Modern World* (Inter-Varsity Press, Downers Grove, 1976), p. 16.
11. Johnston, op. cit., p. 52.
12. *Ibid.,* p. 298.
13. Richard Shaull, 'Towards a Reformulation of Objectives', in Norman A. Horner (ed.), *Protestant Crosscurrents in Mission* (Abingdon, Nashville, 1968), p. 104.
14. Cf. Ludwig Rütti, *Zur Theologie der Mission* (Kaiser, Munich, 1972), pp. 188-9.
15. Quoted in the Johannesburg *Star,* 26th July 1974.
16. Cf. Peter Beyerhaus, *Missions: Which Way?* (Zondervan, Grand Rapids, 1971), p. 79.
17. Shaull, op. cit., p. 98 (with reference to A. Th. van Leeuwen).
18. Cf. *ibid.,* p. 96.
19. Cf. *ibid.,* p. 88-9.
20. Cf. Gregory Baum, 'Is there a Missionary Message?', in G. H. Anderson and T. F. Stransky (eds.), *Mission Trends No. 1* (Eerdmans, Grand Rapids, 1974), pp. 81-6.

CHAPTER 5 (pp.42-49)

1. J. H. Bavinck, *An Introduction to the Science of Missions* (Baker, Grand Rapids, 1960), pp. 11-76.
2. Cf. F. Hahn, *Mission in the New Testament* (SCM, London, 1965), p. 167.
3. Alphons Mulders, *Inleiding in de Missiewetenschap* (Paul Brand, Bussum, 1950), pp. 130-40, 140-85.
4. T. Ohm, *Machet zu Jüngern alle Völker* (Erich Wevel, Freiburg, 1962), pp. 141-320.
5. Cf. also Klauspeter Blaser, *Gottes Heil in heutiger Wirklichkeit* (Kaiser, Munich, 1978), pp. 32-4.
6. Quoted by Blaser, op. cit., pp. 33 and 34 (our translation).
7. F. Hahn, op. cit., p. 20.
8. Cf. the English translation of his epoch-making work, *The Mission and Expansion of Christianity in the First Three Centuries* (Harper, New York, 1961), pp. 36-43.
9. Cf. also J. Verkuyl, *Contemporary Missiology: An Introduction* (Eerdmans, Grand Rapids, 1978), p. 90.
10. Cf. D. J. Bosch, *Die Heidenmission in der Zukunftsschau Jesu* (Zwingli Verlag, Zürich, 1959).

CHAPTER 6 (pp.50-57)

1. Cf. for instance F. E. Deist, 'The Exodus Motif in the Old Testament and the Theology of Liberation', *Missionalia,* vol. 5, no. 2 (Aug. 1977), pp. 58-69: C. J. Labuschagne, 'De Godsdienst van Israel en de Andere Godsdiensten', *Wereld en Zending,* vol. 4, no. 1 (1975), pp. 4-16.

2. For the development outlined here, with references, see Bosch, *Heidenmission* (op. cit., Chapter 5, note 10), pp. 31-5.

3. Cf. J. Verkuyl, *Contemporary Missiology* (op cit., Chapter 5, note 9), pp. 96-100.

4. *Ibid.*, pp. 99-100.

5. Cf. Albert Nolan, *Jesus before Christianity* (David Philip, Cape Town, 1976), p. 21.

6. Cf. J. Jeremias, *Jesus' Promise to the Nations* (SCM, London, 1959), pp. 41-6; and W. Grundmann, *Das Evangelium des Lukas* (Evangelische Verlagsanstalt, Berlin, 1974), pp. 118-23.

7. For arguments in favour of this translation, see Jeremias, op. cit., pp. 41-6.

8. Jeremias's interpretation of this passage has been refuted by Hugh Anderson, 'The Rejection at Nazareth Pericope of Luke 4:16-30 in Light of Recent Critical Trends', *Interpretation,* vol. 18, no. 3 (July 1964), pp. 266-70. The more recent discoveries at Qumran, however, tend to vindicate Jeremias's views: see R. Martin, *New Testament Foundations,* vol. 2 (Eerdmans, Grand Rapids, 1978), p. 255. Cf. also A. A. Trites, *The New Testament Concept of Witness* (Cambridge University Press, Cambridge, 1977), p. 71.

9. Cf. Jeremias, op. cit., pp. 45-6.

10. Cf. M. Hengel, 'Die Ursprünge der christlichen Mission', *New Testament Studies,* vol. 18, no. 1 (1971), pp. 35-6.

11. Cf. E. Jansen Schoonhoven, *Variaties op het Thema Zending* (Kok, Kampen, 1974), p. 26.

12. Verkuyl, *Contemporary Missiology,* p. 104.

CHAPTER 7 (pp.58-70)

1. Cf. Mercia Eliade, *The Myth of the Eternal Return* (Princeton University Press, 1974).

2. Cf. G. von Rad, *Weisheit in Israel* (Neukirchener Verlag, Neukirchen, 1970), pp. 165-81, ET *Wisdom in Israel* (SCM, London, 1972).

3. D. T. Niles, *Upon the Earth* (Lutterworth, London, 1962), pp. 242-3.

4. L. Newbigin, *The Finality of Christ* (SCM, London, 1969), p. 50.

5. Cf. Arthur Weiser, *Introduction to the Old Testament* (Darton, Longman & Todd, London, 1961), pp. 83, 87.

6. Cf. also Heinrich Kasting, *Die Anfänge der urchristlichen Mission* (Kaiser, Munich, 1969), p. 129.

7. Cf. H. W. Huppenbauer, 'Missionanische Dimension des Gottesvolkes im Alten Testament', *Zeitschrift für Mission,* vol. 3, no. 1 (1977), pp. 40-1.

8. 'Jésus et les paiens', in Sundkler-Fridrichsen, *Contributions à l'étude de la Pensée Missionaire dans le Nouveau Testament* (Uppsala 1937), p. 36.

9. Cf. further Bosch, *Heidenmission* (op. cit., Chapter 5, note 10), pp. 86-92.

10. R. Martin-Achard, *A Light to the Nations* (Oliver and Boyd, London, 1962), p. 78.

11. Cf. Schuyler Brown, 'The Two-fold Representation of the Mission in Matthew's Gospel', *Studia Theologica,* vol. 31, no. 1 (1977), pp. 21-32.

12. Cf. also H. Kasting, *Die Anfänge der urchristlichen Mission*, pp. 35-6.
13. Cf. B. J. Malina, 'The Literary Structure and Form of Matt. XXVIII 16-20', *New Testament Studies*, vol. 17, no. 1 (1970-1), pp. 87-103.
14. *I Believe in the Great Commission*, p. 23.
15. A. Schlatter, *Der Evangelist Matthäus* (Calwer, Stuttgart, 1948), p. 23 (our translation). See also Peter O'Brien, 'The Great Commission of Matthew 28:18-20. A Missionary Mandate or not?' *The Reformed Theological Review*, vol. 35, no. 3 (Sept.-Dec. 1976), pp. 66-78.
16. Cf. also J. D. Kingsbury, 'The Composition and Christology of Matt. 28:16-20', *Journal of Biblical Literature*, vol. 93, no. 4 (Dec. 1974), pp. 576-7.
17. Cf. Wiard Popkes, 'Zum Verständnis der Mission bei Johannes', *Zeitschrift für Mission*, vol. 4, no. 2 (1978), pp. 63-9.

CHAPTER 8 (pp. 71-74)

1. Cf. Dirk H. Odendaal, *The Eschatological Expectation of Isaiah 40-66 with Special Reference to Israel and the Nations* (Presbyterian and Reformed Publ. Co., Philadelphia, 1970).
2. Cf. Horst Baum, *Mut zum Schwachsein—in Christi Kraft* (Steyler Verlag, St. Augustin, 1977).
3. *The Validity of the Christian Mission* (Harper & Row, New York, 1972), p. 92.
4. Cf. N. P. Moritzen, *Die Kirche als Mission*, (Jugenddienst Verlag, Wuppertal-Barmen, 1966), p. 30.
5. Hans von Campenhausen, 'Das Martyrium in der Mission' *Kirchengeschichte als Missionsgeschichte*, vol. I (Kaiser, Munich, 1974), p. 71 (our translation).

CHAPTER 9 (pp. 75-83)

1. See also Allison A. Trites, *The New Testament Concept of Witness* (Cambridge University Press, Cambridge, 1977), pp. 35-47.
2. Cf. R. E. Clements, *Old Testament Theology. A Fresh Approach* (Marshall, Morgan & Scott, London, 1978), pp. 94-6.
3. H. Rzcpkowski, 'The Theology of Mission', *Verbum SVD*, vol. 15, no. 1 (1974), p. 80.
4. Quoted in Gerald Anderson (ed.), *Christian Mission in Theological Perspective* (Abingdon, Nashville, 1967), p. 223.
5. J. Jeremias, *Jesus' Promise* (op. cit., Chapter 6, note 6), p. 70.
6. L. Newbigin, 'The Church as Witness', *Reformed Review*, vol. 35, no. 1 (March 1978), p. 9.
7. See H. Kasting, *Die Anfänge der urchristlichen Mission* (Chr. Kaiser, Munich, 1969), pp. 109-23. Kasting shows that it were Judaistic elements in the early Church, not the 'official' early Church herself, which tended to limit salvation to Israel. At a later stage, especially after the first century, the 'unofficial', Judaistic position increasingly became the accepted one in Jewish Christianity. That attitude would ultimately become one of the factors leading

to the end of Jewish Christianity (see the paragraph on 'The Church and the Jews' in Chapter 11 below).

CHAPTER 10 (pp. 86-92)

1. Niebuhr, *Kingdom* (op. cit., Chapter 3, note 8), p. 1.

2. H.-W. Gensichen, *Glaube für die Welt* (Gerd Mohn, Gütersloh, 1971), pp. 13-16.

3. Cf. also J. M. van der Linde, 'De Zending als kritische Factor in de Geschiedenis', in *Kerk aan het Werk* (Agon Elsevier, Amsterdam, 1973), pp. 52-87.

4. Cf. for instance Stephen Neill, *A History of Christian Missions* (Penguin Books, Harmondsworth, 1964).

5. *Kirchengeschichte als Missionsgeschichte* (Chr. Kaiser, Munich), Vol. I, 1974 (on the early Church), Vol. II/1, 1978 (on the early Middle Ages).

6. Vol. I, pp. 421-46; Vol. II/1, pp. 507-42.

7. *Machet zu Jüngern alle Völker* (Wevel, Freiburg i.B., 1962), pp. 75-121.

CHAPTER 11 (pp. 93-101)

1. G. Rosenkranz, *Die christliche Mission* (Chr. Kaiser, Munich, 1977), pp. 24-42.

2. *International Review of Missions,* vol. 41 (1952), p. 325.

3. Cf. Feitse Boerwinkel, *Einde of Nieuw Begin?* (Ambo, Bilthoven, 1974), p. 61.

4. Cf. Rosenkranz, op. cit., p. 61.

5. Cf. the collection of essays by Allen, published under the title *The Ministry of the Spirit* (Eerdmans, Grand Rapids, 1962).

6. *Pentecost and Missions* (Lutterworth, London, 1961).

7. Cf. Georg Kretschmar, 'Das christliche Leben und die Mission in der frühen Kirche', *Kirchengeschichte als Missionsgeschichte,* vol. I (1974), pp. 94-128.

8. For the fundamental missionary dimension of Baptism, cf. John H. Piet, *The Road Ahead: A Theology for the Church in Mission* (Eerdmans, Grand Rapids, 1970), pp. 69-83, for that of Holy Communion, cf. Piet, op. cit., pp. 84-93 and David J. Bosch, *Die Heidenmission in der Zukunftsschau Jesu* (1959), pp. 175-84.

9. G. Rosenkranz, op. cit., p. 71 (our translation).

10. Cf. M. Green, *Evangelism in The Early Church* (Hodder & Stoughton, London, 1973), pp. 178-93.

11. Cf. A. von Harnack, *The Mission and Expansion of Christianity in the First Three Centuries* (Harper, New York, 1961), pp. 147-98.

12. *Ibid.,* p. 69.

13. See also note 7 of Chapter 9.

CHAPTER 12 (pp.102-114)

1. Cf. H.-D. Kahl, 'Die ersten Jahrhunderte des missionsgeschichtlichen Mittelalters', in *Kirchengeschichte als Missionsgeschichte,* vol. II/1 (1978), p. 20.

2. C. E. Braaten, *The Flaming Center,* p. 50.

3. Cf. Kahl, op. cit., pp. 36-59.

4. Cf. *ibid.,* pp. 40, 48-52, 72.

5. Cf. Reinhard Schneider, 'Politisches Sendungsbewusstsein und Mission', in *Kirchengeschichte als Missionsgeschichte,* vol. II/1, pp. 227-48.

6. Cf. Kahl, op. cit., pp. 62-71.

7. 'Christlich-jüdische Konfrontation im kirchlichen Frühmittelalter', in *Kirchengeschichte als Missionsgeschichte,* vol. II/1, pp. 397-441.

8. Cf. E. R. Hardy, 'The Mission of the Church in the First Four Centuries', in *History's Lessons for Tomorrow's Mission* (WSCF, Geneva, n.d. (1960)), pp. 29-38.

9. Cf. Anastasios Yannoulatos, 'Monks and Mission in the Eastern Church during the Fourth Century', *International Review of Missions,* no. 230 (April 1969), pp. 208-26.

10. G. S. M. Walker, 'St. Columban: Monk or Missionary?' in G. J. Cummings (ed.), *The Mission of the Church and the Propagation of the Faith* (Cambridge University Press, London, 1970), p. 43.

11. G. Rosenkranz, *Die christliche Mission* (op. cit., Chapter 11, note 1), p. 103 (our translation).

12. Heinz Löwe, 'Pirmin, Willibrord und Bonifatius', in *Kirchengeschichte als Missionsgeschichte,* vol. II/1, pp. 192-226.

13. C. Dawson, *The Making of Europe* (1953), p. 166, quoted by S. Neill, *A History of Christian Missions* (1964), p. 74.

14. J. H. Newman, quoted by C. Dawson, *Religion and the Rise of Western Culture* (Sheed & Ward, London, 1950), pp. 57-8.

15. Cf. also Karl Holl, 'Die Missionsmethode der alten und die der mittelalterlichen Kirche', in *Kirchengeschichte als Missionsgeschichte,* vol. I (1974), pp. 12-17; W. H. C. Frend, 'Der Verlauf der Mission in der Alten Kirche bis zum 7. Jahrhundert', *ibid.,* pp. 44-5.

CHAPTER 13 (pp. 115-119)

1. Neill, *History* (op. cit., Chapter 10, note 4), p. 450. See further *idem, Colonialism and Christian Missions* (Lutterworth, London, 1966).

2. Cf. A. Hastings, *A Concise Guide to the Documents of the Second Vatican Council,* vol. I (Darton, Longman & Todd, 1968), pp. 28-31.

3. Cf. A. Seumois, 'The Evaluation of Mission Theology among Roman Catholics', in G. H. Anderson (ed.), *The Theology of the Christian Mission* (SCM Press, London, 1961), p. 129.

CHAPTER 14 (pp. 120-139)

1. Cf. John Piet, *The Road Ahead* (Eerdmans, Grand Rapids, 1970), pp. 33-4, 84.

2. Niebuhr, *Kingdom* (op. cit., Chapter 3, note 8), p. 26; cf. also pp. 88-9.

3. Charles L. Chaney, *The Birth of Missions in America* (William Carey Library, Pasadena, 1976), p. 32.

4. R. Marius, 'The Reformation and Nationhood', *Dialog,* vol. 15, no. 1 (Winter 1976), p. 34.

5. H. R. Niebuhr, *Christ and Culture* (Harper, New York, 1956), p. 43; cf. also pp. 217-18.

6. Bellarmin, quoted by Stephen Neill, *A History of Christian Missions* (1964), p. 221.

7. Cf. Rosenkranz, *Die christliche Mission* (op. cit., Chapter 11, note 1), p. 151.

8. For Lutheran orthodoxy, cf. Erich Beyreuther, 'Evangelische Missionstheologie im 16. und 17. Jahrhundert', *Evangelische Missionszeitschrift,* vol. 18, nos. 1 and 2 (1961) pp. 1-10, 33-43.

9. Cf. Franklin H. Littell, *The Origins of Sectarian Protestantism. A Study of the Anabaptist View of the Church* (Macmillan, New York, 1972). Cf. also Wolfgang Schäufele, *Das missionarische Bewusstsein und Wirken der Täufer* (Verlag des Erziehungsvereins, Neukirchen, 1966) and J. A. Toews, 'The Anabaptist Involvement in Missions', in A. J. Klassen (ed.), *The Church in Mission* (Board of Christian Literature, Fresno, 1967), pp. 85-100.

10. Cf. Erich Beyreuther, *Evangelische Missionszeitschrift,* vol. 18, no. 1 (1961) pp. 38-9.

11. E. Beyreuther, 'Mission und Kirche in der Theologie Zinzendorfs', *Evangelische Missionszeitschrift,* vol. 17, no. 4 (July 1960), p. 110 (our translation).

12. Zinzendorf, quoted by Beyreuther, *Evangelische Missionszeitschrift,* vol. 18, no. 2 (March 1960), p. 40 (our translation).

13. An attempt at a positive critical evaluation of Gützlaff is offered by E. Jansen Schoonhoven, 'Eerherstel voor dr. Karl Gützlaff, zendeling onder de Chinezen van 1827-1851', in *Variaties op het Thema 'Zending'* (Kok, Kampen, 1974), pp. 115-28.

14. Cf. J. C. Hoekendijk, *Kerk en Volk in de Duitse Zendingswetenschap* (n.d. (1948)), pp. 62-75.

15. E. Troeltsch, quoted by Hoekendijk, op. cit., p. 81 (our translation).

16. J. Richter, *Evangelische Missionskunde,* vol. 2 (A. Deichertsche Verlagsbuchhandlung, Leipzig, 1927), p. 40 (our translation).

17. Cf. in this connection the penetrating study by Hans Schärer, *Die Begründung der Mission in der katholischen und evangelischen Missionswissenschaft* (Evangelischer Verlag, Zollikon—Zürich, 1944).

18. Quoted by Schärer, op. cit., p. 9 (our translation).

19. G. Warneck, *Evangelische Missionslehre,* Vol. III/1 (Perthes, Gotha, 1902) p. 258 (our translation).

20. Cf. Hoekendijk, op. cit., pp. 90-5; Schärer, op. cit., and J. Dürr,

Sendende und werdende Kirche in der Missionstheologie Gustav Warneck's (Missionsbuchhandlung, Basel, 1947).

21. M. Kähler, *Schriften zu Christologie und Mission* (Chr. Kaiser, Munich, 1971). Page references in our discussion of Kähler's contribution refer to this publication. Regarding Kähler, cf. also D. J. Bosch, 'Systematic Theology and Mission. The Voice of an Early Pioneer', *Theologia Evangelica*, vol. 5, no. 3 (Sept. 1972), pp. 165-89.

22. Cf. Schärer, op. cit., and G. Rosenkranz, *Die christliche Mission,* pp. 227-31.

CHAPTER 15 (pp. 140-158)

1. Cf. Neill, *History* (op. cit., Chapter 10, note 4), p. 261.

2. Cf. Niebuhr, *Kingdom* (op. cit., Chapter 3, note 8), pp. x, xii, 88-9.

3. See J. J. A. M. Kuepers, *The Dutch Reformed Church in Formosa 1627-1662* (Neue Zeitschrift für Missionswissenschaft, Immensee, 1978).

4. Cf. Sidney H. Rooy, *The Theology of Missions in the Puritan Tradition* (Meinema, Delft, 1965), pp. 60-5.

5. See Charles L. Chaney, *The Birth of Missions in America* (Wm. Carey Libr., Pasadena, 1976), pp. 9-47.

6. Cf. J. A. de Jong, *As the Waters cover the Sea. Millennial Expectations in the Rise of Anglo-American Missions 1640-1810.* (Kok, Kampen, 1970), pp. 1-2, 77, 115, 157-8, 228.

7. See Rooy, op. cit., pp. 310-28.

8. Jonathan Edwards, quoted by Niebuhr, op. cit., p. 145.

9. Chaney, op. cit., p. 83.

10. Cf. R. Pierce Beaver, 'Eschatology in American Missions', in *Basileia. Walter Freytag zum 60. Geburtstag* (Evang. Missionsverlag, Stuttgart, 1961), p. 61.

11. Cf. U. Gäbler, 'Die Anfänge der Erweckungsbewegung in Neu-England und Jonathan Edwards, 1734/1735', *Theologische Zeitschrift,* vol. 34, no. 2, March-April 1978, pp. 95-104.

12. Chaney, op. cit., p. 49.

13. Niebuhr, op. cit., p. 118.

14. Cf. Ian Bradley, *The Call to Seriousness. The Evangelical Impact on the Victorians* (Jonathan Cape, London, 1976).

15. Niebuhr, op. cit., p. 121.

16. Cf. David O. Moberg, *The Great Reversal* (Scripture Union, London, 1972), pp. 30-34.

17. Quoted by A. H. Oussoren, *William Carey, especially his Missionary Principles* (Sijthoff, Leyden, 1945), p. 29.

18. Cf. Chaney, op. cit., p. 271; see also pp. 274-6.

19. *Ibid.,* p. 269.

20. *Ibid.,* p. 155.

21. *Ibid.,* p. 295.

22. Cf. P. Gerard Damsteegt, *Foundations of the Seventh-Day Adventist Message and Mission* (Eerdmans, Grand Rapids, 1977), p. 11.

23. Niebuhr, op. cit., p. 177.

24. *Ibid.,* p. 176.

25. See especially Damsteegt, op. cit.

26. Cf., apart from Damsteegt's thorough study, the contribution of his fellow-adventist, Gottfried Oosterwal, *Mission in einer veränderten Welt* (Advent-Verlag, Hamburg, n.d.).

27. Quoted by Niebuhr, op. cit., p. 192. See there for a further characterisation of the 'Social Gospel' movement.

28. Niebuhr, op. cit., p. 192.

29. *Ibid.*, p. 195.

30. *Ibid.*, p. 193.

31. Moberg, op. cit., p. 42.

32. J. A. Scherer, 'Ecumenical Mandates for Mission', in Norman A. Horner (ed.), *Protestant Crosscurrents in Mission* (Abingdon, Nashville/New York, 1968), p. 20.

CHAPTER 16 (pp. 159-18|1)

1. Cf. H. Frick, *Die evangelische Mission* (Bonn/Leipzig, 1922), p. 387.

2. See further I. P. C. van 't Hof, *Op Zoek naar het Geheim van de Zending*. In Dialoog met de Wereldzendingsconferenties 1910-1963 (Veenman, Wageningen, 1972), pp. 27-31.

3. Cf. Gerald H. Anderson, *The Theology of Missions: 1928-1958* (University Microfilms, Ann Abor, 1960), pp. 6-11.

4. Cf. van 't Hof, op. cit., pp. 46-54.

5. W. R. Hogg, *Ecumenical Foundations* (Harper & Brothers, New York, 1952), p. 98.

6. W. H. Temple Gairdner, *Edinburgh Conference 1910* (Edinburgh 1910), p. 137.

7. See especially his *Living Religions and a World Faith* (Macmillan, New York, 1940), pp. 190-208.

8. For a rendering of the key paragraphs in this report, see Jerald D. Gort, 'Jerusalem 1928: Mission, Kingdom and Church', *International Review of Mission*, no. 267 (July 1978), pp. 278-81; see also Anderson, op. cit., pp. 40-80.

9. Cf. van 't Hof, op. cit., pp. 66-70.

10. See further van 't Hof, op. cit., pp. 82-90; Anderson, op. cit., pp. 61-80.

11. German original: 'Die Theologie und die Mission in der Gegenwart.' It was first published in the journal *Zwischen den Zeiten* (1932).

12. Cf. J. Aagaard, 'Some Main Trends in Modern Protestant Missiology', *Studia Theologica*, vol. 19 (1965), pp. 238-59.

13. See van 't Hof, op. cit., p. 125. For an excellent survey of the Tambaram conference, cf. E. Jansen Schoonhoven, 'Tambaram 1938', *International Review of Missions*, no. 267 (July 1978), pp. 299-315; see also G. H. Anderson, op. cit., pp. 121-80.

14. See further Dieter Manecke, *Mission als Zeugendienst* (Brockhaus, Wuppertal, 1972), especially pp. 231-63.

15. See Wiedenmann's thorough study, *Mission und Eschatologie*. Eine Analyse der neueren deutschen evangelischen Missionstheologie (Bonifacius-Druckerei, Paderborn, 1965).

16. Cf. Holsten's book, *Das Kerygma und der Mensch* (Kaiser, Munich, 1953).

17. M. Warren, *The Truth of Vision* (Canterbury Press, London, 1948), p. 53.

18. W. Manson, 'Mission and Eschatology', *International Review of Missions* (1953), pp. 390-1.

19. For an evaluation of Whitby's contribution to the theology of mission, see Feliciano V. Carino, 'Whitby: Partnership in Obedience', *International Review of Mission*, no. 267 (July 1978) pp. 316-28; van 't Hooft, op. cit., pp. 138-54; Anderson, op. cit., pp. 188-200.

20. Many of Hoekendijk's shorter contributions on this subject were published in the volume *The Church Inside Out* (SCM Press, London, 1966). A valuable and fair assessment of Hoekendijk is offered by L. A. Hoedemaker, 'De oorspronkelijkheid van het Apostolaat', *Nederlands Theologisch Tijdschrift*, vol. 30, no. 2 (April 1976), pp. 141-54. Cf. also Manecke, op. cit., pp. 107-61.

21. For a remarkable contemporary evaluation of events in China, see David M. Paton, *Christian Mission and the Judgment of God* (SCM Press, London, 1953).

22. J. Aagaard, 'Some Main Trends in Modern Protestant Missiology', *Studia Theologica*, vol. 19 (1965), p. 249. For a good theological evaluation of Willingen, see Rodger C. Bassham, 'Seeking a Deeper Theological Basis for Mission', *International Review of Missions*, no. 267 (July 1978), pp. 329-37; van 't Hof, op. cit., pp. 155-77; Anderson, op. cit., pp. 219-75; Wilhelm Andersen, *Towards a Theology of Mission* (SCM Press, London, 1955), pp. 34-44.

23. See in this respect Helmut Rosin, *Missio Dei* (Inter-University Institute for Missiology and Ecumenics, Leyden, 1972).

24. Cf. Ralph D. Winter, 'Ghana: Preparation for Marriage', *International Review of Missions*, no. 267 (July 1978), pp. 338-53; Max Warren, 'The Fusion of I.M.C. and W.C.C. at New Delhi: Retrospective Thoughts after a Decade and a Half', in *Zending op Weg naar de Toekomst*. Essays aangeboden aan Prof. Dr. J. Verkuyl (Kok, Kampen, 1978), pp. 190-202.

25. Warren, op. cit., pp. 194, 196.

26. Cf. Winter, op. cit., p. 349.

CHAPTER 17 (pp.182-195)

1. For literature on Orthodox Theology of mission, cf. James J. Stamoolis, 'A Selected Bibliography of Eastern Orthodox Mission Theology', *Occasional Bulletin of Missionary Research*, vol. 1, no. 3 (July 1977), pp. 24-7.

2. M. Mildenberger, *Denkpause im Dialog*. Perspektiven der Begegnung mit anderen Religionen und Ideologien (Otto Lembeck, Frankfurt, 1978). See also S. J. Samartha (ed.), *Faith in the Midst of Faiths*. Reflections on Dialogue in Community (World Council of Churches, Geneva, 1977).

3. Cf. H.-W. Gensichen, *Glaube für die Welt* (Gerd Mohn, Gütersloh, 1971), pp. 219-20.

4. R. Winter, *International Review of Missions*, no. 267 (July 1978), p. 351.

5. Cf. H. Berkhof, *Christelijk Geloof* (Callenbach, Nijkerk, 1973), p. 432.

6. Cf. K. Bockmühl, *Was heisst heute Mission?* (Brunnen Verlag, Basel, 1974), p. 14.

7. Cf. Kaj Baago, 'The Post-Colonial Crisis in Missions', *International Review of Missions,* no. 219 (July 1966), pp. 322-32; Georges Khodr, 'Christianity in a Pluralistic World', *Ecumenical Review,* vol. 32, no. 2 (April 1971), pp. 118-28.

8. See D. J. Bosch, 'Crosscurrents in Modern Mission', *Missionalia,* vol. 4, no. 2 (Aug. 1976), esp. pp. 75-84. Cf. also John H. Kromminga, 'Evangelical Influence on the Ecumenical Movement', *Calvin Theological Journal,* vol. 11, no. 2 (Nov. 1976), pp. 148-80.

9. See for instance Rudolf Thaut, 'Evangelisation Heute—Ein Vergleich der Dokumente von Lausanne, Rom und Nairobi', *Oekumenische Rundschau,* vol. 26, no. 4 (Oct. 1977), pp. 451-8.

CHAPTER 18 (pp. 198-201)

1. Stephen Neill, *The Church and Christian Union* (Oxford University Press, London, 1968), p. 75.

2. Karl Barth, *Church Dogmatics* IV/1 (T. and T. Clark, Edinburgh, 1956), p. 737.

3. Cf. Gensichen, *Glaube* (op. cit., Chapter 17, note 3), esp. pp. 80-96, 168-86. See also G. F. Vicedom, *Die missionarische Dimension der Gemeinde* (Luth. Verlagshaus, Berlin, 1963).

4. Cf. D. van Swigchem, *Het Missionair Karakter van de Christelijke Gemeente volgens de Brieven van Paulus en Petrus* (Kok, Kampen, 1955).

CHAPTER 19 (pp. 202-211)

1. Harold Lindsell, 'A Rejoinder', *International Review of Missions,* no. 216 (Oct. 1965), p. 439.

2. J. S. Murray, 'The Mission and the Ministry of the Church', *International Review of Missions,* no. 205 (Jan. 1963), p. 29. (Murray defines 'mission' as proclamation and 'ministry' as service.)

3. E. Trueblood, *The Validity of the Christian Mission* (Harper and Row, New York, 1972), p. 98.

4. See A. J. R. McQuilkin, 'The Foreign Missionary—a Vanishing Breed?' in A. F. Glasser and others: *Crucial Dimensions in World Evangelization* (Wm. Carey Library, Pasadena, 1976), pp. 293-305.

5. Ronald J. Sider, *Evangelism, Salvation and Social Justice* (Grove Books, Bramcote, 1977), p. 18.

6. J. D. Gort, 'Gospel for the Poor?', in *Zending op Weg naar de toekomst.* Essays aangeboden aan Prof. Dr. J. Verkuyl (Kok, Kampen, 1978), p. 106.

7. Stephen C. Knapp, 'Mission and Modernization', in R. Pierce Beaver (ed.), *American Missions in Bicentennial Perspective* (Wm. Carey Library, Pasadena, 1977), pp. 146-209.

8. Cf. I. J. du Plessis, *Christus as Hoof van die Kerk en Kosmos* (Groningen, 1962).

9. Cf. H. Berkhof, *Christ and the Powers* (Herald Press, Scottdale, 1962), and John H. Yoder, *The Politics of Jesus* (Eerdmans, Grand Rapids, 1972), esp. pp. 135-62.

CHAPTER 20 (pp. 212-220)

1. Cf. in this connection, among others, John H. Yoder, *The Politics of Jesus* (Eerdmans, Grand Rapids, 1972).
2. Cf. H.-R. Weber, 'God's Arithmetic', in G. H. Anderson and T. F. Stransky (eds.), *Mission Trends No. 2* (Eerdmans, Grand Rapids, 1975), pp. 64-7.
3. See Orlando E. Costas, *The Church and its Mission* (Tyndale House, Wheaton, 1974), p. 90.
4. G. Winter, quoted by Ronald J. Sider, *Evangelism, Salvation and Social Justice* (1977), p. 6.
5. P. G. Aring, *Kirche als Ereignis* (Neukirchener Verlag, Neukirchen, 1971), p. 101 (our translation).
6. See Braaten, *Flaming Center* (op. cit., Chapter 4, note 9), pp. 115-19. Cf. also Johannes Triebel, *Bekehrung als Ziel der missionarischen Verkündigung* (Verlag der ev.-luth. Mission, Erlangen, 1976), pp. 101-221.
7. Cf. however par. 20 of the Nairobi document 'Confessing Christ Today'.
8. Cf. Braaten, op. cit., pp. 45, 101-2, 144.
9. Stott, *Christian Mission* (op. cit., Chapter 4, note 10), p. 18.
10. Cf. Gensichen, *Glaube* (op. cit., Chapter 17, note 3), pp. 168-9.
11. J. B. Metz, *Kirche im Prozess der Aufklärung* (Kaiser, Munich, 1970), p. 82 (our translation).
12. Cf. Braaten, op. cit., pp. 151-2.
13. Cf. esp. Harvie Conn's reaction to a contribution by David C. Jones, 'Who are the Poor?' in *Evangelical Review of Theology,* vol. 2, no. 2 (Oct. 1978), pp. 229-35, as well as Gort (op. cit., Chapter 19, note 6), pp. 81-8.
14. Cf. in this respect the exceptionally illuminating article by Gort (op. cit., Chapter 19, note 6), esp. pp. 88-103.
15. Sider, op. cit., p. 11. Cf. also pp. 14-16.
16. Cf. H. Berkhof, *Christelijk Geloof* (Callenbach, Nijkerk, 1973), pp. 432, 434.
17. J. Aagaard, 'Some Main Trends in Modern Protestant Missiology', *Studia Theologica,* vol. 19 (1965), p. 259.

CHAPTER 21 (pp. 221-229)

1. Cf. also Roger D. Haight, 'Mission: The Symbol for Understanding the Church Today', *Theological Studies,* vol. 37, no. 4 (Dec. 1976), pp. 620-49.
2. Braaten, *Flaming Center* (op. cit., Chapter 4, note 9), p. 117.
3. Cf. S. Knapp, 'Mission and Modernization', in R. Pierce Beaver (ed.), *American Missions in Bicentennial Perspective* (1977), pp. 167-9.
4. The two documents were published in one volume (World Council of Churches, Geneva, 1968).
5. Barth, *Church Dogmatics* IV/3 (op. cit., Chapter 18, note 2), pp. 571-5.

6. Lesslie Newbigin, 'The Future of Missions and Missionaries', *Review and Expositor,* vol. 74, no. 2 (Spring 1977), p. 217.

7. Alfred C. Krass, 'On Dykes, the Dutch and the Holy Spirit', *Milligan Missiogram,* vol. 4, no. 4 (Summer 1977), p. 5.

8. For van Ruler's contribution in this respect, see further Krass, op. cit., pp. 12-13.

9. Knapp, op. cit., p. 168.

10. For the centrality of the concept 'witness' in the New Testament, cf. A. A. Trites, *The New Testament Concept of Witness* (Cambridge University Press, Cambridge, 1977), esp. p. 222.

11. R. Sider, *Evangelism, Salvation and Social Justice* (1977), p. 19.

12. H. Kraemer, *The Christian Message in a Non-Christian World* (Edinburgh House Press, London, 1947), p. 433. Cf. also J. Nxumalo, 'Church as Mission', *Journal of Theology for Southern Africa,* no. 26 (March 1979), pp. 39-49.

13. Sider, op. cit., pp. 17-18.

14. Quoted by Paul Löffler, 'The Confessing Community', *International Review of Missions,* no. 264 (Oct. 1977), p. 341.

15. E. Castro, 'Liberation, Evangelism, and Development: Must we Choose in Mission?', *Occasional Bulletin of Missionary Research,* vol. 2, no. 3 (July 1978), p. 88.

16. Sider, op.cit., p. 20.

CHAPTER 22 (pp. 230-238)

1. Cf. Peter Beyerhaus, *Missions: Which Way? Humanization or Redemption?* (Zondervan, Grand Rapids, 1971), p. 79; and Knapp (op. cit., Chapter 21, note 3), p. 159-62.

2. Barth, *Church Dogmatics* IV/1 (op. cit., Chapter 18, note 2), p. 652.

3. Cf. Jürgen Moltmann, *Theology of Hope* (SCM Press, London, 1974), p. 195.

4. Cf. B. H. Willeke, 'Mission und die Zeichen der Zeit', *Zeitschrift für Missions- und Religionswissenschaft,* vol. 62, no. 3 (July 1978), pp. 169-82.

5. Cf. M. Warren, *I Believe in the Great Commission* (Hodder & Stoughton, London, 1976), pp. 139-47.

6. Cf. H. Berkhof, *Christ the Meaning of History* (John Knox Press, Richmond, 1966), pp. 194-205.

7. Cf. J. Miguez y Bonino, 'An Approach to the Discussion of Tradition in a Heilsgeschichtliche Frame of Reference', in *Oikonomia. Heilsgeschichte als Thema der Theologie* (Herbert Reich Verlag, Hamburg, 1967), pp. 295-301.

8. Cf. Arnold Toynbee, reference in Braaten, op. cit., p. 127.

9. Cf. Martin Kähler, *Schriften zu Christologie und Mission* (1971), pp. 67, 159, 459-60.

10. Cf. J. Moltmann, op. cit., p. 83.

11. F. Kollbrunner, *The Splendour and Confusion of Mission Today* (Mambo Press, Gwelo, 1974), p. 20.

12. Cf. Werner Bieder, *Das Mysterium Christi und die Mission* (EVZ Verlag, Zurich, 1964), p. 46.

13. Cf. Oscar Cullmann, *Salvation in History* (SCM Press, London, 1967), pp. 183-4.

14. C. Braaten, op. cit. (Chapter 4, note 9) p. 47.

15. J. Aagaard, 'Some Main Trends in Modern Protestant Missiology', *Studia Theologica*, vol. 19 (1965), p. 256.

16. Cf. Karl Barth, *Church Dogmatics* IV/3 (op. cit., Chapter 18, note 2), pp. 928-942, under the heading 'Life in hope'.

17. Cf. H.-W. Heidland, 'Das Defizit an Eschatologie', *Deutsches Pfarrerblatt*, vol. 74, no. 1 (1974), pp. 7-11.

CHAPTER 23 (pp. 239-248)

1. See in this connection particularly Lesslie Newbigin, *The Relevance of Trinitarian Doctrine for Today's Mission* (Edinburgh House, London, 1963) and J. Lopéz-Gay, 'Trinitarian, Christological and Pneumatological Dimensions of Missions', *Omnis Terra*, no. 87 (Nov. 1977), pp. 14-27.

2. Cf. F. W. Dillistone, 'The Holy Spirit and the Christian Mission', in G. H. Anderson (ed.) *The Theology of the Christian Mission*, pp. 269-80.

3. Cf. R. Allen, *The Ministry of the Spirit* (Eerdmans, Grand Rapids, 1962), and H. Boer, Pentecost and Missions (Lutterworth, London, 1961).

4. H. Berkhof, *Christelijk Geloof* (Callenbach, Nijkerk, 1973), pp. 346-9 (our translation).

5. Cf. J. C. Hoekendijk, quoted by D. Manecke, *Mission als Zeugendienst* (Brockhaus, Wuppertal, 1972), p. 113.

6. A. C. Krass, 'Calling the Nations to Faith and Obedience', *Milligan Missiogram*, vol. 4, no. 4 (Summer 1977), p. 21. See also his *Five Lanterns at Sundown* (Eerdmans, Grand Rapids, 1978).

7. Cf. F. Boerwinkel, *Einde of Nieuw Begin?* (Ambo, Bilthoven, 1974), pp. 67-72.

8. Cf. P. F. Theron, *Die Ekklesia as Kosmies-Eskatologiese Teken* (D. R. C. Booksellers, Pretoria, 1978), pp. 69-73.

9. J. H. Bavinck, *An Introduction to the Science of Missions* (Baker, Grand Rapids, 1961), p. 303.

SELECT BIBLIOGRAPHY
ON THE
THEOLOGY OF MISSION

Aagard, J., 'Some Main Trends in Modern Protestant Missiology', *Studia Theologica*, vol. 19 (1965), pp. 238-59

Andersen, W., *Towards a Theology of Mission* (SCM Press, London, 1955)

Anderson, G. H., *The Theology of Missions: 1928-1958* (Univ. Microfilms, Ann Arbor, 1960)

Anderson, G. H. (ed.), *The Theology of the Christian Mission* (SCM Press, London, 1961)

Anderson, G. H. (ed.), *Christian Mission in Theological Perspective* (Abingdon, Nashville, 1967)

Aring, P. G., *Kirche als Ereignis.* Ein Beitrag zur Neuorientierung der Missionstheologie (Neukirchener Verlag, Neukirchen, 1971)

Barth, K., 'Die Theologie und die Mission in der Gegenwart', *Theologische Fragen und Antworten,* vol. 3 (Evang. Verlag, Zollikon-Zürich, 1957), pp. 100-26

Barth, K., *Church Dogmatics* IV/3 (T. & T. Clark, Edinburgh, 1962)

Bavinck, J. H., *An Introduction to the Science of Missions* (Baker Book House, Grand Rapids, 1961)

Beyerhaus, P., *Missions: Which way?* (Zondervan, Grand Rapids, 1971)

Beyerhaus, P., *Allen Völkern zum Zeugnis.* Biblisch-theologische Besinnung zum Wesen der Mission (Brockhaus, Wuppertal, 1972)

Blaser, K., *Gottes Heil in heutiger Wirklichkeit* (Otto Lembeck, Frankfurt, 1978)

Blauw, J., *The Missionary Nature of the Church.* A survey of the biblical theology of mission (Eerdmans, Grand Rapids, 1974; Lutterworth, London, 1974)

Bockmühl, K., *Was heisst heute Mission?* Entscheidungsfragen der neueren Missionstheologie (Brunnen Verlag, Giessen/Basel, 1974)

Bosch, D. J., *Die Heidenmission in der Zukunftsschau Jesu* (Zwingli Verlag, Zürich, 1959)

Braaten, C. E., *The Flaming Center* (Fortress Press, Philadelphia, 1977)

Chaney, C. L., *The Birth of Missions in America* (Wm. Carey, Pasadena, 1976)

Damsteegt, P. G., *Foundations of the Seventh-Day Adventist Message and Mission* (Eerdmans, Grand Rapids, 1977)

Gensichen, H.-W., *Glaube für die Welt* (Gerd Mohn, Gütersloh, 1971)

Hahn, F., *Mission in the New Testament* (SCM Press, London, 1965)

Haight, R. D., 'Mission: The Symbol for Understanding the Church Today', *Theological Studies* vol. 37, no. 4 (Dec. 1976), pp. 620-49

Harnack, A. von, *The Mission and Expansion of Christianity in the First Three Centuries* (Harper, New York, 1961)

Hoekendijk, J. C., *The Church Inside Out* (SCM Press, London, 1966)

Hoekstra, H., *The World Council of Churches and the Demise of Evangelism* (Tyndale House, Wheaton, 1979)

Hof, I. P. C. van 't, *Op zoek naar het Geheim van de Zending*. In Dialoog met de Wereldzendingsconferenties 1910-1963 (Veenman, Wageningen, 1972)

Horner, N. A. (ed.), *Protestant Crosscurrents in Mission* (Abingdon, Nashville-New York, 1968)

Jansen Schoonhoven, E., *Variaties op het Thema 'Zending'* (Kok, Kampen, 1974)

Jeremias, J., *Jesus' Promise to the Nations* (SCM Press, London, 1959)

Johnston, A. P., *The Battle for World Evangelism* (Tyndale House, Wheaton, 1978)

Jong, J. A. de, *As the Waters Cover the Sea*. Millennial Expectations in the Rise of Anglo-American Missions 1640-1810 (Kok, Kampen, 1970)

Kähler, M., *Schriften zu Christologie und Mission* (Chr. Kaiser, Munich, 1971)

Kane, J. H., *Christian Missions in Biblical Perspective* (Baker, Grand Rapids, 1976)

Kasting, H., *Die Anfänge der urchristlichen Mission* (Chr. Kaiser, Munich, 1969)

Knapp, S. C., 'Mission and Modernization: A Preliminary Critical Analysis of Contemporary Understandings of Mission from a "Radical Evangelical" Perspective', in R. P. Beaver (ed.), *American Missions in Bicentennial Perspective* (Wm. Carey, Pasadena, 1977) pp. 146-209

Kraemer, H., *The Christian Message in a non-Christian World* (Edinburgh House Press, London, 1947; Kregel, Grand Rapids, 1961)

Neill, S. C., *A History of Christian Missions* (Penguin Books, Harmondsworth, 1964)

Neill, S. C., *Salvation Tomorrow* (Lutterworth, London, 1976; Abingdon, Nashville, 1976)

Newbigin, L, *The Open Secret. Sketches for a Missionary Theology* (Eerdmans, Grand Rapids, 1978)

Newbigin, L., *The Relevance of Trinitarian Doctrine for Today's Mission* (Edinburgh House Press, London, 1963)

Niebuhr, H. R., *The Kingdom of God in America* (Harper, New York, 1959; first edition 1937)

Ohm, T., *Machet zu Jüngern alle Völker; Theorie der Mission* (E. Wevel, Freiburg, 1962)

Peters, G. W., *A Biblical Theology of Mission* (Moody Press, Chicago, 1972)

Piet, J. H., *The Road Ahead: A Theology for the Church in Mission* (Eerdmans, Grand Rapids, 1970)

Power, J., *Mission Theology Today* (Gill and Macmillan, Dublin, 1970)

Rooy, S. H., *The Theology of Missions in the Puritan Tradition* (Meinema, Delft, 1965)

Rosenkranz, G., *Die christliche Mission.* Geschichte und Theologie (Chr. Kaiser, Munich, 1977)

Rosin, H. H., *Missio Dei.* An Examination of the Origin, Contents and Function of the Term in Protestant Missiological Discussion (Inter-University Institute for Missiological and Ecumenical Research, Leiden, 1972)

Rossel, J., *Mission in a Dynamic Society* (SCM Press, London, 1968)

Rütti, L., *Zur Theologie der Mission* (Chr. Kaiser, Munich, 1972)

Schärer, H., *Die Begründung der Mission in der katholischen und evangelischen Missionswissenschaft* (Evang. Verlag, Zollikon-Zurich, 1944)

SEDOS, *Foundations of Mission Theology* (Orbis, Maryknoll, 1972)

Sider, R. J., *Evangelism, Salvation and Social Justice* (Grove Books, Bramcote, 1977)

Stott, J., *Christian Mission in the Modern World* (Falcon, London, 1975; IVP, Downers Grove, 1976)

Sundkler, B., *The World of Mission* (Lutterworth, London, 1965)

Verkuyl, J., *Contemporary Missiology: An Introduction* (Eerdmans, Grand Rapids, 1978)

Warren, M., *I Believe in the Great Commission* (Hodder & Stoughton, London, 1976; Eerdmans, Grand Rapids, 1976)

Wiedenmann, L., *Mission und Eschatologie.* Eine Analyse der neueren deutschen evangelischen Missionstheologie (Bonifacius-Druckerei, Paderborn, 1965)

INDEX OF PERSONAL NAMES

GENERAL INDEX

INDEX OF BIBLICAL REFERENCES